THE HISTORY OF THE
US AIR FORCE

THE HISTORY OF THE
US AIR FORCE

BILL YENNE

Exeter Books

NEW YORK

A BISON BOOK

Page 1: An F-86 Sabre-jet unleashes a salvo of 5-inch High Velocity Aerial Rockets (HVAR) over the test range at Nellis AFB. During the early 1950s the HVAR was one of the US Air Force's principal air-to-air weapons.

Page 2-3: As the sun sets over the Nevada hills, ground crews rest near a line of TAC A-10 'Warthogs' on the ramp at Nellis AFB during a *Red Flag* exercise.

Below: SAC B-52Ds (left and background) and B-52G (right) photographed from the top of a C-5A in the huge hangar at AFLC's San Antonio Air Logistics Center at Kelly AFB.

Picture Credits

Unless otherwise specified all illustrations are Official US Air Force photographs.

American Graphic Systems Archives 18

Boeing Airplane Company 28-29, 31 (both), 35, 39, 42-43, 145 (bottom right), 159 (bottom right), 168, 169, 218-19

© **George Hall** 2-3, 103, 110-11, 112, 138-39, 139, 146-47, 186 (top), 188

National Aeronautics and Space Administration 215

National Air and Space Museum, Smithsonian Institution 19, 20 (both), 23 (bottom)

USAF via Bausch 86 (bottom right, both)

US Department of Defense 191

© **Bill Yenne** 7, 9 (all 3), 10 (all 3), 11, 14 (all 3), 15 (both), 27 (all 3), 34 (bottom), 36 (top), 40 (top), 41, 47 (bottom), 48-49 (bottom 6), 52, 78 (above), 81 (top), 82, 105, 109, 113, 116 (both), 117, 119 (top), 120, 130(both), 131 (both), 151, 153, 154, 162 (both), 163 (both), 166-67, 167 (top), 170 (both), 171, 175, 183, 184, 186-87, 187 (top), 191 (bottom), 195, 196, 203 (bottom), 205, 209, 212, 213, 216 (top), 222

All charts, graphs and maps were compiled, designed and drawn by the author.

Edited by Robin Sommer and Susan Garratt.

Acknowledgments
The author would like to thank First Lieutenant Peter Meltzer, Deputy Chief of the Air Force Office of Public Affairs (Magazines and Books); George Hall for the use of his pictures; and Carol Yenne for typing the manuscript.

CONTENTS

PROFILES OF THE MAJOR COMMANDS

A PORTRAIT OF THE US AIR FORCE

A PORTRAIT OF THE US AIR FORCE

The United States Air Force was officially created on 18 September 1947 but had existed as an air arm of the US Army since 1 August 1907, when the Aeronautical Division of the US Army Signal Corps was established. The independent US Air Force is the successor of the US Army Air Forces, an autonomous air arm that became the largest air force in history during World War II with 2,373,292 personnel and 787,757 aircraft (1944). Today the US Air Force has about 600,000 personnel, making it still the world's largest air force in terms of manpower. The USSR is next, with about 550,000 in its Air Defense Forces, Long Range Aviation and Frontal Aviation. The Peoples' Republic of China is third with 500,000; India, France, Great Britain and the Federal Republic of Germany each have around 100,000. In terms of aircraft, the US Air Force is in third place worldwide with about 3700 combat aircraft (out of a total inventory of 7300), against 7500 combat aircraft for the USSR (excluding 755 in naval aviation). China has nearly 5500 combat aircraft (excluding about 800 in naval aviation). In fourth place is the US Navy (including US Marine Corps Aviation) with about 1800 combat aircraft. The air forces of India, France, Great Britain, Germany, Poland and Israel form a second tier of strength – between 500 and 700 combat aircraft each. While the Soviet Union and China have enhanced their statistics by retaining many planes built in the fifties, half the US Air Force inventory consists of aircraft built since 1970.

Of the roughly 7300 aircraft in the US Air Force inventory, 42% are tactical (interceptors, fighters, attack planes), 23% trainers, 12% transports, 8% aerial refueling tankers, 5% strategic bombers, 3% helicopters, and the remainder range from reconnaissance and electronic warfare to utility and observation.

This active inventory is complemented by an additional 450 aircraft flown in the Air Force Reserve (AFRES) and another 1600 assigned to the Air National Guard (ANG). Of these 2050 additional aircraft, 70% are tactical, 19% transports, 7% aerial refueling tankers, with the rest including trainers, observation planes and helicopters. The US Air Force and its reserve forces maintain only a small number of helicopters for utility and search-and-rescue purposes. The bulk of America's military helicopters are assigned to the US Army. Under the 1947 executive order that separated the US Air Force (formerly the US Army Air Forces) from the US Army, the latter retained only light observation and transport aircraft, but was permitted to build up its helicopter fleet for short-range transportation and attack functions. This fleet, presently numbering around 8000 helicopters, outnumbers the US Air Force helicopter fleet by a ratio of 34 to 1.

Of the nearly 600,000 uniformed personnel in the US Air Force, 82% are enlisted airmen and 18% are officers. Nearly three-quarters of US Air Force personnel are sergeants and 15% are officers under the rank of lieutenant colonel. The greatest number of officers in any career area are pilots and navigators,

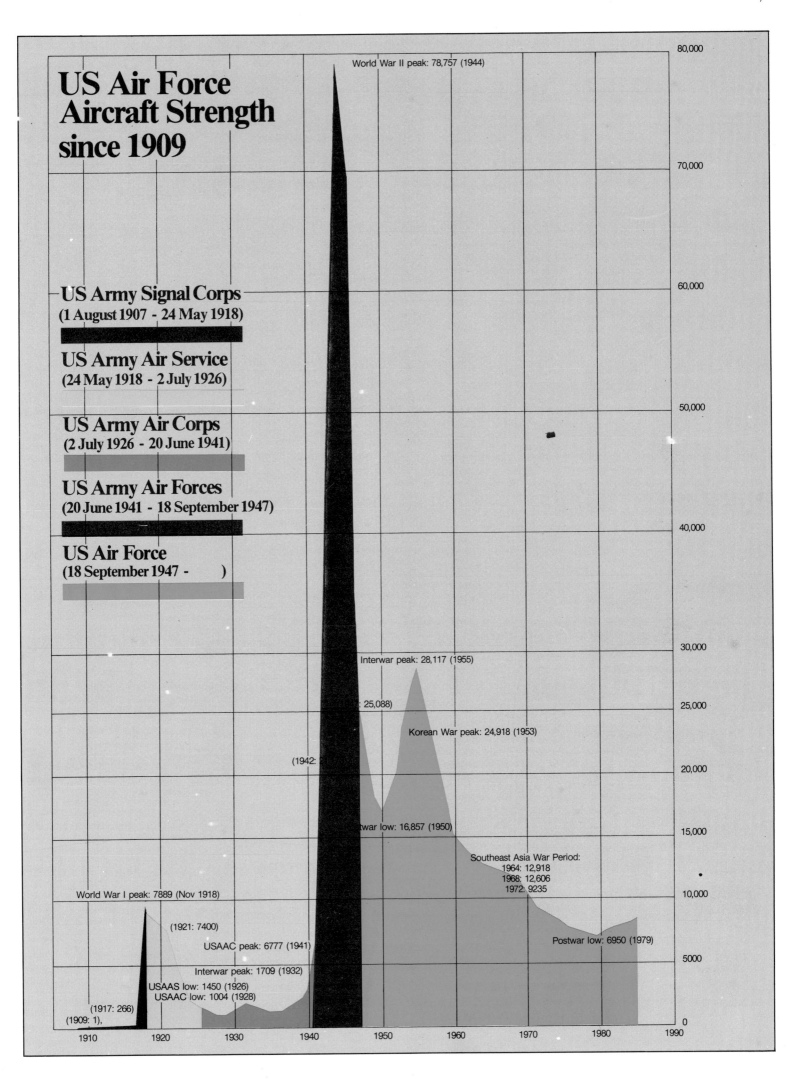

US Air Force Aircraft Strength since 1909

US Army Signal Corps
(1 August 1907 - 24 May 1918)

US Army Air Service
(24 May 1918 - 2 July 1926)

US Army Air Corps
(2 July 1926 - 20 June 1941)

US Army Air Forces
(20 June 1941 - 18 September 1947)

US Air Force
(18 September 1947 -   )

World War II peak: 78,757 (1944)

Interwar peak: 28,117 (1955)

25,088)

Korean War peak: 24,918 (1953)

(1942:

twar low: 16,857 (1950)

Southeast Asia War Period:
1964: 12,918
1968: 12,606
1972: 9235

World War I peak: 7889 (Nov 1918)

(1921: 7400)

USAAC peak: 6777 (1941)

Postwar low: 6950 (1979)

Interwar peak: 1709 (1932)

USAAS low: 1450 (1926)
USAAC low: 1004 (1928)

(1917: 266)
(1909: 1),

80,000
70,000
60,000
50,000
40,000
30,000
25,000
20,000
15,000
10,000
5000
0

1910   1920   1930   1940   1950   1960   1970   1980   1990

The Commanders of the US Army Air Service

Maj Gen William Kenly (Chief, Div of Military Aeronautics)
    20 May 1913–22 Dec 1918
Maj Gen Charles Menoher (Chief of the Air Service)
    23 Dec 1918–4 Oct 1921
Maj Gen Mason Patrick (Chief of the Air Service)
    5 Oct 1921–1 July 1926

Chiefs of the US Army Air Corps

Maj Gen Mason Patrick	2 July 1926–12 Dec 1927
Maj Gen James Fechet	14 Dec 1927–19 Dec 1931
Maj Gen Benjamin Foulois	19 Dec 1931–21 Dec 1935
Maj Gen Oscar Westover	22 Dec 1935–21 Sept 1938
Gen H H Arnold 29 Sept	1938–20 June 1941

The Commanders of the US Army Air Forces

Gen H H Arnold (Chief of the AAF) 20 June 1941–8 March 1942
Gen H H Arnold (Commanding
    General AAF)   9 Mar 1942–28 Feb 1946
Gen Carl Spaatz (Commanding
    General AAF) 1 Mar 1946–25 Sept 1947

Chiefs of Staff of the US Air Force

Gen Carl Spaatz	26 Sept 1947–29 Apr 1948
Gen Hoyt Vandenberg	30 Apr 1948–29 June 1953
Gen Nathan Twining	20 June 1953–30 June 1957
Gen Thomas White	1 July 1957–30 June 1961
Gen Curtis LeMay	30 June 1961–31 Jan 1965
Gen John McConnell	1 Feb 1965–31 July 1969
Gen John Ryan	1 Aug 1969–31 July 1973
Gen George Brown	1 Aug 1973–30 June 1974
Gen David Jones	1 July 1974–30 June 1978
Gen Lew Allen, Jr.	1 July 1978–30 June 1982
Gen Charles Gabriel	1 July 1982–

Secretaries of the Air Force

Stuart Symington	18 Sept 1947–24 Apr 1950
Thomas Finletter	24 Apr 1950–20 Jan 1953
Harold Talbott	4 Feb 1953–13 Aug 1955
Donald Quarles	15 Aug 1955–30 Apr 1957
James Dougles, Jr.	1 May 1957–10 Dec 1959
Dudley Sharp	11 Dec 1959–20 Jan 1961
Eugene Zuckert	24 Jan 1961–30 Sept 1965
Harold Brown	1 Oct 1965–15 Feb 1969
Robert Seamans, Jr.	15 Feb 1969–14 May 1973
John McLucas	18 July 1973–23 Nov 1975
James Plummer (Acting)	24 Nov 1975–1 Jan 1976
Thomas Reed	2 Jan 1976–6 Apr 1977
John Stetson	6 Apr 1977–18 May 1979
Hans Mark	26 July 1979–9 Feb 1981
Verne Orr	9 Feb 1981–

Chief Master Sergeants of the Air Force

CMSAF Paul Airey	3 Apr 1967–1 Aug 1969
CMSAF Donald Harlow	1 Aug 1969–1 Oct 1971
CMSAF Richard Kisling	1 Oct 1971–1 Oct 1973
CMSAF Thomas Barnes	1 Oct 1973–1 Aug 1977
CMSAF Robert Gaylor	1 Aug 1977–1 Aug 1979
CMSAF James McCoy	1 Aug 1979–1 July 1981
CMSAF Arthur Andrews	1 Aug 1981–

who number almost 30,000 or nearly a third of the total number of officers in the USAF.

Ten percent of US Air Force officers are women and five percent are black. Of the enlisted personnel, 12% are women and 17% are black. The average age of US Air Force personnel is 34 for officers and 26 for enlisted airmen. Sixty percent of the officers have college degrees, 39% have master's degrees and 2% have doctorates.

THE DEPARTMENT OF DEFENSE

The United States Air Force was established in 1947 by the National Defense Act of that year as one of the nation's three principal military forces within the Department of Defense. The Department of Defense (DoD) is headed by a civilian Secretary of Defense who has full cabinet rank. Under the Secretary of Defense are three civilian Executive Departments – Army, Navy and Air Force – each headed by a Secretary who does not have full cabinet rank. Within each Executive Department are the small Office of the Secretary and a vastly larger military service. Each of these three military services is commanded by a Chief of Staff (in the case of the US Navy, the Chief of Naval Operations). These three plus the Commandant of the US Marine Corps (which is contained within the Department of the Navy) form the five-man Joint Chiefs of Staff (JCS) with the JCS Chairman. These officers are drawn from the service they command, with the chairman's position rotating among the services, and are of four-star rank. At the end of World War II the equivalent JCS positions were held by officers of five-star rank, but no regular service officers have been promoted beyond four-star rank since that time.

THE OFFICE OF THE SECRETARY OF THE AIR FORCE

The Secretary is appointed by the President and has his office, like those of the other Secretaries, at the Pentagon, ten minutes drive from the White House and just across the Potomac River from Washington DC. Geographically it is in the state of Virginia, but its telephone and postal code system are those of the District of Columbia. The Secretary's staff includes an Under Secretary, Assistant Secretaries for (a) Manpower, Reserve Affairs and Installations; (b) Research, Development and Logistics; and (c) Financial Management. Also on the staff are General Counsel, the Auditor General and special assistants, administrative assistants and Deputy Under Secretaries as required. All of the above are civilian appointees, but the Secretary may have US Air Force officers on his staff in such roles as Director of Public Affairs and Director of the Office of Legislative Liaison. The staff is completed by the necessary clerical and administrative personnel.

THE US AIR FORCE AIR STAFF

The military Air Staff commands the US Air Force and is headed by the Chief of Staff, under whom are the Vice Chief of Staff, the Assistant Vice Chief and Assistant Chiefs for Information, Intelligence, and Studies and Analysis. Other Air Staff members are the Judge Advocate General, Surgeon General, Chief of Air Force Chaplains, Director of Administration, Chief of the Air Force Reserve and Director of the Air National Guard. All of the above are officers of General rank but the staff includes civilian scientists and one enlisted man, the Chief Master Sergeant of the Air Force.

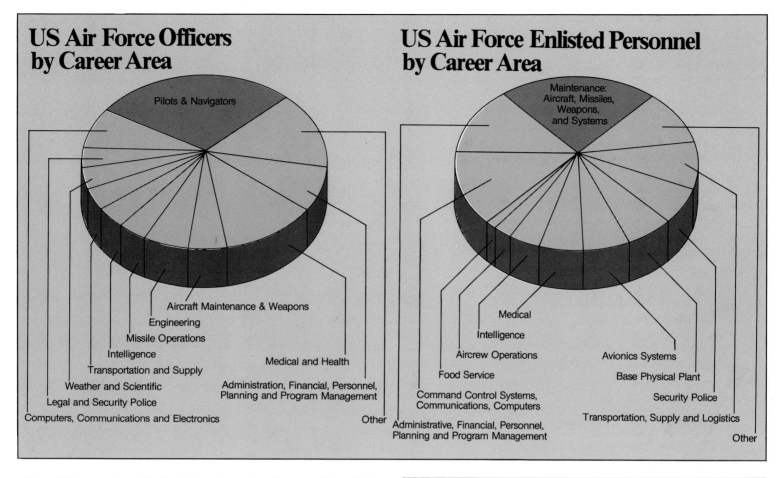

US Air Force Officers by Career Area

Pilots & Navigators

Aircraft Maintenance & Weapons
Engineering
Missile Operations
Intelligence
Transportation and Supply
Weather and Scientific
Legal and Security Police
Computers, Communications and Electronics

Medical and Health
Administration, Financial, Personnel, Planning and Program Management
Other

US Air Force Enlisted Personnel by Career Area

Maintenance: Aircraft, Missiles, Weapons, and Systems

Medical
Intelligence
Aircrew Operations
Food Service
Command Control Systems, Communications, Computers
Administrative, Financial, Personnel, Planning and Program Management

Avionics Systems
Base Physical Plant
Security Police
Transportation, Supply and Logistics
Other

In addition to the Air Staff there are the Comptroller of the Air Force, the Inspector General of the Air Force, and Deputy Chiefs of Staff for (a) Programs and Resources; (b) Research Development and Acquisition; (c) Manpower and Personnel; (d) Plans and Operations; and (e) Logistics and Engineering.

Together, the Office of the Secretary, the Air Staff and the National Guard Bureau are staffed by about 2700 uniformed and 2000 civilian personnel.

The Air Staff, like the Office of the Secretary, is head-quartered at the Pentagon, and is also supported by two Air Force Bases (AFB) in the Washington DC area: Bolling AFB in the District of Columbia and Andrews AFB 11 miles southeast of the capital near Suitland, Maryland. Both bases are assigned to the Military Airlift Command (MAC) but have been host to a number of other major commands over the years including the Strategic Air Command (SAC) and the now defunct Continental Air Command and Headquarters Command. Andrews AFB, though a MAC base, today houses the headquarters of the Air Force Systems Command (AFSC). Bolling AFB and the adjoin-ing Anacostia Naval Air Station (NAS) were once the major landing fields in the District of Columbia, but the runways have long since been inoperative. Andrews AFB, on the other hand, serves as the major military airfield in the area with tenants including the Air Force Reserve, Air National Guard and Naval Air units, as well as MAC's 89th Military Airlift Wing (MAW) operating VC-137 (Boeing Model 707) VIP executive aircraft. These include *Air Force One*, the personal plane of the President of the United States.

BASIC ORGANIZATION

Within the Department of the Air Force and under the Air Staff there are three basic components to the full-time USAF: Major Commands, Direct Reporting Units (DRU) and Separate Operating Agencies (SOA) totalling

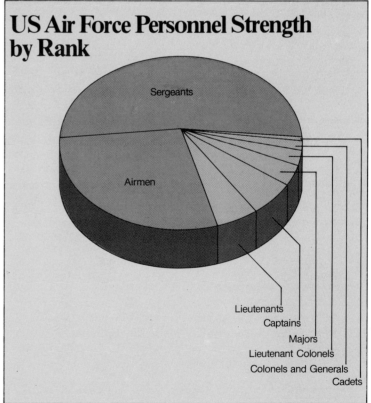

US Air Force Personnel Strength by Rank

Sergeants
Airmen
Lieutenants
Captains
Majors
Lieutenant Colonels
Colonels and Generals
Cadets

nearly 600,000 uniformed and 250,000 civilian personnel. The largest number (91%) are assigned to twelve Major Commands. Of the 750,000 total personnel in the Major Commands, 26% are civilians compared to 69% in the DRUs and SOAs.

In addition to the three full-time components of the US Air Force there are just over 200,000 Reserve personnel in the Air National Guard and Air Force Reserve, which would bring the total personnel strength of the Air Force to slightly more than a million if all were called up at the same time.

THE DIRECT REPORTING UNITS

The Direct Reporting Units total about 40,000 personnel and include the Air Force Technical Application Center (AFTAC) which has DoD responsibility to maintain facilities and personnel for detecting and monitoring nuclear detonations in the atmosphere, underground and in outer space. AFTAC was established for this purpose in 1947 by JCS chairman General Dwight D. Eisenhower and was responsible for discovering the first Soviet atomic test in September 1949, when an AFTAC sensor aboard an RB-29 over the North Pacific detected the Russian fallout. AFTAC is currently headquartered at Patrick AFB, Florida with squadrons at McClellan AFB, California, Wheeler AFB, Hawaii and Lindsey AS in Germany; there are 19 detachments and 50 equipment locations worldwide.

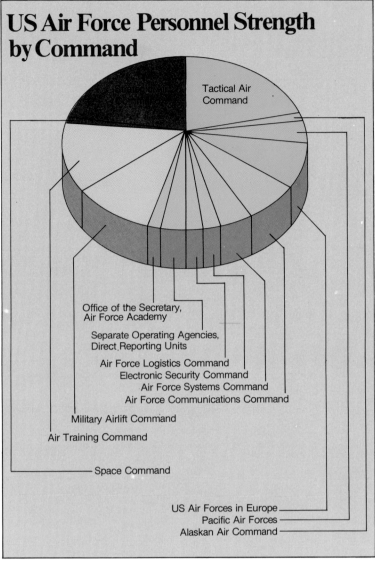

US Air Force Personnel Strength by Command

Above: Most of the personnel in the US Air Force are assigned to the Major Commands, with over three quarters of them assigned to the flying commands, which are divided between training and transport (yellow), strategic (red), and tactical (blue).

Above left: There is probably no more familiar landmark at stateside Air Force bases than the ubiquitous checkered water tower.

US Air Force Insignia of Rank

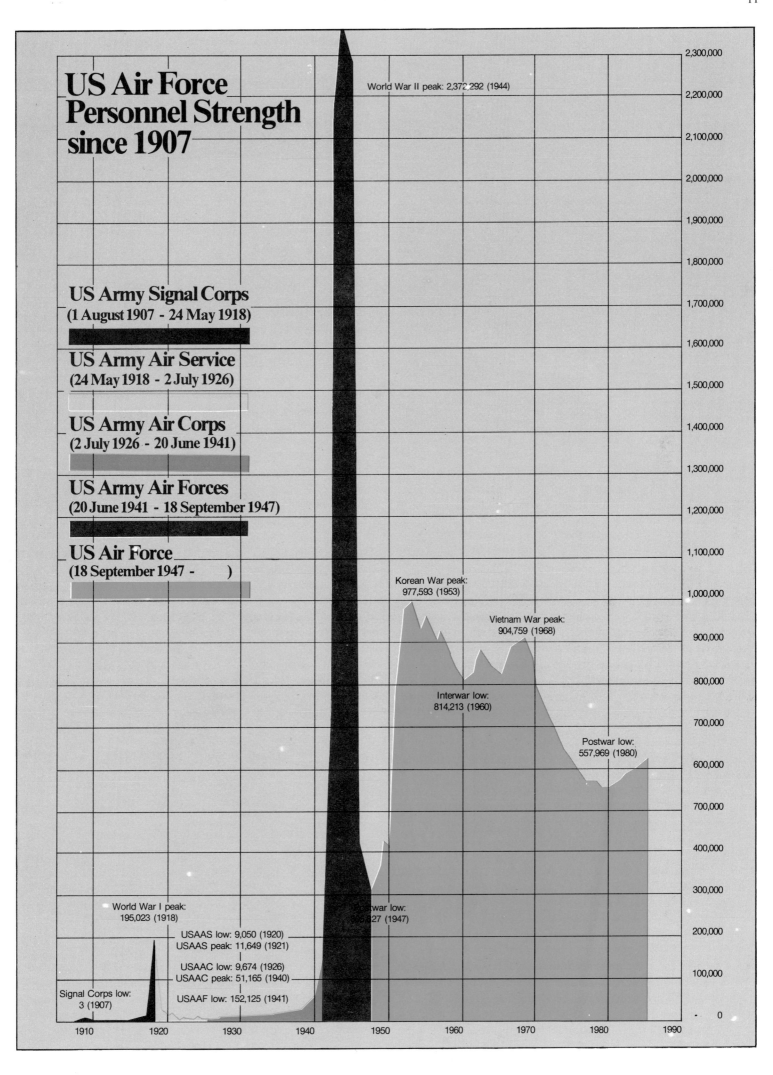

US Air Force Personnel Strength since 1907

US Army Signal Corps
(1 August 1907 - 24 May 1918)

US Army Air Service
(24 May 1918 - 2 July 1926)

US Army Air Corps
(2 July 1926 - 20 June 1941)

US Army Air Forces
(20 June 1941 - 18 September 1947)

US Air Force
(18 September 1947 -   )

World War II peak: 2,372,292 (1944)

Korean War peak:
977,593 (1953)

Vietnam War peak:
904,759 (1968)

Interwar low:
814,213 (1960)

Postwar low:
557,969 (1980)

Postwar low:
305,827 (1947)

World War I peak:
195,023 (1918)

USAAS low: 9,050 (1920)
USAAS peak: 11,649 (1921)

USAAC low: 9,674 (1926)
USAAC peak: 51,165 (1940)

USAAF low: 152,125 (1941)

Signal Corps low:
3 (1907)

1910   1920   1930   1940   1950   1960   1970   1980   1990

2,300,000
2,200,000
2,100,000
2,000,000
1,900,000
1,800,000
1,700,000
1,600,000
1,500,000
1,400,000
1,300,000
1,200,000
1,100,000
1,000,000
900,000
800,000
700,000
600,000
700,000
400,000
300,000
200,000
100,000
0

Left: A cadet sailplane flies over the heart of the Academy campus at the foot of the Rampart range.

Right: The Eagle and Fledglings statue with the Academy's 17-spired chapel in the background.

The Air Force Academy is also a Direct Reporting Unit. With the creation of an independent US Air Force in 1947, its leaders, who had come up through the ranks of the US Army, many of them via its Military Academy at West Point, recognized the need for an Air Force Academy. Established by Act of Congress, signed into law by President Dwight D Eisenhower on 1 April 1954, the Air Force Academy joined West Point, Annapolis and the Coast Guard Academy as one of four service academies. Later, in 1954, Secretary of the Air Force Harold Talbott appointed a commission to help him select a permanent site. It considered 580 sites in 45 states, narrowing these prospective locations to three, from which Talbott selected one near Colorado Springs, Colorado.

The first Air Force Academy class began its academic career in temporary facilities at Lowry AFB in Denver in July 1958, as construction began on the Academy campus. The Cadet Wing made its move to the nearly complete campus in August 1958, and the first class of 207 graduates was commissioned as second lieutenants in June 1959 with the Academy's degree program accredited by the Commission of Colleges and Universities of the North Central Association of Colleges and Secondary Schools. In 1964 President Lyndon Johnson signed a bill authorizing the Cadet Wing to increase its students from 2529 to 4417. On 7 October 1975 President Gerald Ford signed legislation permitting women to enter the nation's military academies, and the first female cadets entered the Air Force Academy in June 1976, graduating in May 1980. The Academy has graduated over fifteen thousand officers including a future Medal of Honor winner, seventeen who would become generals, and two who would become combat aces. Among its graduates have been

nearly ten thousand pilots, of whom several have been selected as astronauts for the space program.

Cadet training includes professional military studies and training, leadership, aviation science and flight training in gliders as well as T-43 and T-41 aircraft. The cadet honor code is 'We will not lie, steal, cheat, nor tolerate among us anyone who does.' The fourth part of the code is considered its backbone, but is also its most controversial provision. It has resulted in occasional scandals whereby cadets had to choose, in a damned-if-we-do-damned-if-we-don't way, whether or not to turn in cheating classmates. Cadets found guilty of violating the code are expected to resign from the Academy.

Parachuting or sky-diving is also part of the training program at the Academy. The school's parachute demonstration team, Wings of Blue, competes annually in intercollegiate competitions, winning first place in the 40-school national competition nearly every year since they became involved. In addition to the competitions, the Wings of Blue put on about 40 public demonstrations each year. The cadets compete in intercollegiate athletics through their teams, whose mascot is the 'Fighting Falcon.' More than a mascot, the birds are integral to the unusual extracurricular program in falconry. Under special permits issued by the US Fish and Wildlife Service and the Colorado Division of Wildlife, the Academy acquired and bred wild prairie falcons for use by cadets in demonstrations. Since 1974 the prairie falcons used have been bred in captivity, most of them at the Academy; no wild birds have been captured. In demonstrations the falconer whirls a rectangular leather lure, with meat attached, on a ten-foot cord. The bird has learned to strike the swiftly moving lure in mid-air, with the meat as its reward. The Academy usually has about ten Colorado prairie falcons and one or two white gyrfalcons. The most famous of these was Baffin, named for the bay in Canada where she was captured, with the permission of the Canadian Government, in 1965. She was an important part of campus life for 13 years until her death in 1978. In July 1980 a fourth white gyrfalcon succeeded Baffin as the school's official mascot. Named Glacier, he was captured on the Seward Peninsula in Alaska by an Academy search team and has since become a feature of many Air Force Academy functions.

SEPARATE OPERATING AGENCIES

While each of the Major Commands and DRUs occupies a specific niche, the SOAs, totaling about 20,000 military and civilian personnel, provide services to all the Commands across the full breadth of the service.

The Air Force Accounting and Finance Center (AFAFC), based at Lowry AFB, Colorado, is the centerpiece of a computerized global network of over a hundred Accounting and Finance Offices (AFO) that issue payrolls and conduct billings and collections. Over a million active-duty US Air Force personnel and retirees, plus 165,000 reservists, get their regular paychecks via the AFAFC with a better than 99% record for accuracy. The center handles all the monies appropriated to the USAF by Congress and maintains trust fund accounts for Department of Defense foreign military sales.

The Air Force Audit Agency (AFAA) operating out of Norton AFB, California, under direction of the Auditor General in the Secretary's office, evaluates the economy and effectiveness of

MAN'S FLIGHT
THROUGH LIFE IS
SUSTAINED BY THE
POWER OF HIS
KNOWLEDGE

The Superintendents of the Air Force Academy

Lt Gen Hubert Harmon	27 July 1954–27 July 1956
Maj Gen James Briggs	28 July 1956–16 Aug 1959
Maj Gen William Stone	17 Aug 1959–30 June 1962
Maj Gen Robert Warren	1 July 1962–30 June 1965
Lt Gen Thomas Moorman	1 July 1965–31 July 1970
Lt Gen Albert Clark	1 Aug 1970–31 July 1974
Lt Gen James Allen	1 Aug 1974–31 July 1977
Lt Gen Kenneth Tallman	1 Aug 1977–16 June 1981
Maj Gen Robert Kelley	16 June 1981–

Air Force operations. The AFAA is composed of three Directorates – Aquisition and Logistics (based at Wright-Patterson AFB, Ohio), Forces and Support Management and Field Activities (both at Norton AFB).

The Air Force Commissary Service (AFCOMS) operates from a headquarters at Kelly AFB, Texas, and fifteen other sites in the US as well as two overseas regions (Europe and the Pacific). AFCOMS purchases and provides food for all authorized Air Force appropriated-fund dining facilities. Many commissaries feature delicatessans and on-site full-service bakeries with the latest in technology, including laser scanners to read universal product codes (bar coding) at the check-out counter. The commissaries offer their wares at the lowest possible prices consistent with covering their overhead and operating costs. AFCOM's motto is 'We serve where you serve.'

The Air Force Engineering and Services Center (AFESC) based at Tyndall AFB, Florida, provides the Air Force worldwide with a broad range of basic support services. These include readiness and contingency operations, facility energy, environmental planning, fire protection, installation operation and maintenance, food service, billeting and civil engineering. AFESC has Regional Civil Engineers based in Atlanta, San Francisco, Dallas and at Norton AFB to provide support for construction projects ranging from housing and dining halls to runways and missile support facilities. Among AFESC's recent activities have been a two-year study of USAF engineering requirements in wartime, developing rapid runway repair procedures utilizing crushed stone and fiberglass -reinforced polyester covers, and development of a system to remove trichloroethylene and other volatile organic chemical wastes from contaminated groundwater.

The mission of **the Air Force Inspection and Safety Center (AFISC)** at Norton AFB is to assess USAF fighting capability and resource management for the Commands. AFISC divisions include the Directorates of Aerospace Safety, Inspection, Nuclear Surety (at Kirtland AFB, New Mexico), and Medical Inspection, plus the Offices of Management Support and Data Automation. AFISC supports the Air Force Inspector General through the Office of the Assistant for Inquiries and Complaints operating their Computerized Complaints Data Collection System.

The Air Force Intelligence System (AFIS) based in Washington DC gathers, evaluates and disburses intelligence information for Air Force Headquarters and USAF field commanders worldwide and supplies intelligence for the Defense Department. While the USAF has been involved in such activities since its inception in 1947, the AFIS was not established as an SOA until 27 June 1972. Among its Directorates are Operational Intelligence, Target Intelligence, Security and Communications

Above: The 65-ton Oshkosh P-15, developed by AFESC, is the flagship of the USAF fire-protection fleet. It is powered by two 430 hp diesel engines.

Below: The Air Force in the railroad business. Fuel and supplies arrive by rail and are often shuttled around larger bases by switch engines. Some cars also carry training and technical facilities between bases.

Management, Intelligence Data Management, Attaché Affairs, Intelligence Reserve Forces, Soviet Affairs and Evasion and Escape/Prisoner of War Matters. The AFIS Special Studies Division gathers and analyzes data about foreign camouflage concealment and deception techniques.

The Air Force Legal Services Center (AFLSC), also in Washington DC, is under the Judge Advocate General. AFLSC functions as the Air Force's in-house law firm, handling claims for and against the Air Force, legal aid, labor law, and other matters. AFLSC provides legal services for the USAF ranging from patent and copyright protection to court-martial. Within AFLSC are the Divisions of Military Justice, Defense Services, Trial Judiciary, Government Trial and Appellate Counsel, Claims and Tort Litigation and General Litigation. AFLSC also includes the Court of Military Review and a Special Assistant for Clemency and Rehabilitation Matters.

The Air Force Manpower and Personnel Center (AFMPC) is headquartered at Randolph AFB, Texas; its commander also serves as the Assistant Deputy Chief of Staff for Manpower and Personnel on the Air Staff. AFMPC administers Air Force programs covering the lives and careers of USAF personnel and their families. Its objective, summed up in the AFMPC motto 'Responsive to the Mission – Sensitive to the People,' is to see that the right people are in the right places at the right time, with optimum attitude and morale. AFMPC's areas of activity include libraries, sports, child care, recreation, re-enlistment, retirement, voting assistance and awards and decorations, to name a few.

The Air Force Medical Service Center (AFMSC), headquartered at Brooks AFB, Texas, was established in July 1978 under the Deputy Surgeon General of the Air Force for Operations. The AFMSC oversees health-care policy and practice and USAF medical research. There are two AFMSC Directorates: Health Care Support and Professional Services.

The Air Force Office of Security Police (AFOSP) was estab-

15

lished as SOA in September 1979 at Kirtland AFB in New Mexico, under the command of the already existing office of Air Force Chief of Security Police who is answerable in both roles to the Inspector General of the Air Force. The AFOSP operates theAir Force Security Clearance Office in Washington and is concerned with all issues relating to the security of Air Force bases, personnel, systems and aircraft. While AFOSP has only about a hundred people, the worldwide Security Police Force that they support totals nearly 39,000. In peacetime the Security Police Force (known as Air Police until 1967) functions much like a civilian police force. In wartime, with much tighter security imposed and enemy attack on USAF facilities possible, it would function more like an Army or Marine combat unit, with Air Base Ground Defense its primary mission. The tools of the Security Policeman's trade range from civilian-type police cars to armored vehicles, from a wide variety of small arms to K-9 working dog teams.

The Air Force Office of Special Investigations (AFOSI), headquartered at Bolling AFB, DC, provides the Air Force and its Commands with investigative services including antiterrorist operations, counterintelligence, forensics, personnel protection and polygraph. More than half of AFOSI's activities deal with criminal investigations; about a third deal with fraud in contracts, computer systems, property disposition etc. AFOSI antiterrorist activities are credited for a decline in terrorist attacks against USAF personnel in recent years.

The Air Force Operational Test and Evaluation Center (AFOTEC) at Kirtland AFB, New Mexico, is charged with testing Air Force procedures, systems, and hardware under operational conditions. The center has four detachments based at Edwards AFB, California; Eglin AFB, Florida; Nellis AFB, Nevada; and Kapuan AS in Germany. The headquarters structure co-ordinates and supports the test teams, operating at about two dozen field sites around the world, with the test team personnel generally drawn from the Major Commands.

Above: An assortment of Security Police vehicles in familiar Air Force blue, including both pickups and vans.

Below: The AFOSI headquarters at Bolling AFB in the District of Columbia.

The Air Force Service Information and News Center (AFSINC) headquartered at Kelly AFB, Texas, is the in-house communications department, providing information for Air Force as well as Army personnel through both print and broadcast media. Answerable to the Director of Public Affairs in the Office of the Secretary of the Air Force, AFSINC was founded in June 1978 and merged with the Air Force Hometown News Center one year later. The Army Hometown News Center became part of AFSINC in October 1980. AFSINC is composed of four Directorates: Administration & Resources, Internal Information, Armed Forces Radio & TV and Army & Air Force Hometown News. The Radio and TV Directorate manages all Air Force broadcasting throughout the Pacific, in Alaska, Europe, Greenland and the Middle East.

THE US AIR FORCE BAND

The Air Force Band has individual ensembles servicewide that provide entertainment at Air Force functions, air shows and off-base concerts. The ensembles range from the 702nd Air Force Band (the Strategic Air Command Band) at Offutt AFB, a full 60-piece band, to small ensembles like the Strolling Strings and the Singing Sergeants, who are based near Air Force Headquarters. Musical styles represented range from the traditional marching bands and drum and bugle corps to rock and soul groups.

Like many Air Force traditions, the Band had its roots in the Army. The US Army Band was officially formed in 1921 from remnants of the American Expeditionary Force Headquarters Band that had been formed at Chaumont, France, during World War I. By World War II, the USAAF had its own bands, from which the USAF Band would be derived. There is probably no wartime Air Force Band more famous than the USAAF Band, Europe, under the direction of Major Glenn Miller.

Before the war, Glenn Miller was one of the top Big Band leaders in the country: in 1939 he had had two enormous hits with *Tuxedo Junction* and *In the Mood*. By 1940 one of every three nickels shoveled into an American jukebox went to play a Glenn Miller song. In 1942, with the United States at war, Miller joined the USAAF and was sent to England where he took charge of the USAAF Band, Europe. It was Major Miller's idea to give the troops the kind of music they wanted to hear, and his group was immensely popular. On 16 December 1944, he set out by air from a USAAF base in the South of England en route to a show in Paris. He was never seen again. His plane was presumed lost in the English Channel.

The USAAF band broke up a year later, but in 1950 the US Air Force formed a new band, called the Airmen of Note, dedicated to perpetuating the Glenn Miller/Big Band sound. In 1953 the Airmen portrayed the Miller Band in the movie *The Glenn Miller Story*. For over thirty years, the Airmen of Note have been one of the most popular units in the US Air Force Band, playing Big Band concerts in 25 countries on four continents and around the United States. Based at Bolling AFB, the Airmen were described by *Downbeat* Magazine as 'One of the best bands anyone interested in big band jazz or good dance music can hope to hear today.'

Left: Colonel Arnold Gabriel, Commander and Conductor of the US Air Force Band, directs the band in a concert at the Jefferson Memorial in Washington, DC. Colonel Gabriel is one of the world's most widely traveled directors, having conducted in all 50 states and 45 foreign countries since he assumed his command in 1964.

Below: An Army Air Forces band in concert at Colfax Army Air Field during World War II. North American T-6 trainers and Douglas C-47 transports are visible in the background.

Right: The Airmen of Note pose in a hangar with a World War II era P-38. Organized to perpetuate the 1940s Big Band sound, the Airmen of Note are the only organization in the USAF to wear USAAF uniforms.

AMERICAN AIR POWER BEFORE THE US AIR FORCE

EARLY AERONAUTICS

The first commentary on air power by an American was written by the preeminent stateman Benjamin Franklin less than a year after the United States had won its war of independence. Franklin, serving as American envoy to France, had been on hand when Jean de Rozier made the first manned ascent in a balloon in Paris on 15 October 1783, and had made his first reference to the military potential of balloons in a letter dated 21 November 1783. Franklin observed that an army could employ balloons for functions 'Such as elevating an engineer to take a view of an enemy's army, works, etc, conveying intelligence into or out of a beseiged town, giving signals to distant places, or the like.'

Much more than a politician, Franklin was also a journalist, an inventor and a man of great foresight. In January 1783 he wrote that the balloon's potential in warfare was 'of great importance, and what may possibly give a new turn to human affairs. . . . Five thousand balloons, capable of raising two men each, could not cost more than five ships of the line; and where is the prince who can afford to so cover his country with troops for its defense as that ten thousand men descending from the clouds might not in many places do an infinite deal of mischief before a force could be brought together to repel them?'

Daring aeronauts had been experimenting with balloons in Europe for a number of years when the Frenchman Jean Pierre Blanchard made the first ascent in the United States in Phila-

delphia on 9 January 1793. In attendance were not only President George Washington, but four future presidents: John Adams, Thomas Jefferson, James Madison and James Monroe. Blanchard was aloft for almost an hour and rose to an altitude of nearly a mile.

While the balloon was still regarded as a curiosity in America, the French had already made note of the military potential observed by Franklin a decade earlier. In 1794 the first military air service, the French Aerostatic Corps, was born. Staffed by energetic and imaginative men a hundred years ahead of their time, the corps first saw action on 26 June 1794 in the Battle of Fleurus, Belgium, directing artillery and generally overseeing the defeat of the Austrian forces under the Prince of Saxe-Coburg. The world's first air force went on to serve with some success until it was disbanded by Napoleon in 1799.

It was not until the Civil War that the United States would officially take up the notion of an aerial corps, but it was not for want of an occasional proposal. During the Seminole War in 1841, when the US Army was engaged in a protracted fight with the Seminole Indians in the Florida Everglades, Army Colonel John Sherburne suggested to Secretary of War Joel Poinsett that balloons could help infantry columns locate Indian camps: they could be sent aloft at night to spot the Seminole campfires, without the Indians' awareness. Poinsett complimented Sherburne for his idea but placed approval of the scheme with General W K Armistead, the Army Commander in Florida, who rejected it out of hand. The war was soon over and Sherburne's

'commendable idea' remained just that.

The first documented instance of a proposal to use a balloon as an American combat weapon came in the course of the assault on Veracruz in 1846 during the Mexican War. General Winfield Scott's invasion troops were pinned down by the fort of San Juan de Ulloa at Veracruz and needed a way out to punch through to Mexico City. The troops had been bottled up for several months, with both the Army and the Navy making unsuccessful attempts to secure the fort. Then a Pennsylvania balloonist named John Wise (who would later attempt to secure money from Congress for a transatlantic balloon voyage) came forward. Wise suggested that he could float a balloon over the forests out of range of enemy artillery and drop 'a thousand percussion bombshells' on the castle of Veracruz. In retrospect, the tactic might have worked, but in fact the War Department, in typical bureaucratic style, chose to ignore Wise. Ultimately the issue became moot when Scott's ground forces succeeded in taking the citadel.

The point worth making in these two anecdotes goes beyond the ingenuity and foresight of Sherburne and Wise. At the heart of both is the beginning of a pattern of official opposition to air power that stymied its advocates right up to the eve of the creation of the Air Force in 1947.

It was not until 1861, in the first months of the Civil War, that the US Army first enlisted the services of aeronauts and their 'bags of air.' Among them were John Wise, who volunteered his services again: this time his offer was accepted. Another balloonist, James Allen, was also enlisted and both were placed at

Far left: Benjamin Franklin was the first American statesman to see a future in air power.

Above: The French Aerostatic Corps in action at Fleurus, Belgium in 1794. It was air power's first application in warfare.

the disposal of General Irvin McDowell. Mishaps plagued their first operations, but Wise succeeded in observing Confederate lines and obtained useful reconnaissance information on 24 July in the wake of the first Battle of Bull Run. McDowell was pleased and sent him on another scouting mission a few days later, only have the balloon break free of its moorings; it had to be shot down. Wise had now lost favor with the top brass and he threw up his hands in disgust, abandoning the balloon for a cavalry mount.

Meanwhile the flamboyant Thaddeus S C Lowe, the 29-year-old Ohio aeronaut, had made the first aerial reconnaissance behind enemy lines on 20 April, purely by accident. He was preparing for a transatlantic flight and had taken off that morning on a practice flight from Cincinnatti that took him to Unionville, South Carolina. Lowe was taken prisoner by Confederate civilians and held until someone recognized him as being *the* Thaddeus Lowe, a famous aeronaut and not a Yankee spy. He was released with a safe-conduct pass and allowed to return home across Confederate lines. Lowe decided to forgo the adventure of crossing the great water for that of serving in the great war. He offered his services and those of his balloon, *Enterprise*, to President Lincoln. Lowe was Lincoln's guest at the White House and on 18 June, in a demonstration in Washington,

Lincoln received the first telegraph message from an airship. Lowe had achieved a great milestone in the history of air power by taking his case directly to the President. Coming down strongly in favor of developing balloons for military service, Lincoln personally asked crusty General Winfield ('Old Fuss and Feathers') Scott, now commander of the Union Army, to 'See Professor Lowe . . . about his balloon.'

Scott refused Lowe's repeated attempts to see him, and it took the President's personal intervention to bring the general around. Under duress, Scott finally ordered that Lowe be given 'everything he needs to set up an aeronautical service on land and sea.' As of 19 June 1861, with James Allen's first flight, the

Balloon Corps of the Army of the Potomac was a reality, and the United States had its first air service.

On 2 August 1861, after the failed attempts of Wise and the others, Lowe and his corps were given their initial task to build the Army's first balloon, the *Union*. By 24 September Lowe was aloft with his aerial telegraph and was directing artillery fire. By the end of the year the Balloon Corps had expanded dramatically, with numerous aeronauts signed up and seven balloons – *Union, Intrepid, Eagle, Constitution, Excelsior, United States* and *Washington* – completed or on order.

Over the next two years, the aeronauts proved the practical worth of the corps, making thousands of flights (Chief Aeronaut Lowe himself made more than 3000) observing Confederate lines and directing artillery. Though successful in the field, the Balloon Corps was doomed to logistical and administrative failure. There had never been a coherent plan for its placement in the command structure. In the beginning it was attached to the Topographic Engineers, but on 31 March 1862 control was transferred to the Quartermaster Corps and a year later to the Corps of Engineers. Meanwhile there had never been a decision on the rank of the aeronauts, numerous paydays were missed, expense money became snarled in red tape and the Quartermaster Corps was prone to commandeering the Balloon Corps' horses and wagons. Because they had no specified place in the command structure, the corps always found themselves in last place in the supply line, and without any specified rank, Lowe had to scrounge supplies or dip into his own pocket. The transfer of Lowe's air service to the Engineers was really its death knell. A 40% salary cut was imposed – despite the fact that the pay-checks often didn't arrive at all. On 7 May 1863 Lowe resigned and the corps was disbanded. The war would last another two years, but the great promise shown by the nation's first air corps had receded into history.

By the mid-1880s balloon corps had found their way into the military services of all the major European Powers, but for the US Army it was officially a dead issue. It was not until General Adolphus Greely became commander of the Army Signal Corps in 1891 that things began to change. Greely, who had taken an interest in balloons, methodically researched their potential and ultimately hired carnival aeronaut William Ivy. Ivy became a sergeant and his balloon became the *General Myer*. The *General Myer* burst and was replaced with a new balloon, which was on hand when the Spanish American War broke out in 1898. Signal Corps Lieutenant-Colonel Joseph Maxfield and Sergeant Ivy were ordered to sail for Cuba with two 'Balloon Companies,' which at that time consisted of themselves and the single balloon. They arrived in Cuba with 27 men, a damaged balloon and no hydrogen generator.

Ivy repaired the balloon and it was filled with bottled hydrogen. After several tentative flights it was in position to help direct artillery fire and observe the Spanish positions during the 1st July assault on San Juan Hill. The battle was a turning point in the war, and some say that the balloon played a decisive part in the American victory by helping to direct fire and locating an alternate route of attack. There are others who claim the balloon was actually a hindrance, helping to draw fire to American positions. In any event, it was severely punctured and could not be used again.

Even as balloon flights were becoming common-place, men around the world were tinkering with the notion of powered, manned, heavier-than-air flight. Samuel Pierpont Langley of the Smithsonian Institution had been working on the problem for some years before he was able to get a steam-powered model to fly in 1896. With the moral support of both General Greely and inventor Alexander Graham Bell, Langley obtained a grant of $50,000 from the War Department in 1898 to build a full-scale, powered and manned flying machine. Charles Manly, a promising engineering student from Cornell, was commissioned to build a gasoline engine. By October 1903 the craft was ready to fly, but its first attempt, on 7 October, was unsuccessful. On 8 December they tried again, and again the vehicle crashed before it was airborne. This second failure was the end of the government's attempt to achieve heavier-than-air flight. Many who had long thought it impossible now felt vindicated.

Ironically, even as the War Department was closing its ledger book on Langley's costly mishap, the private sector was flourishing amid the icy gales that buffeted a small nowhere on the North Carolina coast called Kill Devil Hill. On 17 December 1903 a pair of bicycle shop owners from Ohio climbed that uncelebrated knoll outside the town of Kitty Hawk to try their hands at conquering the obstacles to powered flight. By the middle of that cold December day, Wilbur and Orville Wright had accomplished powered flight not once but four times, with the last trial covering 852 feet and lasting 59 seconds. For the first time in history, a manned machine had risen from the ground, traveled under its own power and landed successfully.

The British Government took an immediate interest in the experiments of the Wright brothers, to the extent of offering to

Above: General James Allen, the Signal Corps' first Air Chief (1907-13).

buy their machine in 1904. The Wrights declined, hoping instead to elicit some interest among officials in their own capital. The War Department, perhaps still smarting from the Langley affair, took a decidedly arm's-length approach to the Wrights, despite their now having made over a hundred successful flights in several machines. It was not until the Aero Club of America went directly to President Theodore Roosevelt that the Board of Ordnance and Fortification issued a Signal Corps Specification for a heavier-than-air machine on 27 December 1907.

Even as the War Department was finally negotiating with the Wrights, the long years of air-power advocacy by General Greely and his successor, Brigadier General James Allen, were coming to fruition. On 1 August 1907, Chief Signal Officer Allen signed the confidential War Department directive establishing the Aeronautical Division of the Signal Corps to oversee matters pertaining to military application of 'ballooning, air machines and all kindred subjects.' That day marked the establishment of the first permanent air service in American military history, which would evolve and change for forty years until it became, on 18 September 1947, the United States Air Force.

A PERMANENT AIR SERVICE

For several years during the Civil War, the United States had its first officially sanctioned, though short-lived, aviation service in the US Balloon Corps; it was half a century before the Aeronautical Division of the Signal Corps took its place in the roster of America's military forces. The

Left: Benny Foulois as an Air Service Captain in France, 1918. He was the Signal Corps' first pilot, learning to fly from the Wright Brothers, and later went on to serve as Chief of the US Army Air Corps between 1931 and 1935.

Right: Early air chiefs: General George Scriven, Signal Corps Air Chief from 1913 to 1917: the highly decorated General George Squier, last Signal Corps Air Chief who served between February 1917 and May 1918; General William Kenley, the first USAAS Chief who served through the peak of World War I and until 22 December 1918; and General Mason Patrick, who oversaw the transition of the US Army Air Service into the US Army Air Corps in July of 1926 (*see chart on page 8*).

Aeronautical Division would grow and change, but there was now a permanent air service. Speaking in 1982 on the 75th anniversary of the establishment of the Aeronautical Division and the 35th anniversary of the US Air Force, chief of Staff General Charles Gabriel recalled that:

In August 1907 the Army Signal Corps assigned an officer, two enlisted men, and a civilian clerk to its new Aeronautical Division. In the summers of 1908 and 1909, the Wright Flyer thrilled thousands of spectators who watched at Fort Myer as Wilbur and Orville Wright flight-tested improved versions of their 1905 model. It was not until August 1909 that the Army finally accepted "Aeroplane Number 1.' Three months later, the nation temporarily lost its total air strength when the plane crashed.

As the only officer on flying duty in early 1910 [Lieutenant Benjamin Foulois] taught himself how to fly in the only plane the Army had. Foulois received instruction from the Wrights by mail, becoming the first correspondence-school pilot in history. The Wrights later sent him an instructor to help with the hardest part . . . landing. Over the next months and years, the young air pioneers trained hard and developed tactics to turn the airplane into an effective military weapon. They did the best they could with what they had, and worked hard to show the Army and Navy how air power could contribute to joint operations.

Lieutenant Foulois, whose career grew with the new Army air arm, and who as a Major General was Chief of the Air Corps for four years in the mid-thirties, did not remain the only pilot for long. Though the Aeronautical Division started with three uniformed personnel in 1907, there was an average of 25 people in the division between 1908 and 1912; in 1913 that number was up to 114. Nevertheless, despite its invention in the United States, heavier-than-air aviation was growing much faster in

Europe than in America. In England the Royal Flying Corps had already been established, and there were many more pilots on the Continent than in the US. The fledgling birdmen in the US Army petitioned hard for an expanded service and were rewarded by an Act of Congress (2 March 1913) that authorized the Signal Corps to add pilots and to pay them at a higher scale for their time aloft. A year later the number of authorized pilots was increased again, and on 18 July 1914 the Aeronautical Division officially became the Aviation Section of the Signal Corps.

On 5 March 1913, three days after it had been authorized to expand, the Aeronautical Division had issued Field Order Number 1, establishing what was to be the First Provisional Aero Squadron. But due to a typographical error on the part of an anonymous but perhaps foresighted clerk, the word 'provisional' was not inserted. The First Aero Squadron was established at the air field near Texas City, Texas, on Galveston Bay under Captain Charles Chandler. The early Wright Pusher was soon joined in the First's inventory by the Curtiss D, the Burgess H and the Martin TT seaplane. In search of good weather in which to learn the art of flying their fragile craft, the First moved in early 1914 from the Texas Gulf Coast to San Diego, California, where the Signal Corps Aviation School was established.

Meanwhile, the Imperial Powers of nineteenth-century Europe had blustered their way to the brink of war. As these great nations dropped over the edge into the seething cauldron of 20th-century warfare, their forces included pilots and their flying machines for the first time. While there were more aeroplanes per se in France, the Germans had a larger air force – 500 aircraft, more than double the number available to the Royal Flying Corps. The Aviation Section had fewer than 20.

As millions of men went to war under the withering firepower of enormous fighting machines on Europe's center stage, the United States was being drawn into a brushfire war in its own backyard, reminiscent of the Indian wars of fifty years before. A Mexican bandit turned revolutionary and folk hero, Francisco 'Pancho' Villa, had recently been ousted after two years as dictator of Mexico and was riding with his outlaw gang in Northern Mexico. Since the United States had recognized the new government formed by his former cohort Carranza, Pancho Villa had no qualms about occasionally crossing the border on one of his raids. On 8 March 1916 he came north on a raid against the town of Columbus, New Mexico, in which 17 Americans were killed. The War Department promptly ordered General John J 'Blackjack' Pershing, commanding the Presidio of San Francisco, to proceed south and form a military expedition to capture the legendary *bandito*. Among the forces placed at Pershing's disposal was the First Aero Squadron, back in Texas at Fort Sam Houston and commanded by Major Benny Foulois. America's first air squadron was going into its first conflict, albeit in an observatory role. The eight Curtiss JN-2s and JN-3s of the First arrived in Columbus three days after the Villa raid and were ordered south into Mexico. On the flight to Casas Grandes,

about a hundred miles south of the border, two of the 'Jennys' crashed and the others, already the worse for wear, ran afoul of sandstorms that seriously jeopardized their airworthiness. Moreover, the Villa gang was holed up in the 12,000-foot mountains of the high Sonora desert plateau country, an altitude at which the JN-3s could not function. When the Pershing expedition ended five months later, the results of America's first 'air war' were disappointing. Pancho Villa was still at large, and the only two JN-3s to come out of Mexico were written off as no longer safe. Nevertheless, the First Aero Squadron had logged 346 hours on 540 courier and reconnaissance missions.

Less than a year later the United States was pulled into the Great War in Europe – World War I. While air combat over the Continental trenches and steppes had developed into something of an art, the Aviation Section was scarcely better equipped than it had been a year earlier for the foray into Mexico. Of more than 1100 men in the section, only 35 were pilots. The inventory of fewer than 300 planes did not include a single combat aircraft. The United States faced the reality of going to war with an enemy far superior in aviation technology, and changes would have to be made quickly. From the creation of the Aeronautical Division in 1907 through the time of the Mexican incursion, the US Army

had spent a little more than half a million dollars on aviation. On 24 July 1917, three and a half months after the declaration of war, President Woodrow Wilson signed the Aviation Act of 1917, which budgeted over six hundred million dollars for military aviation. This huge increase in spending bolstered not only the Aviation Section, but the American aircraft industry as well. While manufacturers geared up, the Army sent Colonel Raynal Bolling to Europe for a first-hand look at what would be required of the air units joining the American forces. What he saw was American pilots flying French and British planes of a type superior to what American industry could design and produce in the limited time available. Thus it was decided that the United States would not build pursuit aircraft, but would concentrate on trainers and reconnaissance planes while American fighter pilots flew SPADs and Nieuports. The principal aircraft produced in the US during this period were the Curtiss JN-4, a descendant of the planes Foulois had flown into the Sonora Desert, and the British-designed de Havilland DH-4, built in America by license.

On 24 May 1918, six weeks after American pilots shot down ther first enemy aircraft in combat, the Army decided to take its air arm out from under the wing of the Signal Corps and make it a new unit equal in importance in the military organization. The

Below: The Curtiss JN series 'Jennys' were the first aircraft to be built in large numbers for the Signal Corps.

US Army Air Service was born. The first Commander of the USAAS, Major General William Kenley, himself a pilot, now held a rank equivalent to that of his old boss, Chief Signal Corps Officer Major General George Squier.

While Kenley was attending to his new duties in Washington, the star of his field commanders was on the rise. When General John Pershing of Pancho Villa campaign fame, now commander of the American Expeditionary Forces, arrived in France, he had on his advisory board as air officer a young major named Billy Mitchell, who was to become one of the most outspoken advocates of the air-power doctrine in the postwar years. Mitchell soon became Air Commander for the Zone of Advance, and by October 1918 was a Brigadier General and Chief of the Air Service for the entire Army Group. Throughout the period, as American air power grew steadily, Mitchell continued to press for a more vigorous use of that power in an offensive or strategic way. Pershing steadfastly continued to think of air power (beyond the dog-fighting air-superiority role) as supportive of ground offensives, rather than as an offensive force in itself.

In the air-superiority role, American pilots were riding the crest of the battle tide now running in favor of the Allies. In all, American aviators shot down only 781 enemy aircraft and 73 balloons, but among them were some standouts. Twenty-two of the 71 American aces had more than ten victories, and Captain Eddie Rickenbacker of the famous 94th ('Hat in the Ring') Aero Squadron scored 26. By the end of the war, 11 November 1918, the personnel strength of America's air arm had increased from 311 two years before to 195, 023 – an increase of over 6000%!

The halcyon days of 1918 were not to last. America was determined that the Great War was indeed to be the 'war to end all wars' and disarmed accordingly. The isolationists prevailed. The League of Nations, an idea carefully conceived and nurtured by President Wilson, was embraced by the world but rejected by Congress at home. The domestic aircraft industry went into a tail-spin, as vast quantities of surplus Army Jennies were dumped on the civilian market. The Air Service remained intact, but its strength in 1919 had fallen to only 13% of its wartime peak, though it was still considerably ahead of prewar levels.

On the other hand, among those 9050 men who remained in 1920 were a hard core of young officers who had come out of the war convinced that air power represented the future of American military might. The staunchest advocate was Billy Mitchell. Mitchell and like-minded airmen had some important allies in the Secretary of War's Cromwell Commission, which proposed, after a careful study of the recent air war, that a separate air force on a par with the Army and Navy should be created, as Britain had done in June 1918 when the Royal Flying Corps became the Royal Air Force. But opposition was enormous. The Navy saw its battleships as the nation's first line of defense, and would

tolerate no competition for that role from bombers. General Pershing's own commission on the question agreed with the general that air power should stay under Army control. Secretary of War Baker concurred, but authorized an expansion of the Air Service and better flight pay. He also ordered that Air Service squadron commanders, some of whom were still cavalry officers, must all be pilots.

Mitchell, now Assistant Chief of the Air Service, wanted more. Air Service units were still subordinate to Army field commanders, and he wanted them independent. While the War and Navy Departments were intransigent, public attention was attracted to the flamboyant Mitchell, who had become something of a celebrity. Congress was also intrigued and compelled the reluctant Navy to allow Mitchell a chance to prove his claim – which the Navy disputed – that Air Service bombers could sink a battleship. The Navy organized tests in which Mitchell's bombers attacked some captured German ships, including the battleship *Ostfriesland*, off the mouth of Chesapeake Bay. Mitchell's bombers sank the ship, but the War and Navy De-

partments were unmoved. Additional experiments two years later were also successful, and Mitchell became more and more outspoken, while the military establishment grew increasingly irritated with him. In September 1925, in the wake of the tragic crash of the airship *Shenandoah*, Mitchell accused the authorities of 'criminal negligence.' This was about all they could take from the plucky Mitchell. He was promptly court-martialed, convicted and suspended from duty for five years. Air power's foremost prophet became its foremost martyr. Mitchell resigned his commission and devoted himself, until his death in February 1936, to the crusade for air power through the public press.

While Mitchell was in the headlines, others were at work behind the scenes, refining air tactics and building a professional service within a service. In December 1925, the same month that Mitchell was convicted by court-martial, the Lambert Congressional Committee called for the establishment of a single Defense Department combining the US Army, Navy and Air Force as coequals. At the same time the Morrow Board, appointed by President Calvin Coolidge, also turned in its report,

which rejected the notion of a separate air force, but did advocate that the Air Service be upgraded to Corps status, with the appointment of an Assistant Secretary of War for Air. On 2 July 1926 Congress passed the Air Corps Act creating the US Army Air Corps, with General Staff representation and an increased budget designed to bring USAAC strength to 1800 aircraft and 20,000 men in five years. Since the demobilization peak of 1919, the Air Service had never had more than 11,649 men in uniform (1921); the new Air Corps began with only 9674. Personnel strength would increase steadily, but it would be twelve years before it topped 20,000.

In December 1931 Major General Benjamin Foulois, the Army's first pilot and a long-time advocate of air power, became Chief of the Air Corps. Soft-spoken where Billy Mitchell had been outspoken, he began to lobby for more Air Corps autonomy. In 1934 the Baker Board joined a long line of commissions to take up the question of a separate air force and report in favor of the status quo. A notable voice of dissent on the Baker Board was that of Shell Oil Company executive and pilot James Doolittle, whose air-power stance would be confined eight years later in the skies over Tokyo. The Baker Board did, however, support the notion of establishing a General Headquarters Air Force to centralize command of the Air Corps, rather than having its command structure entangled with that of ground forces. The GHQ Air Force was established at Langley Field, Virginia, under command of Brigadier General Frank Andrews, in charge of all tactical Air Corps units; authority for training and logistics remained under control of General Foulois as Chief of USAAC. This arrangement was not without a potential for interservice conflict, since the GHQ commander did not have direct control of his training and supply services. The situation would not be resolved for another four years, by which time the Air Corps and the nation were facing a far more serious threat from without.

With the Czechoslovakian crisis of mid-1938, the eyes of the world were focused on Germany and her military might. In a few short years Germany had gone from a defeated and demoralized empire, beset by anarchy and hyperinflation, to a prosperous and highly ordered society with a military force that seemed second to none. Special attention was focused on the German Air Force, the Luftwaffe, with its modern aircraft and prestigious position within the German command structure. In his January 1939 message to Congress, President Franklin D Roosevelt, the former Navy Secretary, remarked on this and cited the need to expand the capabilities of America's Air Corps, which now ranked sixth in strength among the world's air forces. Eight months later the Germans put their Luftwaffe to the practical test in Poland, and the world teetered into the abyss of the 20th century's second world war.

The Luftwaffe was instrumental in the attack against Poland and, half a year later, on Scandinavia and Benelux. When France fell on 22 June 1940, and Germany squared off against England in the Battle of Britain, the role of air power in modern warfare was no longer theoretical: official attitudes toward it changed overnight. Though there was still some isolationist opposition, the prevailing mood favored a rapid expansion of American air power. All Europe seemed doomed to fall under the shadow of the swastika, and there was a strong sense of urgency. General Henry H 'Hap' Arnold, now Chief of the Air Corps, found himself in the position not of having to beg for men and planes, but rather of being begged to demand more of them. In 1938, when Arnold took command of the Air Corps, personnel strength stood at 21,089. Two years later it had more than doubled, and by December 1941 it had increased nearly seventeenfold to 354,000. During the same period the number of bases more than quintupled and training facilities proliferated, as did (with generous new tax advantages) aircraft factories in the private sector. At the time France fell in June 1940, military aircraft production in the United States stood at a little more than 400 units per month. By the end of 1941 the figure was up to 2464 and rising. Of the 22,077 planes produced during the period, 6756 went to Britain, 4034 to the US Navy and 9932 to the Air Corps. It was just the beginning, however belated.

AN AUTONOMOUS AIR SERVICE

In early 1941, with the frenetic growth in size and activities of the Air Corps, there was a clear need for organizational changes. General Arnold found in Army Chief of Staff General George Marshall a leader more willing than his predecessors to allow a measure of independence. On 20 June 1941, under the War Powers Act of 1941, President Roosevelt signed the executive order permitting Marshall to create the US Army Air Forces – an autonomous, if not independent, air arm, with

Arnold as chief. Six months later Arnold's position was changed to Commanding General, USAAF, and he gained a seat on the Joint Chiefs of Staff and the Allied Combined Chiefs of Staff. Meanwhile, Secretary of War Henry Stimson appointed Robert Lovett to the long-vacant post of Assistant Secretary of War for Air. By executive order, the new autonomy was designed to last only until six months after cessation of hostilities, but neither Marshall nor Arnold saw it as anything but permanent. Hap Arnold now commanded an organization still closer to the kind of air force envisioned by the earlier air-power pioneers.

General Headquarters Air Force came back under direct control of the Air Corps Chief. Tactical and Air Defense units in the continental United States were divided geographically into four numbered Air Forces, with the First and Second in the northeast and northwest quadrants of the country and the Third and Fourth in the southwest and southeast. Separate Commands similar to the Commands of today's US Air Force were established to oversee such duties as training and maintenance, while the Ferry Command supervised delivery of lend-lease aircraft to Britain.

Among the other subsidiary commands of the USAAF were regional commands in US possessions in the Pacific. The Hawaiian Air Force was established in November 1940, and a year later the Far East Air Force was set up in the Commonwealth of the Philippines. When the Japanese launched the surprise air attacks against Hawaii and the Philippines on 7 and 8 December 1941 that brought the United States into World War II, these Commands bore the brunt of the initial attack. While the US Naval base at Pearl Harbor was the primary target in the attack on Hawaii, Hickam, Bellows and Wheeler Army Air Fields were also high on the list. Across the Pacific in the Philippines, Clark Field was a primary objective of Japanese raiders.

Throughout the 18 months prior to December 1941, the USAAC/USAAF had grown and expanded at a far greater rate than could have been imagined just a few years earlier, but faced with a global war, the pressure was on to grow even faster. As operations spread around the world, the idea of numbered air forces, previously used only in the continental United States, was extended to USAAF tactical forces worldwide. The Far East Air Force, which had relocated to Australia when the Japanese captured the Philippines, was redesignated the Fifth Air Force and the Hawaiian Air Force became the Seventh. When USAAF strength increased in the Western Pacific in 1944, the Thirteenth, born in the jungles of the Solomon Islands and nicknamed the Jungle Air Force, combined with the Fifth under the Far East Air Forces, into which the Seventh would also be incorporated. Within the Far East Command, the Thirteenth was assigned to Guadalcanal and the Solomons; the Fifth directed its attention westward toward New Guinea and the Philippines, with the objective of recapturing Clark Field north of Manila, its former home base and now the major Japanese air base for the entire region.

For the Hawaii-based Seventh, it was the island-hopping campaign in the vastness of the Central and Western Pacific. Picking themselves up from the humiliation of Pearl Harbor, the Seventh took part in the victory at Midway and helped spearhead the drive up through the Marshall Islands, the Carolines, the Marianas, Iwo Jima and ultimately Japan itself.

A month after the United States entered the war, the USAAF began to establish units in Europe for conduct of the war against Germany. The Eighth Air Force was established in England, where it merged with the RAF Bomber Command to form the Allied Strategic Air Forces that conducted the strategic air offensive against Germany and Occupied Europe. The Ninth Air

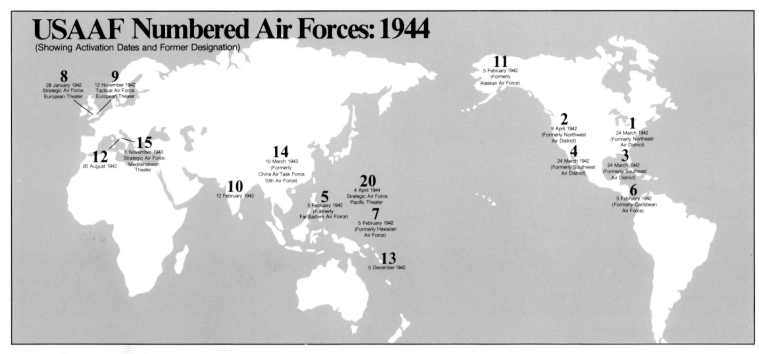

USAAF Numbered Air Forces: 1944
(Showing Activation Dates and Former Designation)

11
5 February 1942
(Formerly
Alaskan Air Force)

8
28 January 1942
Strategic Air Force,
European Theater

9
12 November 1942
Tactical Air Force,
European Theater

15
1 November 1943
Strategic Air Force,
Mediterranean
Theater

12
20 August 1942

14
10 March 1943
(Formerly
China Air Task Force,
10th Air Force)

10
12 February 1942

20
4 April 1944
Strategic Air Force,
Pacific Theater

5
5 February 1942
(Formerly
Far Eastern Air Force)

7
5 February 1942
(Formerly Hawaiian
Air Force)

13
5 December 1942

2
9 April 1942
(Formerly Northwest
Air District)

1
24 March 1942
(Formerly Northeast
Air District)

4
24 March 1942
(Formerly Southwest
Air District)

3
24 March 1942
(Formerly Southeast
Air District)

6
5 February 1942
(Formerly Caribbean
Air Force)

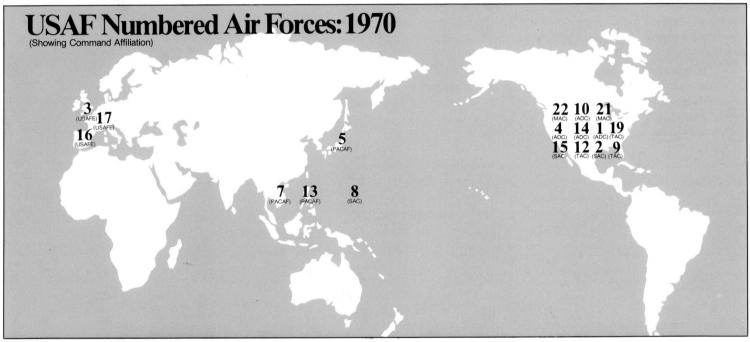

USAF Numbered Air Forces: 1970
(Showing Command Affiliation)

3
(USAFE)

17
(USAFE)

16
(USAFE)

5
(PACAF)

7
(PACAF)

13
(PACAF)

8
(SAC)

22
(MAC)

10
(ADC)

21
(MAC)

4
(ADC)

14
(ADC)

1
(ADC)

19
(TAC)

15
(SAC)

12
(TAC)

2
(SAC)

9
(TAC)

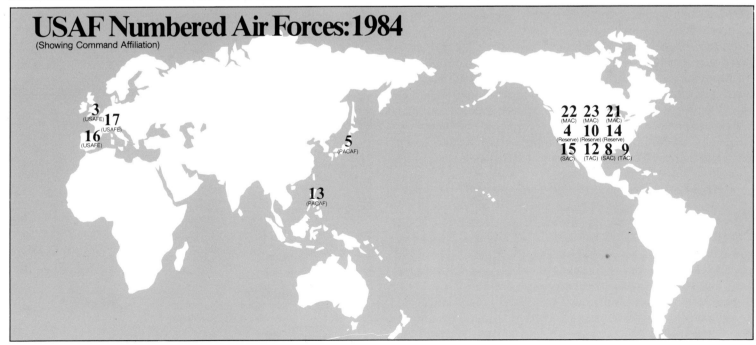

USAF Numbered Air Forces: 1984
(Showing Command Affiliation)

3
(USAFE)

17
(USAFE)

16
(USAFE)

5
(PACAF)

13
(PACAF)

22
(MAC)

23
(MAC)

21
(MAC)

4
(Reserve)

10
(Reserve)

14
(Reserve)

15
(SAC)

12
(TAC)

8
(SAC)

9
(TAC)

Left: A Martin B-26 Marauder medium bomber of the Twelfth Air Force over St Tropez, France during Operation *Anvil* in August 1944. The Twelfth was born in the North African desert and went on to serve in Italy and France.

Below: General Arnold and General Chennault inspect some of the latter's shark-faced Curtiss P-40s in China during General Arnold's round-the-world inspection tour in 1943. Chennault's China Air Task Force was first attached to the Tenth Air Force, but became the Fourteenth Air Force in March 1943.

Force joined the RAF Middle East in Egypt to form the Allied Middle East Air Forces. Across North Africa the Twelfth Air Force was formed from components of the Eighth when it joined the RAF to form the Northwest Africa Air Forces. While the Twelfth remained in the Mediterranean Theater, following the Allied advance to Sicily and then Italy, the Ninth moved to England where it became the tactical complement to the strategic Eighth Air Force. The Ninth went on to play a key role in the Normandy invasion in June 1944 and in maintaining air supremacy over the battlefields of Western Europe until the end of the war.

With the strategic bombing campaign underway from England involving the RAF Bomber Command and the USAAF Eighth Air Force, a new Strategic Air Force, the Fifteenth, was established in Italy. Its role was to conduct a campaign against targets in Italy, Southern Germany, Southern France, Austria and other targets like the huge petroleum complex at Ploesti, Rumania.

On the far side of the world in the Asian subcontinent, the Tenth Air Force was being formed. Major General Lewis Brereton, late of the retreating Far East Air Force, arrived in Ceylon in February 1942 with six planes and some currency wrapped in an army blanket, to establish the Tenth Air Force as the USAAF operating Command for the China/Burma/India Theater. In the least publicized theater of the war, the Tenth attacked Japanese positions in the jungles and rivers of Southeast Asia, frequently striking targets in and around Rangoon and Bangkok. As the Allied advance into Burma began in 1943, the Tenth was overhead providing cover. Through it all one of the most difficult ongoing air operations in the theater, and perhaps in the entire war, was the Air Transport Command airlift of supplies supported by the Tenth from India over the Himalayas to China. The 'Hump,' as it came to be known, was one of the most treacherous air routes in the world and a supply link vital to maintaining operations in China.

Across the Hump in China, American pilots had been fighting the Japanese since before Pearl Harbor as members of the American Volunteer Group under Brigadier General Claire Chennault. The AVG, better known as the 'Flying Tigers' because of their shark's-mouth-decorated P-40s, had been the first real threat to the Japanese since they invaded China in the thirties. Though overwhelmingly outnumbered, the Flying Tigers exacted a severe toll in men and planes from the frustrated Japanese by flying hit-and-run, guerrilla-style missions, catching the enemy off guard.

Below: A playful P-38 Lightning flirts with a formation of B-17 Flying Fortress heavy bombers.

Right: 'Finito Benito, Next Hirohito' reads the slogan painted on the back of this Fifteenth Air Force B-25 Mitchell medium bomber seen over the Gulf of Naples in 1944. The reference is to Italian dictator Benito Mussolini, whose demise was imminent, and Japanese emperor Hirohito, whose empire would be gone the following year but who would survive another four decades.

Bottom: One of General Hoyt Vandenberg's Ninth Air Force P-47 Thunderbolts on a snow-covered runway in France during the winter of 1944-45. A top fighter-bomber, the P-47 dropped 113,963 tons of bombs as against 20,139 dropped by the second-place P-38.

GENERAL HENRY HARLEY ARNOLD
USAAF Commanding General during World War II

'Hap' Arnold was born on 25 June 1886 in Gladwyn, Pennsylvania, and served as Commander of the US Army Air Corps and the US Army Air Forces between 29 September 1938 and 28 February 1946. During his tenure, Arnold saw the USAAF through all of World War II and ended it presiding over the largest air force in history.

Graduating from the US Military Academy at West Point on 14 June 1907, Arnold's first assignment was with the 29th Infantry in the Philippine Islands. He returned to the United States in October 1909 and served at Governor's Island, New York, until April 1911, when he was assigned to the Aeronautical Division of the Signal Corps and sent to Dayton, Ohio, for flight training in the Wright Flyer. Upon completing his training, he became a flight instructor at the Signal Corps Aviation School at College Park Maryland. On 1 June 1912 he established a new altitude record of 6540 feet in a Burgess-Wright aircraft. After another tour in the Philippines (1913-16) he was sent to the Panama Canal Zone in February 1917 to help organize a pursuit squadron for the defense of the Canal. When World War I broke out in Europe, he was brought to Washington and placed in charge of the Information Service of the Signal Corps Aviation Division. In February 1918, with the temporary rank of Colonel, he became Executive Officer and later Assistant to the Director of Military Aeronautics. After the war he became Supervisor of the US Army Air Service Western District at Coronado, California.

On 30 May 1919 Arnold became Air Officer of the Ninth Corps Area based at the Presidio of San Francisco; on 30 June 1920 he was promoted to a permanent rank of Captain. In 1925 he became Chief of the Information Division of the Office of the Chief of the Air Service in Washington. The creation of the US Army Air Corps on 2 July 1926 found Captain Arnold in command of the Air Corps detachment at Marshall Field, Fort Riley, Kansas; on 1 February 1931 he was promoted to Lieutenant Colonel and became Commanding Officer of March Field near Riverside, California. Between 19 July and 20 August 1934, he led a ten-plane bomber squadron from Washington, DC, to Fairbanks, Alaska, a difficult feat for that era and one for which Arnold was awarded the Distinguished Flying Cross.

On 11 January 1936 he left March Field to become Assistant Chief of the USAAC in Washington, and two months later was promoted to the permanent rank of Colonel. Two years later (29 September 1938) he became Chief of the USAAC and Deputy Chief of Staff for Air, with the temporary rank of Major General. With creation of the US Army Air Forces on 20 June 1941, he became Chief of the USAAF with permanent rank of Major General. On 9 March 1942 his title was changed to Commanding General, USAAF. He was promoted to the temporary rank of General (four star) on 19 March 1943 and to General of the Army (five stars) on 21 December 1944. The four-star rank was made permenant on 23 March 1946, and on 7 May 1949, by Act of Congress, he became the first and only permanent General of the Air Force.

During World War II General Arnold sat on the Joint Chiefs of Staff as commander of the nearly two-and-a-half-million-man USAAF. In 1942 he received the Distinguished Service Medal for his command of a 77-hour flight from Bolling Field, DC, through the war-torn South Pacific to Brisbane, Australia. In early 1943 he made a 35,000-mile, globe-circling inspection tour of the world's battlefronts, from North Africa through the Middle East to India, China and the Pacific. During this tour he joined President Roosevelt in attending the unconditional surrender conference at Casablanca, where he also received the decoration *Ouissam Alaovite* from the Sultan of Morocco. After World War II he turned command of the USAAF over to his deputy, General Carl Spaatz, on 28 February 1946. He returned from the service on 30 June 1946 and moved to Sonoma County, California, where he died on 15 January 1950.

During his career, Hap Arnold was awarded the MacKay Trophy for outstanding achievements in aviation in 1912 and again in 1934. He received the Distinguished Flying Cross in 1936 and the Distinguished Service Medal in 1942. Two Oak Leaf Clusters were added to the latter in 1945, in recognition of his wartime leadership and contribution to the war effort. In addition to these decorations, he received the World War II Victory Medal, three theater ribbons and foreign decorations and awards from Brazil, England, France, Mexico, Morocco, Peru, and Yugoslavia. General Arnold was also the author of a number of books on aviation, including *The Bill Bruce Series* (1928), *Air Men and Aircraft* (1929), *This Flying Game* (with General Ira Eaker, 1936), *Winged Warfare* (1941), *Army Flyer* (1942) and *Global Mission* (1949).

Because they were initially cut off from the outside world, the AVG continued to operate independently of the USAAF for over six months after the United States entered the war. On 4 July 1942 the AVG was incorporated into the slightly larger China Air Task Force, part of the Tenth Air Force. With American markings instead of Chinese, and with a more regular flow of supplies, Chennault's Flying Tigers continued to pick away at the Japanese. Finally, in March 1943, the CATF was sufficiently supplied and equipped to be upgraded to numbered status; it was redesignated the Fourteenth Air Force. For the duration, when other commands were achieving numerical superiority in their theaters, the Fourteenth fought as an underdog. While the Japanese were losing in the Pacific, the Fourteenth tenaciously harassed them in China. Often fighting from improvised bases spread across a rugged 5000-mile front, the Fourteenth constantly disrupted rail and boat traffic along the coasts of Japanese-occupied China. In the skies over the vast Asian mainland, the Fourteenth shot down nearly eight enemy aircraft for every one they lost.

While the United States was bent on taking the war to the enemy, concern grew about possible enemy action against the US and its possessions. With German U-Boats active in the Caribbean, and the probability of another air attack like that on Pearl Harbor, the Panama Canal was particularly vulnerable. Air units had been based in the Canal Zone since 1917. In fact, young Hap Arnold, then a captain, had commanded a pursuit squadron at the Atlantic entrance in 1917. Because of the canal's strategic importance, the Air Corps had created the Panama Canal Air Force in October 1940 (changed to the Caribbean Air Force in August 1941); in February 1942 it became the Sixth Air Force. The Sixth became active not only in defense of the canal but in antisubmarine warfare. Later in the war, it conducted tactical training in the Canal Zone for the USAAF as well as various Latin American air forces, particularly that of Brazil.

In Alaska the new Alaskan Air Force became the Eleventh Air Force, joining land and naval forces of both the United States and Canada in defense of Alaska and in retaking the Aleutian Islands that had been occupied by the Japanese. In July 1943 Eleventh Air Force bombers based in the liberated Aleutians launched the first land-based air attacks on Japanese territory with raids on the northern Kurile Islands. Plans to use the Alaska-based Eleventh for the strategic air offensive against Japan were shelved in favor of using the newly formed Twentieth Air Force operating from the Marianas Islands in the Pacific,

where the weather was far more conducive to air operations.

The Twentieth Air Force was activated on 4 April 1944 for the sole purpose of conducting the strategic air offensive against Japan. The Twentieth was the only USAAF component to receive the giant Boeing B-29 Very Heavy Bomber. The B-29 Stratofortress was the largest strategic bomber ever built, with a far greater range than any other. It had been one of Hap Arnold's pet projects since the late thirties when earlier, smaller heavy bombers were barely off the drawing boards; now it was a reality. Arnold's objective was to use the B-29 to demonstrate that a major world power, Japan, could be defeated by air power. Arnold felt that a strategic offensive using B-29s would negate the need for the planned invasion of Japan. The Twentieth Air Force was unlike the other fifteen in that it reported directly (via Arnold) to the Joint Chiefs of Staff, rather than being under the operational control of a theater commander. This was by design: Arnold intended the organization to be prototypical for the postwar Air Force he envisioned. By the early months of 1945, the Twentieth had inflicted severe damage on the Japanese home islands and on the nation's war economy. In August the Twentieth made history as the only unit ever to use nuclear weapons in wartime.

Above: The crew of the Eighth Air Force B-17 Flying Fortress 'Hell's Angels' after the plane's 31st mission over Europe.

Below: After 48 missions, 'Hell's Angels' had downed 18 German fighters.

Top: General Spaatz (seated, center) at his headquarters with Generals Ralph Royce (note his RAF wings), Hoyt Vandenberg and Hugh Knerr.

Above: Ninth Air Force Commander Vandenberg during a press conference at his field headquarters in northern France, 1944.

AIR-POWER COMMAND AND THE USAAF

In 1942, despite the reorganization that accompanied creation of the USAAF, the Army Field Manual still called for air units under operational control of the ground-force commander. The inherent fallacy in this directive, which would not be fully recognized until the USAAF got into combat, was that it disallowed the need to gain air superiority over the theater of operations. It can be said, as indeed it has, that the fundamental basis for the organization of air power in a theater came out of the first American experiences over the sands of North Africa in the fall of 1942. At that time the Twelfth Air Force, organized as an Air Support Command, was assigned to the Second American Corps to cover the invasion of Northwest Africa. The British had assigned RAF 242 Group to support their First Army. At the same time, Egypt-based units of the RAF and the USAAF were not co-ordinated with those in Northwest Africa. The Luftwaffe on the other hand, despite serious supply problems, was well organized and a serious adversary. Because they were attempting to provide ground support before gaining air superiority, Allied planes were easy pickings for the Germans and consequently failed in their ground-support mission as well.

Losses both on the ground and in the air were severe, and Allied air commanders went to work formalizing a new command structure. It was presented at the Casablanca Conference in January 1942 and approved by President Roosevelt and Prime Minister Churchill. The cornerstone of the new structure was creation of a single unified air command for the entire Mediterranean Theater. The air commander would be RAF Air Marshal Arthur Tedder; under him the newly unified Northwest African

GENERAL CARL ARTHUR SPAATZ
Second USAAF Commanding General, First USAF Chief of Staff

Carl 'Tooey' Spaatz was born on 28 June 1891 in Boyertown, Pennsylvania, and served as Commanding General of the US Army Air Forces and as the first Chief of Staff of the US Air Force between 1 March 1946 and 29 April 1948. He graduated from the US Military Academy at West Point in June 1914 and was assigned to the 25th Infantry at Schofield Barracks, Hawaii, until 13 October 1915 when he was transferred to the Signal Corps Aviation School at San Diego. In June 1916, just after completing his flight training, Spaatz was assigned to the First Aero Squadron which was being sent into Mexico under General John J Pershing to track down the Mexican bandit Pancho Villa. In May 1917 he was promoted to Captain and assigned to the Third Aero Squadron in San Antonio, Texas. With the active entry of the United States into World War I, Spaatz went to France as Commander of the 31st Aero Squadron. On 15 November he was assigned to the American Aviation School at Issoudin where he served continuously, except for a month on the British Front, until 30 August 1918. In September he joined the Second Pursuit Squadron as a pursuit pilot and flight leader; serving in combat for barely two months he managed to shoot down three German Fokkers and was awarded the Distinguished Service Cross.

After the war Captain Spaatz served in California and Texas, becoming Assistant Air Service Officer for the Western Department in July 1919. On 1 July 1920 he was promoted to Major and placed in command of Kelly Field, Texas, on 5 October of the same year; he served there until February 1921. Then he became commander of the First Pursuit Group at Ellington Field, Texas, and later at Selfridge Field, Michigan, until 24 September 1924. In June 1925, after graduating from the Air Corps Tactical School, Langley Field, Virginia, he was assigned to the Office of the Chief of the Air Corps in Washington. In January 1929 Spaatz commanded the aircraft *Question Mark*, which set an endurance record of 150 hours 50 minutes by means of aerial refuelling, for which he was awarded the Distinguished Service Cross.

Between May 1929 and June 1933, in a transition from fighters to bombers, Spaatz served as commander of the Seventh Bombardment Group and later the First Bombardment Wing at Rockwell and March Field in California. On 10 June 1933, he became Chief of the Air Corps Training and Operations Division. He enrolled in the Command and General Staff School at Fort Leavenworth, Kansas, in August 1935 and emerged the following June as a Lieutenant Colonel. In November 1939, with the temporary rank of Colonel, he was sent to Britain as a special military observer.

In January 1942 with the temporary rank of Major General he was assigned as Chief of the USAAF Combat Command in Washington. In May 1942 he became commander of the Eighth Air Force and was transferred to England to prepare for the American strategic bombing of Germany. On 1 December 1942, with the permanent rank of Colonel, Spaatz took command of the Twelfth Air Force in North Africa. Three months later, with the temporary rank of Lieutenant General, he assumed command of the Northwest African Air Force, which incorporated the Twelfth. After the Germans had been driven out of North Africa and the invasion of Italy was launched, General Spaatz became deputy commander of the Mediterranean Allied Air Forces, incorporating both the Twelfth and Fifteenth Air Forces.

In January 1944 he returned to England as Commander of the US Strategic Air Forces in Europe, presiding over the strategic air offensive against Germany until that country's defeat. After a brief assignment in Washington, Spaatz was, in June 1945, named commander of the US Strategic Air Forces in the Pacific, where he served during the final two months of the strategic air offensive against Japan. He received the temporary rank of four-star General on 11 March 1945, and was one of few officers present at all three signings of unconditional surrender documents by the enemy – at Rheims, Berlin and Tokyo. In October 1945, with the permanent rank of Major General, he returned to USAAF Headquarters. On 1 March 1946 he became Commanding General of the USAAF, and with the creation of the independent US Air Force, he became its first Chief of Staff on 26 September 1947, serving until 29 April 1948. He retired from the service on 30 June 1948 as a four-star General and became a contributing editor at *Newsweek* Magazine. He died on 14 July 1974.

During his career, General Spaatz was awarded the Distinguished Flying Cross, the Distinguished Service Cross, the Distinguished Service Medal, the Mexican Interior Campaign Ribbon, the World War I ribbon with three bronze battle stars, the European, Pacific and American theater ribbons and the World War II Victory ribbon. His foreign decorations included the French Croix de Guerre, Grand Commander of the British Empire, Russia's Second Order of Suvorov and Poland's *Polonia Restituta* Commander's Cross with Star.

Air Force would be commanded by USAAF General Carl 'Tooey' Spaatz, then commander of the US Twelfth Air Force. Units could now be distributed and deployed where they were most needed.

The first order of business for the new Northwest Africa Air Forces was air superiority. No longer shackled by the old command structure, the NAAF was able to exploit enemy weaknesses. With control of all air units, Spaatz could shift them in any level of concentration to wherever they were most needed. Ultimately, unified command of air power proved decisive in the battle over North Africa. It was the Germans' turn to feel the brunt of well-organized air power.

If North Africa was the proving ground for the practical application of tactical air power, Operation *Overlord*, 18 months later, would provide an opportunity for integrating tactical and strategic air power against a single enemy. Germany had designed and built what it called *Festung Europa*, Fortress Europe, a theoretically impregnable wall of defenses that had kept Allied armies from setting foot on the Continent. Operation *Overlord*, the Allied attempt to breach those defenses with an invasion of northern France, would be the biggest operation of its type ever

undertaken, calling for precise integration of vast land, sea and air forces.

The outline for *Overlord* was drawn up at the Quebec Conference by President Roosevelt and Prime Minister Churchill in August 1943. The plan called for direction by a single Supreme Commander of the Allied Expeditionary Force who would be, despite some reservations on the part of the British, an American. General Marshall, the American Chief of Staff, was the first choice, but Roosevelt felt that he was indispensable in his current post. General Dwight D Eisenhower, who had been supreme commander for the Operation *Torch* landings in North Africa, was named Commander in Chief of Supreme Headquarters, Allied Expeditionary Force (SHAEF). With an American in the top job, the British wanted one of their officers as deputy commander. Eisenhower, to his credit, recognized the importance of air power's role in the operation and selected Air Marshal Arthur Tedder.

Until the spring of 1944 the Allied Strategic Air Forces based in England (RAF Bomber Command and USAAF Eighth Air Force) had conducted an intensifying strategic offensive against targets in the German heartland. The nature of strategic opera-

34

Above: Smoke billows up from an enemy railyard struck by Fifteenth Air Force B-24s in September 1945. These aircraft dropped 452,508 tons of bombs during the war, 29 percent of the total USAAF tonnage.

Right: An Eighth Air Force, First Bombardment Wing, 351st Bombardment Group B-17 during a mission over Germany. The B-17s dropped 640,036 tons of bombs during the war, 41 percent of the total USAAF tonnage.

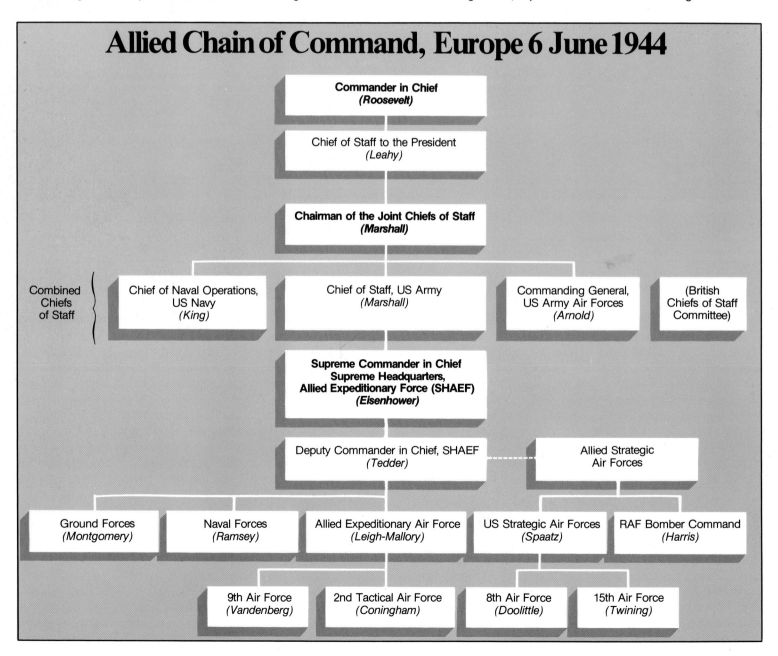

Allied Chain of Command, Europe 6 June 1944

Commander in Chief
(Roosevelt)

Chief of Staff to the President
(Leahy)

Chairman of the Joint Chiefs of Staff
(Marshall)

Combined Chiefs of Staff:

Chief of Naval Operations, US Navy *(King)*	Chief of Staff, US Army *(Marshall)*	Commanding General, US Army Air Forces *(Arnold)*	(British Chiefs of Staff Committee)

Supreme Commander in Chief
Supreme Headquarters,
Allied Expeditionary Force (SHAEF)
(Eisenhower)

Deputy Commander in Chief, SHAEF *(Tedder)* — — — Allied Strategic Air Forces

Ground Forces *(Montgomery)*	Naval Forces *(Ramsey)*	Allied Expeditionary Air Force *(Leigh-Mallory)*	US Strategic Air Forces *(Spaatz)*	RAF Bomber Command *(Harris)*

9th Air Force *(Vandenberg)*	2nd Tactical Air Force *(Coningham)*	8th Air Force *(Doolittle)*	15th Air Force *(Twining)*

Chain of Command, Pacific Theater 1945

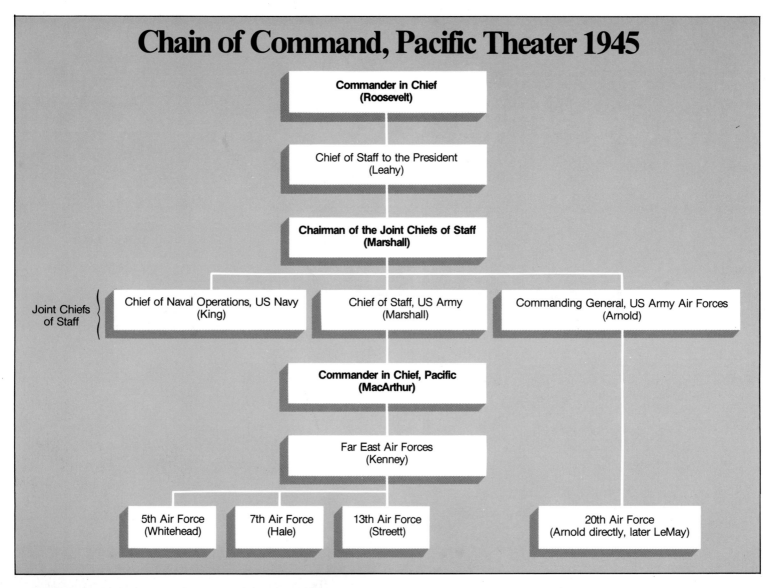

Commander in Chief
(Roosevelt)

Chief of Staff to the President
(Leahy)

Chairman of the Joint Chiefs of Staff
(Marshall)

Joint Chiefs of Staff {

| Chief of Naval Operations, US Navy (King) | Chief of Staff, US Army (Marshall) | Commanding General, US Army Air Forces (Arnold) |

Commander in Chief, Pacific
(MacArthur)

Far East Air Forces
(Kenney)

5th Air Force
(Whitehead)

7th Air Force
(Hale)

13th Air Force
(Streett)

20th Air Force
(Arnold directly, later LeMay)

Above: General Spaatz (left) confers with Far East air chief General George Kenney at the New Grand Hotel in Yokohama shortly after VJ Day.

tions is such that their effects are not seen immediately at the front – strategic targeting involves hitting an enemy's warmaking power at the source. Destruction of a tank factory does not immediately reduce the number of tanks at the front, but its effects will be felt when disabled vehicles cannot be replaced. In spring 1944 this factor was not fully understood, and the fact that bomber forces were only then getting up to strength also led observers to criticize the lack of perceptible results. Therefore, plans were laid to divert the strategic bomber force, placing it under SHAEF (Eisenhower's) control. General Spaatz, now overall commander of the US Strategic Air Forces (including both the Eighth and the Fifteenth), and Arthur Harris of RAF Bomber Command, were strongly opposed to the idea. *Overlord* would require several months of tactical bombing over northern France to pave the way for the invasion; strategic-bomber commanders did not want their planes turned into tactical weapons when they felt close to a decisive moment in the strategic offensive.

Despite objections, both Eisenhower and Arnold felt it was important for all forces to be under operational control of the Supreme Allied Commander. The plan for *Overlord* called for three tactical commanders under Eisenhower, responsible for ground, sea and air operations. The air commander would be RAF Air Marshal Leigh-Mallory, who would direct all units now designated Allied Expeditionary Air Forces (AEAF). After much consideration, with Eisenhower's favorable attitude toward independent air power and the objections of Harris and Spaatz factored in, a compromise was reached. Under the

revised plan, Leigh-Mallory would command only tactical air forces, while Eisenhower would have direct operational control over strategic air forces through his deputy, Air Marshal Tedder. When the invasion came on 6 June 1944, Tedder and Leigh-Mallory co-ordinated their efforts, with Leigh-Mallory managing all activities in the Normandy battle zone but not strategic operations removed from the immediate engagement area. In October 1944, after the Allies had established themselves in France, the AEAF was disbanded with the two tactical air forces and individual army groups placed under SHAEF command (Tedder, via Eisenhower). With SHAEF now devoting its time to control of tactical air power in support of the three Army Groups, Spaatz and Harris could devote their full resources to the strategic air offensive against the heart of the Reich.

In the Pacific the situation was similar, with General Douglas MacArthur as Supreme Commander; he had control of General George Kenney's Far East Air Force – the Fifth, Seventh and Thirteenth. When the Twentieth Air Force was introduced, however, it was not under MacArthur's tactical control, but directly under the joint Chiefs of Staff. Thus the Twentieth was the most independent US Army Air Force and a forerunner of the autonomous postwar USAF.

Above: A formation of B-29 Stratofortresses over a Japanese airfield.

When World War II began the USAAC had 23,455 men and a few hundred planes and ranked sixth in size among the air forces of the world. Five years later the USAAF had 2,372,292 men and nearly 80,000 planes; it was not only the largest air force in the world, but the largest air force the world has seen to this date.

World War II had been a war of air power. Hitler's first lightning jabs into Poland in 1939 had shown the brutal precision and effectiveness of ably wielded tactical aircraft. The USAAF Air Transport Command had demonstrated that vast quantities of material could be airlifted more quickly than transported by land or sea, to locations often inaccessible by other means, as in the case of crossing the Hump into China. Finally, the Twentieth Air Force proved, as airmen from Billy Mitchell to Hap Arnold had known, that air power could be a decisive factor in the defeat of an enemy, saving countless American lives that would otherwise have been lost.

Air power affected the tactics, strategy and logistics of World War II, and altered forever the way in which wars would be fought. The war began and ended in the skies, and ultimately the strongest air force was the USAAF.

A SEPARATE US AIR FORCE

EMERGENT US AIR FORCE INDEPENDENCE

When the Japanese delegation came aboard the battleship USS *Missouri* in Tokyo Bay on 2 September 1945 to sign the instruments of unconditional surrender, it was fitting that the sky should be filled with 435 B-29s, the planes that represented the triumph of American air power. The USAAF had proved it could play a decisive role in modern warfare. Hap Arnold could see in his mind's eye a completely independent postwar US Air Force; he had been working toward that goal since he became Chief of the US Army Air Corps in 1938, even more so since the creation of the USAAF in 1941. Throughout the war he had built up the structure and promoted the careers of those men whom he thought could perpetuate the vision.

In 1944, the same year that they had created the autonomous all-B-29 Twentieth Air Force under their own control, the Joint Chiefs of Staff had appointed a Special Committee for Reorganization of National Defense to look into the question of overall postwar command structure. In April 1945, after a year of extensive investigation, the committee recommended – as had many others over the years – that an Air Force be established on a coequal basis with the Army and Navy under a single Department of National Defense. The Navy, in the person of Committee Chairman Admiral James Richardson, dissented. The Navy sensed that as a result of long-range bombers and nuclear weapons, it was losing its former position as America's first line of defense, and feared it would lose its own air fleet as well. The loss of their cabinet-level secretary when the Navy and War

Departments merged could also put them at a disadvantage in lobbying for appropriations.

Displeased with the JCS Committee report, the Navy appointed its own commission: much to the chagrin of Navy Secretary Forrestal, it returned with the same conclusion as the JCS. Beginning with the bill introduced in January by Senator Lister Hill of Alabama, Congress considered in 1945 no fewer than eight bills calling for a single department, including one introduced in October by Senator Edwin Johnson of Colorado, which called for a single Department of Military Security with six branches.

By the end of the year the tide was running in favor of change. In November Eisenhower returned from his triumph in Europe to take the place of George Marshall, who was retiring as Army Chief of Staff. Eisenhower was a firm believer in air power and wasted no time in presenting his view that a separate and independent US Air Force should be created. By now, General Arnold's health was beginning to fail. He had suffered several heart attacks during the war and realized he would be unable to continue for long as Commanding General of the USAAF. By October General Spaatz had returned from overseas to become a Major General. He was assigned to AAF headquarters, where Arnold put him in charge of efforts to bring about the creation of a separate Air Force. Spaatz would succeed Arnold five months later as Commanding General of the USAAF, but he began taking on some of the workload immediately. He devoted his time not only to promoting an independent air force but to planning its internal structure. In the case of the latter, the

Left: General Hap Arnold was the father of the modern USAF and was the only airman to eventually wear five stars.

Above: In the wake of World War II, the B-29 was symbolic of America's unrivaled air power.

groundwork had already been laid. A year earlier Arnold had assigned Brigadier General Laurence Kuter, who had been a member of the team that designed the USAAF before the war, to set up a planning group for a unit that could succeed the USAAF as a US Air Force. Early in 1945, General Ira Eaker, who had commanded the Eighth Air Force and later the Allied Mediterranean Air Forces, joined Kuter in the planning.

General Arnold retired on 28 February 1946 and Spaatz was sworn in as the USAAF's Commanding General the following day. When Spaatz had arrived in Washington the preceding fall the entity that he wanted to mold into a separate air force was very different from the one he now commanded. From a 1945 peak of 2,282,259 men, the USAAF had diminished to 890,000 by the end of the year and was now down to 450,000. The tens of thousands of aircraft spread across the globe were being sold for scrap. C-47 Skytrains were being sold off for 500 dollars each, to be snapped up by small airlines and ex-USAAF pilots turned entrepreneur. Brand new P-51 Mustangs, the top USAAF fighter during the war, were sold for a few thousand dollars, cheaper (though ironically more plentiful) than some postwar automobile models. The aircraft sell-off would cut too deeply into the muscle, but the demobilization was part of the larger picture of postwar military reorganization into which the airmen were penciling their independent force.

Not the least of the reorganizers was President Harry S Truman who had submitted to Congress (over the grumbling of Navy Secretary James Forrestal) a plan for the now-familiar tripartite Defense Department (December 1945). The Senate Military Affairs Committee took up the matter early in 1946, resulting in Senate Bill 2044 which began its odyssey through both Houses of Congress in April. In May Truman told the War and Navy Departments to prepare for the inevitable.

Over the summer the Joint Chiefs assigned USAAF Major General Lauris Norstad, who had acted as an adviser to the Senate Military Affairs Committee earlier in the year, and Navy Vice Admiral Forrest Sherman, to design a system wherein the Navy air elements could work with a US Air Force toward a common goal within a combat scenario. The result was a quasi-unified command plan, approved by the War and Navy Departments and by the President at the end of the year. The Sherman-Norstad Report was the backbone of the unification bill taken up by the Eightieth Congress in February 1947.

The unification bill was finally passed by Congress and taken by courier to National Airport, where President Truman was boarding his presidential aircraft, the C-54 called *Sacred Cow*, en route to Missouri and the bedside of his dying mother. At a few minutes past noon on 26 July 1947 the President signed into law the National Security Act of 1947, appropriately aboard a USAAF plane. Simultaneously he signed Executive Order 9877, which defined the roles and missions of the three new branches, as well as the nomination of Navy Secretary Forrestal to be the nation's first Secretary of Defense.

The Act provided for three 'executive departments' under the new Department of Defense. These subdepartments, Army, Navy and Air Force (the Marine Corps remained in the Navy Department) would each be presided over by a civilian Secretary

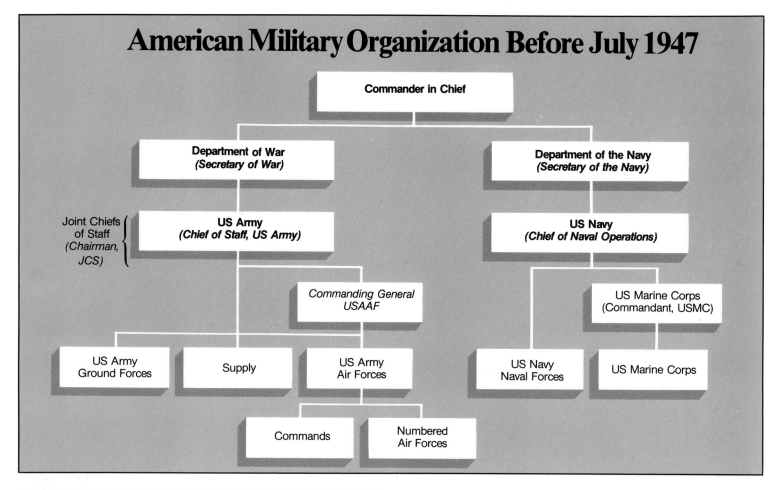

American Military Organization Before July 1947

Commander in Chief

Department of War
(Secretary of War)

Department of the Navy
(Secretary of the Navy)

Joint Chiefs
of Staff
(Chairman,
JCS)

US Army
(Chief of Staff, US Army)

US Navy
(Chief of Naval Operations)

Commanding General
USAAF

US Marine Corps
(Commandant, USMC)

US Army
Ground Forces

Supply

US Army
Air Forces

US Navy
Naval Forces

US Marine Corps

Commands

Numbered
Air Forces

Above: General Arnold presenting the Legion of Merit to Brigadier General Laurence Kuter. General Kuter was involved in the analysis of Billy Mitchell's early air attacks on warships in the 1920s and of Allied and Axis strategic bombing during World War II. After his important work in the creation of the USAF, he went on to command MATS (1948-51), the Air University (1953-55), FEAF (1955-57) and NORAD (1959-62) before his retirement from the Air Force.

and comprise a branch of the Military commanded by a Chief of Staff. The three Secretaries would be members of the new National Security Council, while the Chiefs of Staff would be members of the now-institutionalized Joint Chiefs of Staff. The first Secretary of the Air Force was Stuart Symington, who was the current Under Secretary of War for Air and had himself been among those working toward the goal of an independent Air Force. General Spaatz changed hats and was sworn in as the first Chief of Staff of the US Air Force on 26 September 1947. General Hoyt Vandenberg, Deputy Commander and Chief of the Air Staff, who had served as Commander of the Ninth Air Force during the war, became Vice Chief of Staff on 1 October 1947.

As the sign painters were busy at the Pentagon changing the designations on office doors, the ownership papers of America's military aircraft were also changing hands. The Navy Department retained its carrier-based air fleet, antisubmarine aircraft and Marine Corps Aviation. Across the hall, however, the scene at the Army was reminiscent of a contemporary news photo of a staffer at the national library in British India. British India was about to become independent as two separate countries, India and Pakistan, and the photo's subject was part of a team that had to divide the library's vast collection into two piles, one for India, one for Pakistan. Now everything the Army owned pertaining to aviation had to be evaluated and in most cases turned over to the new Air Force. The list began with aircraft and personnel but also included other items from research and development reports to those paintings in the Official US Army Collection with aircraft and aviation themes. The Air Force would now be responsible for the transport aircraft that would airlift Army personnel over long distances, but the Army would, by compromise, retain a few light aircraft for forward observation and courier work and be permitted to develop its fleet of helicopters for short-distance transportation.

American Military Organization After July 1947

The mission assigned to the Air Force in Executive Order 9877 was largely a product of the planning teams that Hap Arnold had put together during the war and had a firm basis in the kind of Air Force the airmen envisioned. The Air Force was directed to (A) Organize, train and equip air forces for general global and specific theater air superiority, strategic combat, reconnaissance, and airlift and support of Army and Navy forces except in those instances specifically assigned to the Navy air arm; (B) Develop weapons, organization and tactics of an air force, co-ordinating them with those of the other services; (C) Provide planning and execution of missions throughout the world as required by national interests and policies; (D) Co-ordinate Air Defense among the services (the Army would control antiaircraft missiles, the Air Force the interceptors); (E) The Air Force would assist the Army and Navy when necessary by providing supplies and common services.

THE MAJOR COMMANDS

The USAF now had its independence, but it had been no overnight affair. The reorganization efforts that Arnold and Spaatz had presided over just after the war had played a part. Even before the war was over, the organizational entity known as the Major Command had begun to supersede the numbered air forces as the basic building block of the Air Force. A good example was the Far East Air Forces that began as an umbrella for the Fifth and Thirteenth Air Forces, and to which the Seventh was later assigned and, after the war, the Twentieth.

The first important step in the reorganization had come on 21 March 1946, when the Continental Air Forces were divided and redesignated by function. The result was the Strategic, Tactical and Air Defense Commands. The Strategic Air Command began with the Second Air Force but soon gained the famous strategic air forces from the European Theater, the Eighth and Fifteenth. The Tactical Air Command was assigned the tactical Ninth Air Force. On 1 October the Eleventh Air Force became the Alaskan Air Command; the following summer air units assigned to the occupation forces in Europe became the US Air Forces in Europe, another Major Command. The first Major Command established by the new USAF was the Air Materiel Command, created 14 October 1947 to take over the supply and logistics function lost when the service separated from the Army. The Air Transport Command, which had been a separate unit from the numbered air forces, became a Major Command – the Military Air Transport Service – on 1 June 1948. Its mission was to supply transport services to the Air Force and other branches of the military, notably the Army.

Though it was not unique to the Air Force, research and development or R&D became symbolic of the new Air Force, presiding over development of new aircraft and systems in the technology boom that followed the war. To oversee its multiplying facets, the Air Force created the Air Research and Development Command in February 1950.

RESEARCH AND DEVELOPMENT

Even before the end of World War II, it was clear that the immediate postwar period would see an unprecedented explosion in technical fields. During the war aircraft technology advanced at a rate many times faster than had been dreamed of before the war. When the war began, open-cockpit biplanes of a 25-year-old design were common in the world's major air forces. When the war ended, these services were flying jet-propelled aircraft, which Germany had used in combat throughout the last year of the war. This technology explosion was erupting in fields beyond aeronautics: radar had evolved dramatically during the war and guided-missile technology had emerged.

General Hap Arnold once said that World War I had been a war of brawn, World War II a war of logistics and World War III would be a war of brains. He knew at the time – as the world didn't – that nuclear weapons were in the offing, and probably recognized, as Einstein observed, that World War IV would be a war of sticks and clubs if World War III took place. With this in mind, and the shock of Pearl Harbor fresh in his memory, he was bent on making his service a world leader in aviation and defense technology. Arnold was determined not only to end the present war, but to prevent another.

In 1944 he had contacted the Hungarian-born Caltech (California Institute of Technology) scientist Dr Theodore von Karman and asked him to set up a Scientific Advisory Group (SAG), which would bring together scientists and researchers nationwide, from many high-technology fields. One of the first and most important tasks undertaken by von Karman and SAG was a trip to Germany in the wake of the Allied victory to study the breakthrough technology developed by the Germans during the war, including jet propulsion. The Germans had several jet-propelled combat aircraft in service during the war: the Arado Ar-234 bomber, the Messerschmitt Me-262 and Heinkel He-162 fighters and the Messerschmitt's Me-163 rocket-powered interceptor. Of these, the Me-262 was produced in greater numbers, saw more service and was the most advanced. A crucial factor in its success was the swept-wing design. The aerodynamics of swept wings were not fully understood in Britain and the US, and consequently their first operational jet fighters had the traditional straight wings.

George Schairer, an engineer with the Boeing Company, was among the SAG group investigating German facilities. At that same time Boeing was at work on the successor to the famous B-17 and B-29 strategic bombers it had produced for the USAAF during the war; the configuration of a new bomber was not yet decided. After evaluating what he saw in Germany, Schairer decided that Boeing's next bomber would be solely jet-propelled, with swept wings. The result was the sleek B-47 Stratojet.

The Scientific Advisory Group was also looking into the status of German rocket research, where they found two sobering items. The first was development of a successor to the V-2 (technical designation A-4) guided missile that Germany had used against Britain. This new missile, designated A-10, was a two-stage rocket with sufficient range to strike the United States from a launch site in Europe. SAG's second sobering find was that the Russians had not only appropriated vast quantities of rocket data, but had removed scientists and personnel from the principal German rocket test center at Peenemünde on the Baltic coast. The arms race with the Soviets had started even before the Germans had been defeated. At the end of 1945 Dr von Karman and SAG presented their findings to Arnold in a report titled *Science, the Key to Air Supremacy*. Arnold was delighted with the report and made the Scientific Advisory Group a permanent Scientific Advisory Board.

The first obstacle encountered by the new SAB was the familiar one of funding. Postwar demobilization meant that the operational commands were fighting for money, for planes and for the fuel to fly them; it was hard to justify appropriations for research and development when the results would not be visible for many fiscal years. There was, of course, strong Air Force support for R&D. Von Karman remained as a principal scientific

adviser and one of his former Caltech pupils, Brigadier General Donald Putt, was made Director of Research and Development by the Chief of Staff in October 1948. A little over a year later (1 February 1950) the Air Research and Development Command became a Major Command. Two years later the Arnold Engineering Development Center, near Manchester, Tennessee, was dedicated. Named for General Hap Arnold, the man whose foresight had led not only to the independence of the US Air Force, but to its emphasis on R&D, the center is the largest site of its kind in the Western world, supporting all phases of aviation and aerospace research.

AIR FORCE BLUE

Less than a year after he became the first Air Force Chief of Staff, General Spaatz turned over the reins to his Vice-Chief, General Hoyt Vandenberg, who became the US Air Force's first full-time Chief of Staff on 30 April 1948. He would oversee many growing pains. Vandenberg was part of the generation of USAAF officers who came to the forefront during World War II. He had commanded both the Twelfth and Ninth Air Forces and had worked his way through the upper ranks after the war.

While the Air Force had anticipated its independence and had designed a command structure, the new service was still Army-oriented. Most of its commanders had spent their adult lives in the Army. Spaatz had flown in its first air war in Mexico in 1916; Vandenberg himself had joined the Army in the 1920s. When the Air Force inherited the components of the Army Air Force, it was marked by nearly two centuries of tradition. Even the uniform worn by Air Force personnel was an Army uniform, one

Above: Stuart Symington was Undersecretary of War for Air when the US Air Force was created and thus became the first Secretary of the Air Force. Symington later went on to serve as a US Senator from Missouri and in 1960 he made an unsuccessful bid for the Democratic presidential nomination.

Below: With postwar demobilization, much of the USAF's aircraft strength was scrapped or put into storage. These B-29s were mothballed at the Air Materiel Command's Military Aircraft Storage and Disposition Center at Davis Monthan AFB near Tucson. *See page 208 for a discussion of MASDC.*

of Vandenberg's priorities for change. The new blue uniform leaned more toward that of Britain's Royal Air Force than toward the US Army garb. While officers would still be captains, colonels and generals, enlisted men below the grade of sergeant would no longer be corporals and privates, but would be called airmen instead.

The national insignia on aircraft changed also, albeit subtly, with the addition of a red bar in the white fields flanking a white star in a blue circle. This change would be adopted by the Navy, Marines and Army ground forces (for their light planes and helicopters) as well. Pursuit planes had been known as fighters since well before the war; effective 11 June 1948 the prefix *P* was changed to *F*. The P-51 became the F-51, the P-80 the F-80. Photo reconnaissance aircraft formerly designated by the prefix *F* assumed the prefix *R*. The F-13 for example, the reconnaissance version of the B-29, was now the RB-29.

In the post-war years Air Force strength diminished even as reorganization was accomplished. Demobilization was partly to blame; so too was over-reliance on nuclear weapons as a deterrent. Beyond the small number of aircraft that supported occupation forces in Germany and Japan, the Air Force was badly depleted. As of the end of 1947 the Strategic Air Command, the strongest Command, had only 319 B-29s (the only plane capable of dropping nuclear weapons) and 350 fighters, of which only 180 were F-80 jet fighters.

Vandenberg and Secretary Symington began to lobby for increased funding to supply aircraft to the wings and squadrons, many of which existed only on paper. The personnel strength of

Below: Three US Air Force aircraft built by Republic Aircraft are seen at the company's plant in March 1949. From the left are the F-47 (formerly P-47) Thunderbolt of World War II fame, the then-new but ultimately unsuccessful XF-91 Thunderceptor, and the F-84 Thunderjet that would soon be going to war in the skies over Korea.

the Air Force at the time of its creation stood at 305,827, less than that of the USAAF at the time of Pearl Harbor. The prevailing school of thought called on the threat of nuclear war to prevent war. After all, Truman had used it to get the Russians out of Iran. The theory was valid only so long as the United States had a monopoly on nuclear weapons. While men like Major General John Samford, Chief of Air Force Intelligence, predicted that the Russians could produce atomic weapons by the early fifties, others went along with Dr Vannevar Bush of MIT who doubted a Soviet nuclear capability before the late 1960s or early 1970s. The controversy ended with detonation of the first Russian atomic bomb in 1949.

Symington and Vandenberg consistently held that the US needed an adequate conventional military force to prevent a choice between losing a conflict and resorting to nuclear weapons. The debate would live on past their terms in office.

Though Congress was beginning to authorize more money for defense, the rebuilding process was slow. Development of a new generation of aircraft was underway; leap-frogging technology meant that the new generation must be revolutionary. Lockheed, which had produced the famous P-38 Lightning fighter during the war, was responsible for the first operational jet fighter, the P-80 (F-80 as of 1948). Republic, which had given the USAAF the P-47, was developing the F-84 series, a straight-winged fighter that would evolve into a swept-wing aircraft with the F-84F. North American Aviation, which produced the P-51 Mustang, the top USAAF fighter of the war years, was at work on its F-86 Sabre Jet, which would be the first swept-wing fighter for the USAF. With the funding battle and development costs, the personnel strength of the Air Force edged slowly higher. From 305,827 it was up to 419,347 by 1949; in 1950 it had fallen back to 411,277 when there came the surprise many had feared and few had prepared for.

GENERAL HOYT SANFORD VANDENBERG
Second USAF Chief of Staff

Hoyt Vandenberg was born in Milwaukee, Wisconsin, on 24 January 1899 and served as the first full-term Chief of Staff of the US Air Force from 30 April 1948 to 29 June 1953. Vandenberg graduated from the US Military Academy in June 1923, whereupon he attended the Air Service Flying School and Advanced Flying School at Brooks and Kelly Fields in Texas, graduating in September 1924. His first assignment was with the Third Attack Group, whose 90th Attack Squadron he commanded until 1927 when he became a flying instructor at March Field, California. Between May 1929 and September 1931 he served in Hawaii, commanding the Sixth Pursuit Squadron at Schofield Barracks. From Hawaii, Vandenberg returned to the mainland, attending the Air Corps Tactical School (where he later taught), the Command and General Staff School and the Army War College, from which he graduated as a Captain in June 1939. Prior to the US entry into World War II, he served with the Air Corps Plans Division and as Operations and Training Officer to the Air Staff.

In June 1942, with the temporary rank of Lieutenant Colonel, Vandenberg went to England to help plan and organize air operations in North Africa. On 18 February 1943, with the temporary rank of Brigadier General, he became Chief of Staff of the Northwest African Strategic Air Force, with which he flew numerous missions over Tunisia, Sicily, Italy and Sardinia. He was awarded the Silver Star, the Distinguished Flying Cross and the Legion of Merit for his service with the NASAF. In September 1943, after a month at headquarters in Washington, he was assigned to head the Air Mission in Moscow under Ambassador Averell Harriman: he served there until January 1944. Three months later he was designated Deputy Commander-in-Chief of the Allied Expeditionary Air Forces for the Invasion of Europe and assumed command of the Ninth Air Force. For his part in the planning of Operation *Overlord*, the invasion of Europe, he was awarded the Distinguished Service Medal. General Vandenberg, now with the temporary rank of Major General, returned to Headquarters in June 1945, where he served as Assistant Chief of the Air Staff, and later as Director of Intelligence on the War Department General Staff. In June 1946 he was appointed director of the Central Intelligence Agency (CIA), returning to the USAAF a year later as Deputy Commander-in-Chief of the Air Staff. With the creation of the US Air Force, he became Vice-Chief of Staff on 1 October 1947, with the permanent rank of Brigadier General retroactive to 12 December 1942. On 30 April 1948 General Vandenberg succeeded General Spaatz as US Air Force Chief of Staff. In that position he presided over the rebuilding of the postwar Air Force and its activities during the Korean War. He made several trips to Korea and flew over much of Chinese occupied territory in an observation plane to get a first-hand look at the situation.

When the Eisenhower Administration took office in January 1953, the new Secretary of Defense, Charles Wilson, stated his intention to reduce the size of the Air Force. During subsequent Congressional hearings, Vandenberg, now stricken with terminal cancer, did an admirable job of testifying against Wilson. He under-scored the need to maintain a strong conventional Air Force to avoid being painted into the corner of choosing between defeat and recourse to nuclear war in a future conflict.

Vandenberg retired a few months later (30 June 1953) at the end of his second term as Chief of Staff. On 2 April 1954 he died after the painful final bout with his disease. In addition to his American decorations, Vandenberg was honored by Argentina, Belgium, Chile, China, Egypt, Great Britain, Italy, Luxembourg, the Netherlands, Poland and Portugal.

THE US AIR FORCE IN KOREA

THE US AIR FORCE GOES TO WAR

When World War II ended Korea was still part of the Japanese Empire. As with Germany and Austria in Europe, Korea was divided into occupation zones, the north being occupied by Russian forces, the south by the Americans. who also occupied the Japanese home islands. As they did in their zone of Germany and in parts of Eastern Europe, the Russians established a communist government in North Korea, while a Western-style government took over in South Korea. It was soon clear that the two Koreas could not be reunited by political means and North Korea, with the urging of its sponsors in Soviet Russia and Communist China, decided to take another course.

On the morning of 25 June 1950, 135,000 North Korean troops supported by armor crossed the 38th parallel, the demarcation line between the two Koreas. Late on the 25th, with the South Korean capital of Seoul at risk, US Air Force transports were dispatched from Japan to evacuate Americans. The South Korean units, more of a constabulary than a military force, were badly outnumbered and had none of the heavy weapons available to the invaders. On 27 June the United Nations Security Council passed a resolution calling for 'urgent military measures . . . to restore international peace and security' and asked member nations to 'furnish such assistance to the Republic of Korea as may be necessary to repel armed attack.'

General Douglas MacArthur, Commander of US Forces in the Far East, had already ordered the Fifth Air Force to cover the American evacuation and support the South Koreans. On the morning of the 27th a group of Russian-built Yakovlev fighter bombers attacked Kimpo Airfield, where they were intercepted by F-82s of the 68th All Weather Fighter Squadron of the Fifth Air Force based at Itazuke, Japan. The results were unfortunate for the Yaks and the first American air-to-air kill of the Korean War was chalked up by Lieutenant William Hudson. Later that day four Fifth Air Force F-80s shot down a like number of North Korean Il-10 attack bombers, bringing the toll for the first day of the air war over Korea to seven.

On the ground there was no comparable success. The South Korean defenses crumbled and Seoul fell. The Security Council voted on 7 July to establish a unified military command with the United States functioning as operative agent. General MacArthur was named Commander in Chief of the UN Command and the US Eighth Army was introduced into combat to block the North Korean drive to capture the entire Korean Peninsula. Under MacArthur, Air Force General George Stratemeyer was in command of the Far East Air Forces composed of the Fifth in Japan, the Twentieth on Okinawa, the Thirteenth in the Philippines and the Far East Air Materiel Command. The Far East Bomber Command was soon established, largely from SAC B-29s sent out from US bases. Initial targets for all bombers, B-29s and fighters alike, were tactical

Above: A flight of F-86 Sabre Jets of the US Air Force 51st Fighter Interceptor Wing streak toward 'MiG Alley' in Northwest Korea in search of enemy MiG-15s. During the preceding month of September 1952, Fifth Air Force Sabres had downed a record 61 MiGs while losing only four of their own number.

Left: This monsoon-formed lake was not the most ideal taxi-way, but neither was it a sufficient hazard to stop operations of 18th Fighter Bomber Wing F-51s at this Korean air base in September 1951.

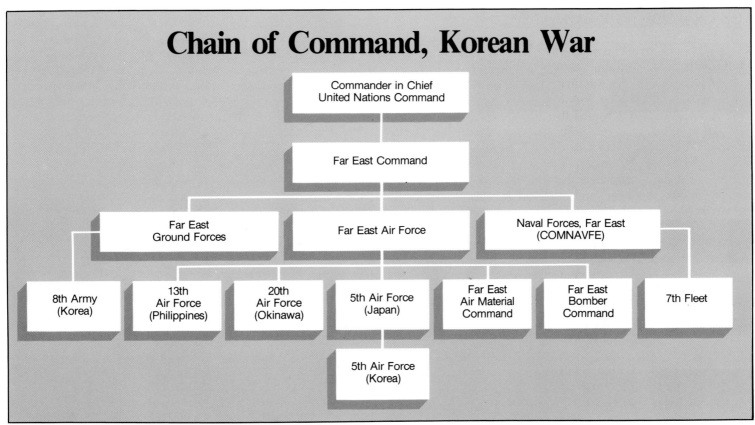

Chain of Command, Korean War

Commander in Chief
United Nations Command

Far East Command

Far East Ground Forces — Far East Air Force — Naval Forces, Far East (COMNAVFE)

8th Army (Korea) — 13th Air Force (Philippines) — 20th Air Force (Okinawa) — 5th Air Force (Japan) — Far East Air Material Command — Far East Bomber Command — 7th Fleet

5th Air Force (Korea)

Below: 'Heavenly Laden,' a 98th Bomb Wing B-29 on the ground in Japan after her 60th mission in April 1951.

due to the pressing need to halt the North Korean advance. Tactical aircraft proved to be more effective against the targets, and by the end of July the B-29s were conducting strikes against strategic targets like railyards, hydroelectric plants and factory complexes in North Korea. By 15 September strategic targets in North Korea had been all but eliminated, and supply lines to North Korean forces in the south had been successfully interdicted by Fifth Air Force fighter bombers and occasional FEAF B-29s. Also on 15 September MacArthur successfully landed his X Corps at Inch'on near Seoul behind enemy lines. At the same time the Eighth Army under General Walker, which had been bottled up at Pusan, counterattacked.

By the first of October Seoul had been recaptured and UN forces had reached the 38th parallel. By 26 October some UN and South Korean units had reached the Yalu River, the North Korean border with Communist China. North Korea had been defeated, its air force destroyed, its warmaking power curtailed. Talk now turned to UN-sponsored elections to reunify the

country. The following day, its job completed, the FEAF Bomber Command was deactivated; the B-29s borrowed from SAC were scheduled to return home.

In the midst of this silver lining was a cloud. There had been growing evidence of Chinese 'volunteers' with the North Korean Army, and on 1 November Chinese MiGs were first encountered by the Fifth Air Force. It was clear that the Chinese were rushing quantities of men and supplies into North Korea to stem the UN advance. The Chinese successfully counterattacked during the last week of November and by 15 December had pushed the UN forces south of the 38th parallel.

The FEAF bomber command was reactivated and sent north again, but now it was a different war in several important ways. First, the UN forces were outnumbered again, this time by the vast manpower reserves of China; second, the FEAF B-29s had not been effectively threatened by the tiny North Korean Air Force, but the Chinese MiG-15 jet fighters were a serious adversary; finally, the FEAF was forbidden, for political reasons to

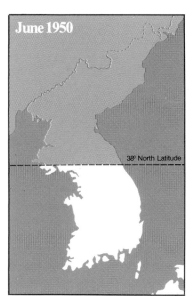

June 1950

38° North Latitude

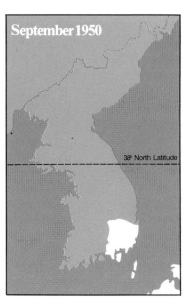

September 1950

38° North Latitude

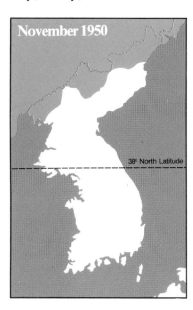

November 1950

38° North Latitude

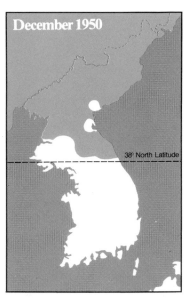

December 1950

38° North Latitude

Below: Chief of Staff Vandenberg addresses airmen at a FEAF base in Japan from the wing of an F-80, 13 July 1950.

attack strategic targets north of the Yalu River in China. Both Stratemeyer and MacArthur wanted to use the B-29s to destroy the Yalu bridges, cutting Chinese supply lines. George Marshall, the World War II Chief of Staff, now Secretary of Defense, had ordered that targets within five miles of the Chinese border could not be bombed. This would permit the Chinese not only access across a formidable natural barrier, but a bridgehead and supply area on the Korean side as well. Under protest, Marshall compromised to permit bombing of the Korean end of the Yalu bridges. Bombing one end of a bridge across a twisting boundary river under prohibition of overflying any Chinese territory in the process was one of the most difficult tasks ever undertaken by the US Air Force. The Chinese MiGs could and did attack American bombers over Korea. MiGs and antiaircraft guns could fire on the B-29s from China without fear of retaliation. It was a grueling task, but the bombers did the job.

On the ground, Chinese forces under Lin Piao made a swift and dramatic advance. The last UN forces in North Korea had

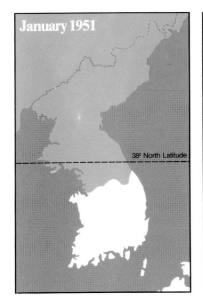

January 1951

38° North Latitude

July 1951 - July 1953

38° North Latitude

US Air Force Medal of Honor Winners of the Korean War

Maj George Davis, Jr (Dublin, Tex) 10 Feb 1952, Sinuiju-Yalu River, North Korea (KIA 10 Feb 1952)
Maj Charles Loring, Jr (Portland, Me) 22 Nov 1952, Sniper Ridge, North Korea (KIA 22 Nov 1952)
Maj Louis Sebille (Harbor Beach, Mich), 5 Aug 1950, Hamch'ang, South Korea (KIA 5 Aug 1950)
Capt John Walmsley, Jr (Baltimore, Md) 14 Sept 1951, Yangdok, North Korea (KIA 14 Sept 1951)

US Air Force Aces of the Korean War

Capt Joseph McConnell, Jr	16	Maj Donald Adams	6.5
Maj James Jabara	15*	Col Francis Gabreski	6.5*
Capt Manuel Fernandez	14.5	Lt Col George Jones	6.5
Maj George Davis, Jr	14*	Maj Winton Marshall	6.5
Col Royal Baker	13*	1st Lt James Kasler	6
Maj Frederick Blesse	10	Capt Robert Love	6
1st Lt Harold Fischer	10	Maj William Whisner, Jr	5.5*
Lt Col Vermont Garrison	10*	Col Robert Baldwin	5
Col James Johnson	10*	Capt Richard Becker	5
Capt Lonnie Moore	10	Maj Stephen Bettinger	5
Capt Ralph Parr, Jr	10	Maj Richard Creighton	5*
Capt Cecil Foster	9	Capt Clyde Curtin	5
1st Lt James Low	9	Capt Ralph Gibson	5
Maj James Hagerstrom	8.5*	Capt Iven Kincheloe, Jr	5
Capt Robinson Risner	8	Capt Robert Latshaw, Jr	5
Lt Col George Ruddell	8*	Capt Robert Moore	5
1st Lt Henry Buttlemann	7	Capt Dolphin Overton, III	5
Capt Clifford Jolley	7	Col Harrison Thyng	5*
Capt Leonard Lilley	7	Maj William Westcott	5

*Pilot also scored victories in World War II that are not included in this total.

Below: US Air Force aircraft of the Korean War, clockwise from top center: the F-80 Shooting Star, the USAF's first jet fighter; the F-82 Twin Mustang, the first USAF plane to down an enemy aircraft in Korea; the F-94 Starfire, an all-weather interceptor introduced late in the war; and in the rear, the superb F-86 Sabre Jet.

F-80C Shooting Star
Manufacturer: Lockheed Aircraft Corporation
First year of service: 1948
Aircraft type: Single-seat jet fighter
Wingspan: 39ft 11in
Length: 34ft 6in
Weight: 16,856lb (gross)
Range: 1380 miles
Service ceiling: 42,750 feet
Top speed: 580mph
Powerplant: (1) 5400lb thrust Allison J33-A-23 turbojet
Armament: Six .50 caliber machine guns

F-82E Twin Mustang
Manufacturer: North American Aviation
First year of service: 1948
Aircraft type: Long-range escort fighter/interceptor
Wingspan: 51ft 3in
Length: 39ft 1in
Weight: 24,813lb (gross)
Range: 2504 miles
Service ceiling: 40,000 feet
Top speed: 465mph
Powerplant: (2) 1600hp Allison V-1710-143/145
Armament/Capacity: Six .50 caliber machine guns, plus 4000lb of bombs or (25) HVAR rockets

F-86F Sabre Jet
Manufacturer: North American Aviation
First year of service: 1952 (F-86A, 1950)
Aircraft type: Single-seat fighter
Wingspan: 37ft 1in
Length: 37ft 6in
Weight: 16,357lb (gross)
Range: 1270 miles (with drop tanks)
Service ceiling: 50,000 feet
Top/Cruising speed: 690mph
Powerplant: (1) 5970lb thrust General Electric J47-GE-27 turbojet
Armament/Capacity: Six .50 caliber machine guns, plus 2000lbs of ordnance

been surrounded at Hungnam and evacuated by sea on Christmas Eve. Seoul fell to the communists for the second time on 4 January 1951 and UN troops were driven farther south.

By mid-February, however, Chinese supply lines through North Korea were stretched thin and under attack by American planes. The tide began to turn: UN forces spearheaded by the American Eighth Army under General Matthew Ridgway rolled back the communist offensive. Seoul was retaken by UN forces in mid-March, and the front returned to the area of the 38th parallel, after nine months of war that had extended it the length of the Korean Peninsula. UN strategy was redirected from unification of Korea toward preventing additional Chinese advances and negotiating a cease-fire in place. For the next two and a half years the front would move very little, as the two sides dug into static defensive positions maintained until the cease-fire was signed on 27 July 1953.

AIR COMBAT IN KOREA

The Chinese intervention in Korea produced a change in air strategy. The MiG-15 was a more potent adversary than anything the North Koreans had put up, one that drastically reduced the effectiveness of the B-29s. As the Air Force had learned in World War II, the priority was achievement of air superiority in the theater of operations. This had been relatively easy against the North Korean Air Force but was quickly lost to the Russian-built MiG-15, a top-of-the-line jet fighter superior to the Fifth Air Force's F-80s and piston-engine F-51s and F-82s. Nevertheless, in the first jet-to-jet air battle of the war, Lieutenant Russell Brown of the 51st Fighter Interceptor Wing, flying an F-80, shot down a Chinese MiG-15 on 8 November 1950. For the most part, though, the F-80s were outmatched. Because they were 100 mph faster than the F-80s, the MiGs could, for example, dive through a formation of bombers escorted by F-80s and escape without being engaged. In a dogfight, the F-80's .50 caliber machine guns were out-classed by the MiG's 37 mm and 23 mm cannons.

Below: 'Miss Jacque II,' a 136th Fighter Bomber Wing F-84, the first Thunderjet to fly 1000 hours, taxis across metal runway matting after having completed an incredible 363 missions against North Korean targets during the all-out interdiction effort codenamed Operation *Strangle.*

The Lockheed F-80 Shooting Star, a product of World War II technology, had been the first jet propelled combat aircraft in service with the USAAF, although the jet-propelled Bell P-59 Airacomet had preceded it experimentally. Designated P-80 (F-80 from 1948) the Shooting Star entered service in early 1945, but the war ended before it could be used in combat. When the Korean War broke out, the Fifth Air Force had 365 F-80Cs in its operational units. They were pressed into service as both interceptors and ground-attack aircraft and served well until the Chinese intervention. In the end, 277 F-80s were lost in Korea, most to ground fire, only 14 in aerial combat.

The North American F-82, the first American aircraft to score a combat victory in Korea, also originated in the previous war. North American's P-51 Mustang had been the top USAAF air-to-air fighter of World War II; when asked to come up with a bomber escort with extremely long range to escort B-29s, North American had the idea of combining two P-51 fuselages on a single wing. The resulting aircraft, the XP-82 Twin Mustang, first flew in mid-1945, too late to get into the war. The first Twin Mustang finally entered USAF Service under the designation F-82E in May 1948 with SAC. When the war in Korea broke out there were 40 F-82s in the Far East Air Forces, assigned to both the Fifth and the Twentieth. In service, though used sparingly, the F-82s performed well, destroying 20 enemy aircraft. Their downfall was to come from a lack of parts. The plane had been produced in fairly small numbers because production delays made it obsolescent when delivered; thus parts were inadequately stocked. As of December 1949 the USAF classified all its aircraft as either first-line or second-line. A new aircraft would be first-line for three years, then revert to second-line status. The F-82 was never classified first-line and was withdrawn from combat in February 1952.

It is ironic that there were more F-51s (former P-51s) in combat in Korea, and they served longer than the F-82s. The F-51s were common early in the war, as Air National Guard units equipped with them were activated. The last F-51 did not leave combat until 26 January 1953.

> **F-84E Thunderjet**
> Manufacturer: Republic Aviation
> First year of service: 1949
> Aircraft type: Single-seat jet fighter/fighter-bomber
> Wingspan: 36ft 5in
> Length: 38ft 6in
> Weight: 22,463lb (gross)
> Range: 1485 miles (1950 miles with drop tanks)
> Service ceiling 43,220 feet
> Top speed: 613mph
> Powerplant: (1) 4900lb thrust Allison J35-A-17 turbojet
> Armament/Capacity: Six .50 caliber machine guns, plus up to 4500lbs of ordnance

While the P-51 had been the top USAAF fighter during World War II, the Republic P-47 Thunderbolt was close, and was certainly the top fighter-bomber. With the dawn of the jet age, Republic, like other leading manufacturers, sought to retain its position by updating successful designs. The result was the jet-propelled P-84 Thunderjet, delivered to the USAAF in February 1947 and reaching operational units as the F-84 a year later. In combat over Korea the straight-winged F-84 was found inferior in speed and maneuverability to the swept-wing MiG-15 and a minor improvement over the F-80. Though the F-84 suffered heavy losses during the first year, it found a niche (not unlike that of the P-47) and by the end of 1951 was being called 'the best ground-support jet in the theater.'

While the F-80 and F-84 were clearly not state of the art jets when the Korean War began, the opposite was true of North American's F-86 Sabre Jet, the Air Force's first swept-wing fighter. It had been operational for only a year when the war broke out. When UN forces lost air superiority to the Chinese, F-86s were rushed to the Fifth Air Force, the first 19 arriving at Korean bases on 1 December 1950. They flew on 16 December and downed their first MiG the following day. There were more MiGs in the theater, and the Sabres had their Korean bases temporarily overrun by the Chinese but F-86s operating from bases in Japan soon regained the advantage for UN forces.

Having attained air superiority the FEAF, supported by F-86s, concentrated on destroying all bases in North Korea capable of supporting MiGs, forcing them to operate largely from bases in the area around Antung, China. To prevent the Russian-built fighters from harassing UN forces farther south, the Fifth Air Force set up combat air patrols and fighter sweeps in the sky south of Antung and the Yalu – it became known as 'MiG Alley.' In the first six months there the F-86s downed 44 MiG-15s and damaged 77, with combat losses of only six planes. The fact that 77 were damaged and not destroyed pointed up the persistent deficiency in American aircraft of the period. While the F-86 and its pilots were decidedly superior to the MiGs, their armament, consisting of six nose-mounted Colt Browning .50 caliber

machine guns was less than ideal for the short target time of a high-speed jet dogfight.

By the fall of 1952, the F-86As were being replaced by F-86Es and F-86Fs with more provision for external fuel tanks, which increased their range. Also introduced on the later F-86s were extended, solid wing leading edges that increased operating altitude (by 4000 feet), speed and rate of climb. Though machine guns were still the basic armament, there was provision for eight High Velocity Aerial Rockets (HVAR). A 20 mm Cannon was tested in combat, though not placed widely into service.

The basic combat air patrol or fighter sweep involved 'gaggles' of F-86s in four-plane cells patroling MiG Alley to lure the enemy into combat or intercept MiGs trying to slip through to

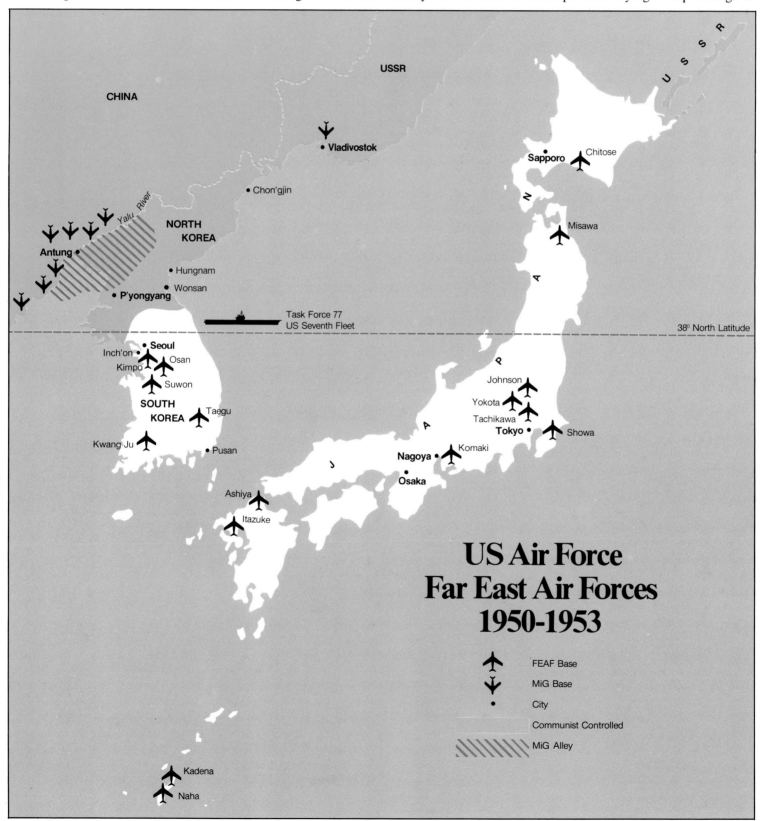

US Air Force
Far East Air Forces
1950-1953

FEAF Base

MiG Base

City

Communist Controlled

MiG Alley

Below: A damaged F-80 was captured making a wheels-up 170 mph landing in this remarkable photo by FEAF planning engineer Frank Hopkins. Note the damage from an enemy shell just above the wing.

Below: The same F-80 seen at left, after a safe landing in a rice paddy. A wheels-up landing on the hard surface of the nearby runway could have been disastrous.

Above: Its hydraulic system shot out over North Korea, this B-26 comes in for a belly landing. No one was injured.

Below: Using the Y in the track as his aiming point, a B-26 bombardier napalms a group of North Korean rail cars south of Wonsan.

Below: MiG masters on patrol. US Air Force F-86s of the 51st Fighter Interceptor Wing prowl MiG Alley in search of the enemy. The 51st was led by Colonel Francis Gabreski, the third-highest-scoring ace of World War II (28 victories), who added six and a half kills to his score in Korea.

Below: A FEAF Fifth Air Force Sabre taxis past a pair of MATS transports (a C-47 and in the foreground a C-54) at a busy Korean airfield during March 1951.

Right: A US Air Force C-119 Flying Boxcar prepares to air-drop supplies to United Nations troops in the rugged mountains of Korea. In Korea transport aircraft turned days into hours in the delivery of essential supplies.

attack F-80 or F-84 fighter bombers. Once engaged, the classic maneuver was to get behind the enemy and attack from the six o'clock position. Most aerial victories in Korea, as in World War II, were from six o'clock and achieved with the forward-mounted machine guns.

The enemy aircraft was almost always the MiG-15, designed and produced in the Soviet Union by the Mikoyan-Gurevich design bureau (hence the initials). The swept-wing MiG-15 was the top Soviet fighter, originating in the same German technology that produced the American swept-wing aircraft. The MiG-15 entered Soviet service in August 1948, and was promptly supplied to Poland and to China before the latter's incursion into Korea. It is no secret that the planes encountered by American pilots in MiG Alley, officially Chinese and North Korean, were often flown by Russian and Polish pilots who were being rotated through the Chinese squadrons for six-week periods for practical combat experience. The Soviet involvement was discovered early in the war when Russian pilots were heard conversing on their radios, a fact that Chief of Staff Vandenberg hastened to point out. It was also reported that one of the Soviet pilots shot down by the Americans was the son of Josef Stalin.

In the final tally, the performance of the American pilots was excellent despite the handicap of restrictive rules of engagement. The F-86 pilots shot down 792 MiGs and lost only 78 Sabres. In all, 1020 enemy aircraft were shot down by the USAF in the Korean War, 839 of them MiG-15s.

The US Air Force flew 716,979 sorties in its first war, firing 183 million rounds of ammunition and 511,329 rockets, dropping 448,366 tons of bombs and nine million gallons of napalm. The sorties destroyed 9417 railroad cars, 869 locomotives and 75,749 vehicles, including 1160 enemy tanks. In addition to the 1020 enemy aircraft confirmed as destroyed, another 182 were probable kills and at least another 1010 were damaged. Against this, the US Air Force lost 104 aircraft of all types in aerial combat, 544 to ground fire and 153 to other causes. Away from the front, the Military Air Transport Service carried 670,000 tons of materiel and 2,700,000 passengers and evacuated 325,000 wounded to hospitals in the States aboard such aircraft as specially fitted Boeing C-97C Stratofreighters.

On the ground, the Korean War was a brutal, frustrating affair, especially from the fall of 1951 to the cease-fire in the summer of 1953, when the situation resembled the hellish trench warfare of World War I. In the air, however, the Korean War was a triumph for American air power and for the men and planes of the new US Air Force.

GENERAL NATHAN FARRAGUT TWINING
Third USAF Chief of Staff

Nathan Twining was born on 11 October 1897 in Monroe, Wisconsin. He began active service in June 1916 with the Third Oregon Infantry on Mexican border duty. In 1917 he entered the US Military Academy, graduating in November 1918. In July 1919 he was assigned to the American Forces in Germany as an observer. His aviation career began in August 1923, when he entered Primary Flying School at Brooks Field, Texas. He graduated from Advanced Flying School at nearby Kelly Field in September 1924 and served as an instructor at Brooks Field for two years until he was transferred to March Field, California. In February 1929 he joined the 18th Pursuit Group at Schofield Barracks, Hawaii.

During the early 1930s he served at several US posts, including duty as an engineering officer with the US Army Air Mail Service. In June 1937 he graduated from the Command General Staff College and was assigned to the San Antonio Air Depot as Technical Supervisor. In August 1940 he was assigned to Washington, where he served at US Air Corps (later USAAF) headquarters until July 1942, when he went to the South Pacific as Chief of Staff to General M F Harmon, Commanding General of Army Forces in the theater. In January 1943 he became Commander of the newly formed 13th Air Force, and on 25 July joint commander of all Allied Air Forces in the South Pacific. In November 1943 he assumed command of the 15th Air Force in Italy and two months later became Commander of the Allied Mediterranean Strategic Air Forces. On 2 August 1945 he succeeded Curtis LeMay as Commander of the Twentieth Air Force in the Pacific, which a few days later dropped the first atomic bomb.

After the war General Twining served as Commander of the Air Materiel Command and of the Unified Alaskan Command. He became USAF Vice-Chief of Staff in 1950 and Chief of Staff of the Air Force on 30 June 1953. On 15 August 1957 General Twining became the first USAF Officer to be named Chairman of the Joint Chiefs of Staff. He retired on 30 September 1960 and stayed on in Washington as Vice-Chairman of the Textbook Division of the Holt, Rinehart and Winston Publishing Company. General Twining died of cardio-pulmonary arrest at Wilford Hall USAF Medical Center, on 29 March 1982 and is buried at Arlington National Cemetery.

GENERAL THOMAS DRESSER WHITE
Fourth USAF Chief of Staff

Thomas D White was born on 6 August 1901 in Walker, Minnesota, and graduated from the US Military Academy on 2 July 1920. His first active duty was with the 14th Infantry at Fort Davis in the Canal Zone. In September 1924 he entered Primary Flying School at Brooks Field, Texas, graduating from Advanced Flying School one year later. After duty with the 99th Observation Squadron at Bolling Field, he was sent to Peking in 1927 where he spent four years learning the Chinese language. Upon his return to the US he was assigned to Air Corps Headquarters. In February 1934 he was named Assistant Military Attaché for Air to Russia and a year later took up the same post in Rome.

In April 1940, after graduating from the Command and General Staff School at Fort Leavenworth, he became Military

Attaché (later Chief of the Military Air Mission) to Brazil. Returning to the United States in March 1942, he served as Chief of Staff of the Third Air Force, headquartered at Tampa, Florida, and in January 1944, he became Assistant Chief of the Air Staff for Intelligence. In September 1944 he went to the South Pacific as Deputy Commander of the Thirteenth Air Force and nine months later became Commander of the Seventh Air Force in Okinawa. In January 1946 he returned with the Seventh to Hawaii; in October 1947 he assumed Command of the Fifth Air Force in Japan.

In October 1948 General White was transferred to the Office of the Secretary of the Air Force in Washington, and in July 1951 he was named USAF Deputy Chief of Staff for Operations. On 30 June 1953 he was promoted to four-star General rank and appointed Vice-Chief of Staff. He became US Air Force Chief of Staff on 1 July 1957. During his tenure, the Air Force test-fired its first air-to-air nuclear rocket, the Genie, over Yucca Flat, Nevada, and became operational with its first Atlas ICBM. General White retired on 30 June 1961 and died on 22 December 1965.

GENERAL CURTIS EMERSON LeMAY
Fifth USAF Chief of Staff

Curtis LeMay was born on 15 November 1906 and graduated from Ohio State University. In 1928 he entered the Army as a flying cadet, completing his training in October 1929. His first tour of duty was with the 27th Pursuit Squadron at Selfridge Field in Michigan. After several tours with fighter squadrons, he transferred to bombers in 1937. LeMay participated in a number of long-range bomber exercises including the first mass deployment of B-17s to South America in 1938.

In 1942 he organized and trained the 305th Bomb Group and led it into combat against Germany. He developed the formation procedures and bombing techniques used by B-17 bomber units throughout the European theater. As Commanding General of the Third Bomb Division, he led the famous B-17 raid on Regensberg in 1943. In July 1944 he was transferred to the Pacific to direct strategic bombing efforts against Japan. After the war, LeMay returned to the US (piloting a B-29 nonstop from Hokkaido to Chicago) to become Deputy Chief of the Air Staff for Research and Development.

In October 1947 he went to Wiesbaden, Germany, to take up command of USAFE. In this position General LeMay organized the Berlin Airlift that supplied the city for a year while it was blockaded by Russian forces. On 16 October 1948 he became Commander of the Strategic Air Command, a post he held for nearly a decade. During this time he built up SAC from remnants of World War II that survived demobilization into an unprecedented all-jet bomber force.

In July 1957 General LeMay became Air Force Vice-Chief of Staff, and on 30 July 1961 Chief of Staff. During his tenure, the first Minuteman ICBM Wing became operational, as did the entire Titan II force. He oversaw the introduction of USAF combat forces in Southeast Asia and formulated the air-war plan that could have – had it been implemented – achieved decisive results against the enemy and ended the war much sooner, saving thousands of American lives.

General LeMay retired on 31 January 1965 but remained active in national defense matters. In 1968 he was selected as the vice-presidential candidate of the American Independent Party. In the election, he and the AIP presidential candidate, George Corley Wallace, gained more of the popular vote than any third-party candidacy in American history, winning five states and nearly ten million votes nationwide. In terms of electoral votes, the AIP earned more than any third-party bid since Theodore Roosevelt's Progressive (Bull Moose) Party came in second in the 1912 election.

GENERAL JOHN PAUL McCONNELL
Sixth USAF Chief of Staff

John McConnell was born in Booneville, Arkansas, on 7 February 1908, and graduated from the US Military Academy at West Point in 1932. He received his pilot's wings in 1933 and served in a variety of operational and administrative positions for the next decade. In November 1944 Colonel McConnell became Chief of Staff of the China/Burma/India (CBI) Air Force Training Command at Karachi, British India. He served for eight months with the Third Allied Tactical Air Force at Comilla, India, taking part in combat operations against the Japanese in Burma. He next became Senior Air Staff Officer in the Southeast Asia Air Command at Kandy, Ceylon, a post he held from September 1944 until June 1945.

After the war, General McConnell was named Senior Air Advisor to the Chinese Government. In 1947 he returned to the United States as Chief of the Reserve and National Guard Division, and in 1950 he went to England as Deputy Commander and later Commander of SAC's Third Air Division. He spent four years as Director of Plans for SAC at Offutt AFB before being named Commander of SAC's Second Air Force in 1957. In 1962, after a year as Vice-Commander-in-Chief of SAC, he was promoted to four-star rank and sent to Europe as Deputy Commander of the unified European Command. He was appointed USAF Vice-Chief of Staff in 1964 and became Chief of Staff on 1 February 1965. During his tenure, General McConnell presided over the buildup of USAF forces in Southeast Asia, to which he made several trips. He retired on 31 July 1969, the same month that the USAF supported the first manned lunar landing.

GENERAL JOHN DALE RYAN
Seventh USAF Chief of Staff

John Ryan was born on 10 December 1915 in Cherokee, Iowa, and graduated from the US Military Academy at West Point in 1938. He received his pilot's wings the following year and served as a flight instructor until January 1942. He went on to serve as Director of Training at Midland Field, Texas, where he was instrumental in establishing an advanced bombardier training school. He served with the Second Air Force at Colorado Springs before being transferred to the Fifteenth Air Force in Italy in February 1944.

He returned to Midland Field after the war and served briefly with the Air Training Command before being assigned to SAC in April 1946. He moved up the ladder in SAC as commander of the 58th Bomb Wing, 509th Bomb Wing, 97th Bomb Wing and the 810th Air Division before becoming Director of Materiel at SAC Headquarters in June 1956. In 1960 General Ryan assumed command of SAC's Sixteenth Air Force in Spain and a year later of SAC's Second Air Force at Barksdale AFB in Louisiana. After a year in Washington as USAF Inspector General, he was named Vice-Commander-in-Chief of SAC in August 1964.

In December 1964 General Ryan became Commander of SAC, and three years later Commander in Chief of PACAF, which he led through the peak of its war effort in Southeast Asia. He became USAF Vice-Chief of Staff in August 1968 and Chief of Staff a year later. During his tenure, the Air Force ended its inconclusive project *Blue Book* study of Unidentified Flying Objects (UFOs) (1969). Gen Ryan retired effective 31 July 1973.

GENERAL GEORGE SCRATCHLEY BROWN
Eighth USAF Chief of Staff

George S Brown was born in Montclair, New Jersey, on 17 August 1918 and graduated from the US Military Academy at West Point in 1941, earning his wings at Kelly Field the following year. That August his group, the 93rd Bomb Group, became the first B-24 wing to join the Eighth Air Force in its strategic offensive against Germany. He received the Distinguished Service Cross for his part in the daring low-level bombing raid on the German petroleum facilities at Ploesti, Rumania (1 August 1943).

In May 1945 Colonel Brown was assigned to ATC as Assistant Operations Officer; the following year he went to ADC to take up a similar role. In May 1952 he became Director of Operations with the Fifth Air Force in Korea. After the Korean War he attended the National War College and held several positions on the Air Staff and in the Office of the Secretary of the Air Force in Washington. In 1963 General Brown became Commander of the MATS Eastern Transport Air Force at McGuire AFB and a year later was selected to organize the JCS Joint Task Force II for weapons-systems testing.

After two years in Washington, DC, General Brown took command of the Seventh Air Force in Vietnam (August 1966). In September 1970 he was named Commander of the Air Force Systems Command at Andrews AFB. On 1 August 1973, the 40th anniversary of the famed Ploesti raid, General Brown became Chief of Staff of the US Air Force. Less than a year later, 1 July 1974, he became Chairman of the Joint Chiefs of Staff, the second USAF officer to hold the position. He retired as JCS Chairman on 21 June 1978.

GENERAL DAVID C JONES
Ninth USAF Chief of Staff

David C Jones was born on 9 July 1921 in Aberdeen, South Dakota, and earned his wings at Roswell Field, New Mexico, in 1943. He was the first USAF Chief of Staff not to have served in combat in World War II and one of two chiefs (the other was Curtis LeMay) who did not attend the US Military Academy at West Point. He did, however serve in combat in the Korean War, flying more than 300 hours of bombing missions over North Korea with the 19th Bomb Squadron out of March AFB. After the Korean War he served with SAC until August 1959, when he enrolled in the National War College in Washington.

Beginning in July 1960 Colonel Jones was assigned to the Pentagon for four years, after which he served for a year with TAC before being assigned to Plans and Operations with USAFE until January 1969. When he left USAFE, General Jones served for six months as Vice-Commander of the Seventh Air Force in Vietnam before taking command of SAC's Second Air Force.

In April 1971 General Jones returned to USAFE as Vice-Commander, being promoted to Commander in August of the same year. On 1 July 1974, he became USAF Chief of Staff, and on 1 July 1978 he succeeded Air Force General George Brown as Chairman of the Joint Chiefs of Staff, a position he held for the next four years.

THE US AIR FORCE IN SOUTHEAST ASIA

GOING TO WAR

In April 1961 the 4400th Combat Crew Training Squadron was activated at Eglin AFB in Florida: in October it was deployed to South Vietnam to train the ramshackle South Vietnam Air Force (RVNAF) in the rudiments of tactical air power as a tool of counterinsurgency. In this way the US Air Force made its unheralded entry into what began as a limited exercise in counterinsurgency, but would become the longest and costliest war in American history.

It began in the jungles and mountains of a remnant of the French Empire adjacent to the South China Sea, where the bulk of the Asian land mass meets the Malay Peninsula and the Indonesian archipelago. It was fought in those rugged backwoods where international boundaries exist only on maps read by the uninitiated, and in the blue tropical skies over those jungles where the cumulus clouds of the monsoon season can be as unmerciful to a million-dollar jet fighter as the most intense ground fire. It would be fought between a force with the best technology in the world but no sense of strategic purpose and a force of limited means but a firm idea of its objective.

That area of Southeast Asia which later became the nations of Vietnam, Cambodia and Laos had been ruled by France as French Indochina from the mid-19th century until World War II. When France was defeated by Germany in 1940, Japan occupied Indochina. When Indochina was liberated from Japanese control

at the end of the war, France attempted to reinstate its rule over the lost colony. An eight-year war ensued between France and various nationalist guerrilla groups, notably the communist Viet Minh led by Ho Chi Minh. The climactic defeat for the French came in 1954 when the Viet Minh overran their garrison at Dien Bien Phu. The French withdrew from Indochina and as a result of accords signed in Geneva in 1954, Vietnam was partitioned at the 17th parallel, the northern part becoming the communist-controlled Democratic Republic of Vietnam under Ho Chi Minh, and the Southern part the Republic of Vietnam, whose first president was Ngo Dinh Diem.

North Vietnam, like North Korea a few years earlier, was bent on unifying the divided nation under ·a single communist government. Unlike the North Koreans, who used an overt conventional attack, Ho Chi Minh and his able military commander General Vo Nguyen Giap waged a protracted guerrilla war similar to that which had dislodged the French. The US, meanwhile, decided to support the noncommunist governments of Southeast Asia, including South Vietnam, to prevent them

Above: Chief of Staff General John McConnell, Marine Corps General Lew Walt and Seventh Air Force commander Joseph Moore confer at Bien Hoa AB in 1965 during one of the Chief's visits to South Vietnam.

Right; US Air Force *Pack Train* C-123s drop South Vietnamese paratroops into Tay Ninh Province during Operation *Phi Hoa II* in March 1963. The C-123s were among the first USAF aircraft to serve in Vietnam.

Above: A veteran of three wars, the B-26 attack bomber, seen here with a C-123 at Korat RTAFB in Thailand with its rocket racks and eight machine guns loaded, was the right plane at the right time for *Farm Gate*.

Below: A Gleaming U-10 observation plane parked on the steel-mesh flight line matting at Korat. Piston-engined aircraft like the U-10 and the T-28s seen behind it were typical of the aircraft committed by the USAF early in the war.

from being pulled into the communist orbit. For this purpose, the Eisenhower Administration sponsored in 1955 the establishment of the Southeast Asia Treaty Organization (SEATO) and began supplying military aid to South Vietnam, as well as neighboring Cambodia, Laos and Thailand. In 1960 North Vietnam established in the jungles and backwaters of South Vietnam that they had infiltrated an entity they called the National Liberation Front (NLF) or Viet Cong (VC). Because it was composed largely of native South Vietnamese and Vietnamese from the north who had come south when the country was partitioned, the NLF had the appearance of an indigenous guerrilla movement. North Vietnam could then conduct the war through the Viet Cong, establishing the fiction that the ensuing guerrilla war was a civil war within South Vietnam. When North Vietnamese regular forces were introduced later it could be said that they intervened in support of one side in this civil war. The fact that the NLF was not a completely independent liberation movement would not be clear until 1975, when the North Vietnamese promptly disbanded the NLF and dissolved South Vietnam after achieving victory through conventional warfare.

In 1961 Soviet Premier Nikita Khrushchev proclaimed that communist influence would be spread around the world by means of 'wars of liberation.' With the Viet Cong already active in South Vietnam, and Soviet aircraft dropping supplies to communist insurgents in Laos, Southeast Asia seemed ripe for picking by such a war. The Kennedy Administration responded by sending both Army Special Forces and Air Force Air Commandos to South Vietnam as 'advisors' to help build a South Vietnamese force to resist the NLF. The 4400th Combat Crew Training Squadron, known as *Jungle Jim*, was the first US Air

Force unit to become involved. After its activation on 14 April, the President authorized deployment of Detachment 2A (11 October 1961) to Bien Hoa AB near Saigon under the designation First Air Commando Group, codenamed *Farm Gate*. The Group was composed of 151 men with eight North American T-28 Trainers refitted as attack aircraft, four World War II vintage Douglas B-26s (previously designated A-26) and four aging C-47 Skytrains, all marked as South Vietnamese aircraft. It was an unimpressive assortment, but *Farm Gate's* stated function was to train the South Vietnam Air Force (RVNAF). Because the training missions were flown de facto in actual combat, and because the US aircraft carried RVNAF markings, missions had to include at least one RVNAF crew member. By the fall of 1961 the Viet Cong controlled large portions of rural South Vietnam and there was a strong need for air support. Given the limited RVNAF capability to fly the missions, and the need to train under combat conditions, *Farm Gate* found itself at war.

The United States, as part of its SEATO commitment, had established in 1955 the Military Assistance Advisory Group, Vietnam (MAAG) to co-ordinate military assistance to South Vietnam. Now, with an active USAF role developing, the Thirteenth Air Force of the Pacific Air Forces (PACAF) set up an advance headquarters (ADVON) on 15 November for its Second Air Division at Tan Son Nhut Airport in Saigon to co-ordinate USAF activities in South Vietnam. Detachments were also established at Nha Trang and Danang Air Bases. Though technically part of the Thirteenth Air Force, based at Clark AB in the Philippines, the Second Air Division ADVON was under operational control of MAAG in Saigon. Also under Second Air Division control were four 15th Tactical Reconnais-

Below: Pilots and ground crews of the 64th Fighter Interceptor Squadron scramble for *Candy Machine* F-102s at Danang AB.

sance Squadron RF-101C Voodoo reconnaissance aircraft deployed to Tan Son Nhut AB between 20 October and 21 November from Kadena AB, Okinawa, under the code name *Pipe Stem*. The four Voodoos, and four that followed from the 45th TRS at Misawa AB, Japan (code name *Able Mabel*), flew 197 photo-reconnaissance missions over South Vietnam and Laos before the end of the year observing Viet Cong supply routes and hideouts.

The *Farm Gate* missions had been underway for a scant two months when it became clear that the need for air support in the field was beyond the capability of the RVNAF, even augmented by *Farm Gate* crews. Thus in December the Joint Chiefs of Staff (JCS), through PACAF, directed development of a tactical air-control system for combat introduction of US Air Force crews flying aircraft with American markings. The system would become effective on New Year's Day 1962 under the code name *Barn Door* and would co-ordinate RVNAF and USAF combat, recon and airlift activities. The US Air Force contingent would include units assigned to the Second Air Division ADVON and those on temporary duty (TDY) in Vietnam from other PACAF units and from Stateside TAC units. On 8 February 1962, MAAG was replaced by the Military Assistance Command, Vietnam (MACV) under US Army General Paul Harkins. MACV was to function as an umbrella group to co-ordinate the growing American military role in South Vietnam. With the situation in Laos also deteriorating, President Kennedy authorized deployment of forces to Thailand as well. This force would be composed of Air Force, Army and Marine units designated Joint Task Force 116. Proposals for a unified Southeast Asia (Thailand-Vietnam) Command directly under the JCS were vetoed by the Commander in Chief, Pacific (CINCPAC), Admiral Harry Felt, who wanted to keep Southeast Asia activities under the Pacific Theater Command rather than establish a new theater command. Thus a Military Assistance Command, Thailand (MACTHAI) absorbed Joint Task Force 116 and was established alongside MACV, both under CINCPAC control. MACTHAI was activated on 13 May 1962, but it was not until Air Force Chief of Staff General Curtis LeMay upgraded the Second Air Division ADVON to reinforced air-division status (8 October) that air units in both countries came under a single unified command.

By the end of 1962 the need for co-ordinated control of air power highlighted an evolving conflict between the Air Force and the US Army. Under Executive Order 9877 (1947) the Army had been permitted to retain light aircraft and helicopters. The Army was now operating its C-7A Caribou twin-engine STOL transports in Vietnam, but did not have the air operations and planning staff needed to control their operations effectively or to co-ordinate them with other – especially Air Force – operations in-country. When this was brought to the attention of CINCPAC, the Caribous were placed under operational control of the USAF Second Air Division Commander. The C-7s would remain US Army property until January 1967, when the 134 remaining Caribous were turned over to the Air Force.

One of the major problems encountered by crews flying the early *Farm Gate* missions was the difficulty or impossiblity of seeing enemy positions hidden in the dense jungle. Air Force planners tackled the problem, and late in 1961 came up with the idea of eliminating the jungle canopy that obscured the view of the ground. Because of moisture and frequent rain, it would be impossible to burn down all the trees (though it would be attempted in Operation *Sherwood Forest* four years later), so it was decided to spray the jungles with a powerful herbicide or weed killer. Six specially modified C-123 transports, equipped with spray bars and chemical tanks, were deployed to Vietnam by TAC via Clark AB. The operation was code named *Ranch Hand* and spraying began on 13 January 1962. The chemical defoliant used was manufactured by Dow Chemical and called *Agent Orange*. Though it was not known at the time, the active ingredient in *Agent Orange*, Dioxin, would ultimately be responsible for dangerous side effects. The legacy of *Agent Orange* was one of the most devastating to be brought home by returning Vietnam War veterans. Many *Ranch Hand* crewmen discovered years later that Dioxin was responsible for sterility in some of them and birth defects in the children of others. Ironically, the *Ranch Hand* operation was never very effective in its mission of destroying Viet Cong hideouts. When the health hazards related to *Agent Orange* were discovered, restrictions placed on its use by the Secretary of Defense resulted in its discontinuation after May 1970. However, the use of *Herbicide White* continued until 16 January 1971. It would be over twenty years before *Ranch* Hand crews would begin receiving govern-

Below: A U-10 of the Fifth Special Operations Squadron out of Nha Trang AB and Bien Thuy AB scatters psychological warfare leaflets over the highlands.

ment compensation for this insidious service-related disability. Coincidentally, the first USAF aircraft lost in Southeast Asia was a *Ranch Hand* C-123 that crashed, killing the three men on board, on 2 February 1962 while spraying defoliant on a Viet Cong ambush site.

Throughout 1961-63 US Air Force activities were geared primarily toward assisting the South Vietnamese Army (ARVN) and Air Force rather than taking a leading air-power role. The mission of *Farm Gate*, which was augmented by 10 B-26s, 5 T-28s and a pair of C-47s, was ground support and related training operations. Prop-driven aircraft were selected because their slower speed made them more suitable for ground support than jets, and because it was felt that the use of jets would give the USAF much too high a profile in the war. In addition to the *Ranch Hand* operations, the USAF C-123s were being used under the code names *Saw Buck* and *Mule Train* as assault transports, to augment RVNAF C-47s in paratroop drops. Two notable operations occurred on 29 June 1962 and 24 March 1963, when up to 16 *Mule Train* C-123s and 10 RVNAF C-47s dropped over a thousand (ARVN) paratroopers in offensive operations northwest of Saigon. Though no jet aircraft were authorized for combat in South Vietnam, the *Able Mable* RF-101C reconnaissance aircraft that had been deployed to Tan Son Nhut with their photo-processing unit continued their recon flights, completing a thousand sorties by December 1962. In addition to the RF-101s, PACAF F-102 all-weather interceptors were brought into Tan Son Nhut and other bases on a rotational TDY basis to safeguard the growing American air presence against the possibility of enemy air attack from North Vietnam. The first F-102s were brought in from Clark AB on 21 March 1962 under the code name *Water Glass* when unidentified radar tracks were detected over South Vietnam. The classified *Water Glass* deployments continued, as did the Operation *Bell Tone* deployments of F-100s and F-102s to Thailand (begun in 1961); when *Water Glass* was compromised in December of 1963, the code name was changed to *Candy Machine*. In June of the following year PACAF *Candy Machine* F-102s were deployed to Danang AB in a more overt demonstration of PACAF deployment capabilities.

While air activities increased in Southeast Asia, the political situation began to deteriorate late in 1963. In Cambodia, Prince Norodom Sihanouk, who had been successfully wooed by the

Below: A RVNAF A-1H Skyraider unleashes a bomb on a Vietcong target.

Soviets, was terminating his agreements with the Americans and being rewarded with four Soviet MiGs and 27 antiaircraft guns. Farther down the Mekong River in Saigon, President Diem, who had ruled South Vietnam for nearly a decade, was assassinated on 1 November and his government overthrown in a coup led by ARVN General Duong Van 'Big' Minh. This created a climate of confusion that encouraged the Viet Cong. Three weeks after Diem was gunned down in Saigon, American President John Kennedy was assassinated in Dallas, Texas, and succeeded by Vice-President Lyndon Johnson. Two weeks to the day after President Kennedy was interred at Arlington National Cemetery, Prime Minister Sarit Thanarat of Thailand was dead and his country ruled by General Thanom Kittikachorn. In less than six weeks leadership of all the major noncommunist powers involved in the conflict in Southeast Asia had changed suddenly and dramatically. Thailand was now under military rule. The

Above: A US Air Force A-1E Skyraider blasts a Vietcong hideout in Kin Trong Province, May 1965.

Below: Helmet in hand, RVNAF pilot Lt Duy Chanh arrives at his Bien Hoa based Skyraider, readied for a 23 November 1963 mission. The RVNAF insignia was similar to that of the USAF, but the sidebars were entirely red on yellow after the South Vietnamese flag, an abbreviated form of which appeared on the tail.

Below: B-57 Canberras, such as this pair seen over the Mekong Delta, were the first USAF jets to fly combat missions in South Vietnam.

Bottom: Defense Secretary Robert McNamara with strongman Khanh, center, at Tan Son Nhut in 1964.

change from Kennedy to Johnson was a radical shift of personalities and leadership styles, and the United States had in Lyndon Johnson the man who, more than any other, would shape America's policy in its longest and costliest war. The change in South Vietnam would also be crucial. From the reasonably stable, if corrupt, Diem regime the country drifted through a succession of erratic military governments (Minh would be ousted by Maj Gen Nguyen Khanh after less than three months in office) that would pave the way for the autocratic Thieu.

It was against this backdrop that the new Johnson Administration set about formulating the policy that would lead to major American involvement in the war in Southeast Asia.

THE GULF OF TONKIN

Through the first half of 1964 the emphasis was on winding down American involvement in South Vietnam. In May Secretary of Defense Robert McNamara was in Saigon, where he restated administration policy that US Air Force personnel would be out of the country in 'a matter of months' and that meanwhile they should limit their activities to providing 'genuine training' only and leave combat operations to the RVNAF. The capabilities of the Second Air Division were wearing thin anyway. The aging prop planes that had come in with *Farm Gate* were starting to fail. The B-26s had been grounded since 11 February when a wing on one of them failed on a combat mission. On 1 April the last of the B-26s were flown

Above: As the setting sun turns the delta rice paddies to rivers of fire, a lone USAF A-1E Skyraider wings home from a mission on the Ca Mau Peninsula south of Saigon.

Far left: A US Air Force C-123 Provider on a *Ranch Hand* defoliation mission about 48 miles east of Saigon in February 1962.

Left: A group of *Ranch Hand* C-123s of the 12th Air Commando Squadron spread their lethal load along a South Vietnam canal. Agent Orange was an amalgram of the common and long-used weed killer 2,4-D and the dioxin-riddled 2,4,5-T developed by Dow and Monsanto.

Above right: Its bomb load expended, a US Air Force A-1E Skyraider rolls down through light cloud cover to make a strafing run against Vietcong positions along the Saigon River south of the South Vietnamese capital.

out to Clark AB, their mission assumed by the T-28 fleet. The attack-modified T-28s were near the end of their usefulness too, and wing failures in combat on 24 March and 9 April led Second Air Division commander Major General J H Moore to note that his Division was 'practically out of business.' By the time of the McNamara visit in May, however, the T-28s had been largely replaced by A-1 Skyraiders, with six RVNAF Squadrons scheduled to be equipped with the newer A-1H as the USAF combat squadrons withdrew.

In June 1964 a high-level strategy conference was held at CINCPAC headquarters in Honolulu. Chairman of the Joint Chiefs of Staff General Maxwell Taylor and Ambassador Henry Cabot Lodge were there; Secretary McNamara flew in from Saigon; Secretary of State Dean Rusk attended, and General William Westmoreland who would soon replace General Harkins as MACV Commander. The conferees, representing the highest levels of the US Government and military, were walking a tightrope between their desire to resolve a conflict against communist aggression to which they were already committed and their wish to avoid getting too deeply involved in a foreign war alongside a nation governed by a revolving door of unstable military strongmen. It was decided that the United States would continue to build up South Vietnamese forces and provide air and ground support while keeping a low profile. Emphasis would be on resolving the conflict on the ground in South Vietnam rather than through use of a decisive strategic air offensive against enemy supply centers in North Vietnam, as had been proposed by USAF Chief of Staff Curtis LeMay. Though the situation would change dramatically two months later, the conference was to set the tone for the next four years based on the situation as it existed in June 1964.

On the night of 2 August 1964 the scenario changed decisively. North Vietnamese torpedo boats attacked the USS *Maddox*, an American destroyer, in the Gulf of Tonkin off North Vietnam.

Two nights later the torpedo boats tangled with the *Maddox* again, and with the destroyer USS *Turner Joy* as well. This represented a serious escalation and General LeMay used the opportunity to call again for a decisive air offensive against the North Vietnamese. The administration did not take up LeMay's idea. President Johnson announced that while 'seeking no wider war' the United States would honor its commitments and would respond to the attacks. On 5 August, under the code name *Pierce Arrow*, US Navy F-8s based on carriers in the Gulf of Tonkin retaliated by bombing North Vietnamese patrol boat bases and fuel storage dumps in southernmost North Vietnam. On the same day PACAF deployed B-57 tactical bombers and F-100s to Bien Hoa AB and Danang AB. Over the next nine days eighteen PACAF F-105 fighter bombers from the 36th Tactical Fighter Squadron at Yakota AB, Japan, deployed to Korat RTAFB, Thailand. On 7 August the US Congress passed the Gulf of Tonkin Resolution, giving the President power to 'take all necessary measures to repel any armed attack against the forces of the United States and to prevent further aggression.' The United States had traded a low profile for a wider war.

THE WIDER WAR

From an earlier prospect of containing the situation, the United States now faced a much-escalated conflict. The Pandora's Box of air raids into North Vietnam had opened, but it was still hoped that a limited response would frighten the North Vietnamese into backing off. Quite the opposite was true. A division of North Vietnamese regulars was being funneled down the Ho Chi Minh Trail infiltration route into South Vietnam. Thirty MiG-15s and -17s were deployed from China into the North Vietnamese air base at Phuc Yen. The enemy was anything but scared off.

On the night of 31 October 1964, Vietcong sappers penetrated the perimeter of Bien Hoa AB near Saigon and set up a mortar barrage in which four Americans were killed and thirty wounded. Many aircraft were destroyed, including five PACAF B-57s. Others, including 13 more B-57s, were damaged. As the acrid smoke gave way to the humid dawn of 1 November, the JCS met in Washington to ponder their options. The Defense Intelligence Agency had earlier drawn up a list of 94 strategic targets

in North Vietnam, whose destruction it was believed would cripple North Vietnam's ability to wage war. It was this list that General LeMay had advocated before Honolulu and again after the Gulf of Tonkin. The JCS decided it was time for this kind of hard-hitting action. A contingency plan was drawn up for a 16-day maximum-effort strategic air offensive against the North, and the plan was presented to Secretary of Defense McNamara and President Johnson for approval. They rejected it. Johnson and McNamara still felt it was necessary only to let the North Vietnamese know they were not immune from attack, and they would see the folly of their ways. The North Vietnamese however, unaffected by the logic of the men in Washington, saw American reluctance as an advance warning and used the time the Johnson Administration gave them to build an immense air-defense network that would cost a great many American lives as the war dragged on.

While the action against North Vietnam was the center of attention, the wider war was engulfing all Southeast Asia. In April 1964 a coup in the Laotian capital of Vientiane by an amalgam of rightists and neutralists under Prime Minister

Souvanna Phouma had provoked stepped-up attacks from the North Vietnamese-sponsored Pathet Lao guerrillas. By 16 May the entire Plain of Jars region of Laos was under Pathet Lao control. American reconnaissance missions over Laos, code-named *Yankee Team*, which had been terminated 18 months earlier, were resumed. On 6 June a US Navy RF-8 reconnaissance plane from *Yankee Team* was shot down by ground fire, followed next day by an F-8 escorting an RF-8. On 8 June 14 PACAF F-100s were dispatched from Clark AB to Danang AB and Takhli RTAFB, making their first strikes against antiaircraft sites in the Plain of Jars on 9 June. On 14 December 1964 PACAF began *Operation Barrel Roll*, involving tactical fighter-bomber missions against targets in Laos. This was the beginning of continuous USAF combat operations in Southeast Asia.

Below: This was the scene at Bien Hoa AB on the morning of 1 November 1964 after the Halloween night Viet Cong attack. Two B-57s were burned to the ground where they sat, while a third parked next to the one on the right lost a wing. Flexible fuel bladders are visible in the lower right, while A-1s are parked around the hangar at the far left. Perimeter defense would be a constant and serious problem for the US Air Force throughout the war years.

Below: The pilot of this 19th Tactical Airlift Squadron C-123K, photographed by Staff Sargeant Andy Sarakon during a mission over South Vietnam in October 1970, has opened his window in deference to the pasty heat rippling up from the jungle below. Camouflage paint schemes on US Air Force aircraft were virtually unknown prior to 1965 when the three-tone scheme visible here was officially adopted for use in Southeast Asia.

ROLLING THUNDER

As 1965 began, the US Air Force found itself no longer an observer and sporadic participant, but deeply engaged in the wider war. The Bien Hoa AB attack had been only the worst of a series of direct attacks on American facilities in South Vietnam. On Christmas Eve 1964, Viet Cong hit the Brink Hotel BOQ in the heart of downtown Saigon with 250-lbs plastic explosive, killing two and wounding 71. The administration was coming to recognize the need for some type of air offensive against North Vietnam in the wake of these attacks. In February 1965 'tit for tat' retaliatory strikes were authorized – air attacks on the North in response to a specific attack in the South. The first of these, code-named *Flaming Dart*, came on 7 and 8 February when USAF and US Navy aircraft struck the communications center at Ninh Linh in the southern panhandle of North Vietnam.

On 1 February Vice Chief of Staff General John McConnell succeeded General LeMay as USAF Chief of Staff. He shared with his predecessor a profound belief in an immediate strategic air offensive against the North. Again the plan was endorsed by the JCS and rejected by the President and Secretary of Defense McNamara. McConnell was able, however, to convince the administration that the restrictions inherent in the strictly retaliatory *Flaming Dart* missions made them inadequate from a tactical standpoint.

The administration gave some ground by removing the 'strictly retaliatory' requirement, but the objectives of air attacks on the North were still narrowly defined by McNamara as: '(A) reduce the flow and/or increase the cost of infiltration of men and supplies from North Vietnam to South Vietnam; (B) make it clear to the North Vietnamese leadership that so long as they continue their aggression against the South they will have to pay a price in the North; and (C) raise the morale of the South Vietnamese people.'

McNamara's outline, approved by the President, paved the way for a tactical rather than strategic air offensive against the North. It would be directed principally at interdicting lines of communication and supply rather than at destroying North Vietnam's ability to wage war. This interdiction campaign would be code-named *Rolling Thunder* – the longest and largest American air operation in Vietnam.

The first *Rolling Thunder* missions were flown by US Navy aircraft of the Seventh Fleet's Task Force 77 on 11 February 1965. The first Air Force participation came with the fifth *Rolling Thunder* strike on 2 March. The bomber force included both B-57s and F-105 fighter bombers, with F-100s flying as escorts. Enemy ground fire proved to be heavier than expected over the target. Three of the F-105s and a pair of F-100s went down; Captain Hayden Lockhart had the dubious honor of being the first US Air Force pilot captured by North Vietnam.

Because of the administration's limited perception of *Rolling Thunder*, it was difficult for Second Air Division and Task Force 77 commanders to obtain clearance to attack anything but logistical targets. If the interdiction campaign were to work, North Vietnamese air defenses had to be neutralized, and the Defense Department would prove persistently timid about authorizing attacks on such targets. One bone of contention between the Navy and Air Force and the administration was Phuc Yen NVPAFB (North Vietnam People's Air Force Base) near Hanoi. Phuc Yen was the biggest interceptor base in North

Left: A Rolling Thunder F-105 of the 354th Tactical Fighter Squadron releases its bombs over North Vietnam.

Vietnam and virtually bristling with MiGs as well as Il-28 light bombers. As such, it was a grave hazard to *Rolling Thunder* pilots. Basic air-power doctrine dictates that the first order of business is to gain air superiority over the combat theater. By recommendation of PACAF Commander General Hunter Harris, Phuc Yen was an obvious early target in the *Rolling Thunder* campaign, and 30 B-52s were armed and ready for a scheduled night strike. The plan, however, was overridden by the authorities in Washington. It would be October 1967 before the President would finally release Phuc Yen for attack. In the intervening 30 months the Phuc Yen MiGs would not rest idle.

The first encounter of the MiG kind came on 3 April 1965. Four Navy F-8Es were flying a mission against the Thanh Hoa Bridge about 30 miles south of Hanoi when they were jumped by MiG-17s. Although one of the F-8s took battle damage, there were no losses; the first aerial combat of the Vietnam War ended in a draw. The following day the Air Force was not so lucky. A strike force of heavily laden F-105s was going north to the same target when it was attacked by a mixed flight of MiG-15s and -17s about 76 miles south of Hanoi. The sluggish F-105s, named Thunderchief but nicknamed 'Thud,' were designed as supersonic fighter bombers and traded off manueverability for speed and bomb capacity. The speedy MiGs were able to get into firing position and a pair of Thuds fell to enemy cannon fire. These were the first USAF losses from air-to-air combat in the war. Though they would be the only USAF losses during 1965, it was a blow to morale.

By this time the Air Force had deployed to Vietnam its top air-superiority fighter, the McDonnell F-4 Phantom, to fly as an escort for the fighter bombers. The Phantom's roots ran back to the Korean War years and a US Navy requirement for a carrier-based fighter/attack plane. The result was the F4H-1 in 1955. In Navy nomenclature of the day F4H translated as the fourth fighter produced for the Navy by McDonnell Douglas (manufacturer's code *H*); the -1 designated the first model F4H to be produced, corresponding exactly to an *A* in USAF nomenclature. When the Air Force expressed an interest in acquiring F4Hs, the Phantom received the USAF designation F-110A. In 1962 the Defense Department merged the Navy and Air Force nomenclature systems, scrapping the more complicated Navy system in favor of the simpler Air Force system. Thus the F4H/F-110 became the F-4 in both services.

In March 1962 the Air Force issued a Military Interdepartmental Purchase Request (MIPR) for the Phantom which it passed to the manufacturer via the Navy, acting as intermediary. The Specific Operational Requirements issued in SOR 200 called for the Air Force Phantom to function across the entire tactical mission range, air support, air superiority, etc., and to be aerial refuelable via the boom method used by the Air Force (which differed from the hose-and-drogue method used by the Navy). The first Air Force Phantoms were designated F-4C, the F-4B being the Navy production version. The first F-4Cs became operational with the 4453rd Combat Crew Training Wing at MacDill AFB, Florida, in November 1963, and with the 12th Tactical Fighter Wing at the same base in January 1964. The first deployments to Southeast Asia came early the following year, with the F-4 going on to become the top American air-superiority fighter of the war.

The first encounter between Phantoms and MiGs took place on 17 June 1965 when US Navy F-4Bs from the carrier USS *Midway* shot down a pair of MiG-17s, scoring the first American aerial victories of the war. The Air Force Phantoms got their first

Right: Another F-105 dropping 750 lb bombs on North Vietnam.

chance at the enemy on the afternoon of 10 July 1965, when a pair of MiG-17s made the mistake of tangling with a flight of F-4Cs of the 45th Tactical Fighter Squadron out of Ubon RTAFB. By now it was known that the enemy tactic for fighter escorts was to time their attack when they knew the F-4s were low on fuel. Today, four Phantoms were purposely running late, flying a *Fluid Four* pattern at an altitude that made them appear on radar like F-105s. The North Vietnamese took the bait and scrambled the MiGs from Phuc Yen. The *Fluid Four* pattern gave way to a *Loose Deuce* formation in which two of the USAF fighters would engage the enemy while the other two covered them. The MiGs broke off their intercept when they sighted the F-4s. The Phantoms lit their afterburners and gave chase, only to have the MiGs turn on them. The MiGs initially outmanuevered the heavier Phantoms and got off some cannon fire at the plane manned by Captains Ken Holcombe and Arthur Clark in the

ensuing dogfight. Holcombe and Clark got inside one MiG's turn, permitting the enemy to overshoot them. They missed their first opportunity to take a shot at the MiG, but maneuvered behind him again after he made an ineffectual pass with cannons blazing. They fired all four of their AIM-9 Sidewinder air-to-air missiles; two connected, and the MiG disintegrated as it dropped into a cloud. The US Air Force had scored its first combat kill of the Vietnam War.

While Holcombe and Clark were wrapped in the contrail of their MiG, the Phantom manned by Captains Thomas Roberts and Ronald Anderson had gone into a Mach 1.4 dive to escape the other. They pulled out of the dive in a four-G (four times the pull of gravity) climb and got into a good position above the MiG. The first Sidewinder exploded off the MiG's port wingtip but did little damage; a second was hastily fired without a radar tracking lock-on and missed. The third AIM-9 exploded just

Above: Running lights ablaze, a flight of F-4Es of the 388th Tactical Fighter Wing out of Korat RTAFB line up behind a SAC KC-135 air refueling tanker to top off their tanks before heading north on a MiG CAP mission. The 388th was organized in April 1966 and earned 17 aerial victories before it was deactivated at the end of 1972.

behind the MiG, and the enemy fighter was swallowed in the blast, which marked the second kill of the war. The four airmen involved received Silver Stars, and the score had been settled for the two F-105s lost in April.

Following the early encounters of spring and summer 1965, the enemy reserved the MiGs for about nine months to reassess tactics and concentrate on building surface-to-air missiles and artillery. The MiG-15s and -17s were at a definite disadvantage against the Sidewinder-toting Phantoms despite their better maneuverability. Consequently, when the MiGs did attack it was to harass unescorted F-105s and force them to jettison their bombs before they got to the target. As of March 1966 the F-4s were flying regular *MiG CAP* (Combat Air Patrol) escort missions with the *Rolling Thunder* F-105s. In April, with north-east monsoon season over, the MiGs were ready to reopen the dogfight season.

A DARING RESCUE IN THE A SHAU

On 10 March 1966 Major Bernard Fisher became the first USAF officer to win the Congressional Medal of Honor in Southeast Asia. A US Special Forces camp in the A Shau Valley of South Vietnam was under attack by 4000 North Vietnamese troops. The northeast monsoon season was still blowing strong and the enemy knew the weather would hamper American air support. The A-1E Skyraiders that did go in faced not only the weather but withering ground fire. One of the Skyraiders was severely damaged and had to make a forced landing on the airstrip in the lower-valley camp. Fisher could see that the pilot had survived but would soon be captured and/or killed. Ignoring the fusillade of ground fire directed from the valley walls above and below, Fisher made a landing on the field, picked up his downed comrade and somehow made it into the air and back to safety.

Above: An aerial view of the A Shau camp taken on 12 March.

Left: A highway bridge 112 miles northwest of Vinh is destroyed by a 750 lb bomb from an F-105 as a second Thud (*upper left*) closes in.

Above: A pair of camouflaged Thuds at work over the southern panhandle of North Vietnam in July 1966.

US Air Force Medal of Honor Winners of the Vietnam War

Capt Steven Bennett (Palestine, Tex) 29 June 1972, Quang Tri, South Vietnam (KIA 29 June 1972)

Col George Day (Sioux City, Iowa) Conspicuous gallantry while POW. Now a retired Colonel living in Shalimar, Fla

Maj Merlyn Dethlefsen (Greenville, Iowa) 10 Mar 1967, Thai Nguyen, North Vietnam. Now a retired Colonel living in Fort Worth, Tex

Maj Bernard Fisher (San Bernardino, Calif) 10 Mar 1966, A Shau Valley, South Vietnam. Now a retired Colonel living in Kuna, Idaho

1st Lt James Fleming (Sedalia, Mo) 26 Nov 1968, Duc Co, South Vietnam. Active Duty at Randolph AFB, Texas

Lt Col Joe Jackson (Newman, Ga) 12 May 1968, Kham Duc, South Vietnam. Now a retired Colonel living in Kent, Washington

Lt Col William Jones, III (Norfolk, Va) 1 Sept 1968, Dong Hoi, North Vietnam. Killed 15 Nov 1969, Woodbridge, Va

A1C John Levitow (Hartford, Conn) 24 Feb 1969, Long Binh, South Vietnam. Now living in Plainville, Connecticut

Capt Lance Sijan (Milwaukee, Wis) Conspicuous gallantry while POW. Died while POW, Jan 1968

Lt Col Leo Thorsness (Walnut Grove, Minn) 19 Apr 1967, North Vietnam. Now a retired Colonel living in Santa Monica California

Capt Hilliard Wilbanks (Cornelia, Ga) 24 Feb 1967 Dalat, South Vietnam. KIA 24 Feb 1967

Capt Gerald Young (Anacortes, Wash) 9 Nov 1967, Da Nang area, South Vietnam. Now a retired Colonel living in Anacortes, Washington

AIR OFFENSIVE COMMAND CONTROL

With the advent of *Rolling Thunder*, the US Navy and Air Force found themselves engaged in the biggest air offensive since World War II. To integrate efforts of the two services in the massive campaign, CINCPAC established the *Rolling Thunder Coordinating Committee* rather than appointing a single overall commander for air operations. PACAF had authority to co-ordinate *Rolling Thunder* but did not receive operational control of the Navy Seventh Fleet carrier aircraft. The Coordinating Committee faced the logistical problem of two air forces under separate operational controls attacking area targets. PACAF's Second Air Division at Tan Son Nhut proposed that the area be divided by time and the two services assigned alternating three-hour intervals to hit any target in North Vietnam. The Committee, however, decided to divide North Vietnam geographically into 'Route Packages,' or navigational sectors. There were seven Route Packages (or Packs) with PACAF covering three that encompassed about 60% of North Vietnam, while the Seventh Fleet got the other four. The Air Force was assigned Route Pack 1 in the southern panhandle of North Vietnam closest to its bases in South Vietnam. Because they had more aerial refueling support, plus the proximity to bases in Thailand, the Air Force was also assigned Route Packs 5 and 6A, deeper in enemy territory. The more limited range of carrier-based aircraft gave the Navy Route Packs 2, 3, 4 and 6B, which were contiguous with the coast of the Gulf of Tonkin where the Seventh Fleet had established its *Yankee Station*.

For political reasons, the Johnson Administration opted to limit *Rolling Thunder* access to targets in the areas of Hanoi, North Vietnam's capital, and Haiphong, the largest port. Bombing would be prohibited for a ten-nautical-mile radius from Hanoi center, and four nautical miles from the center of Haiphong; it would be severely restricted out to 30 nautical miles from the center of Hanoi and ten nautical miles from mid-Haiphong. The stated purpose was to avoid civilian casualties, which it did – but it also gave the enemy an unprecedented break by turning his major strategic targets into sanctuaries. Within them, the North Vietnamese could create, undisturbed, an elaborate air-defense system that would cost the US Air Force dearly in years to come.

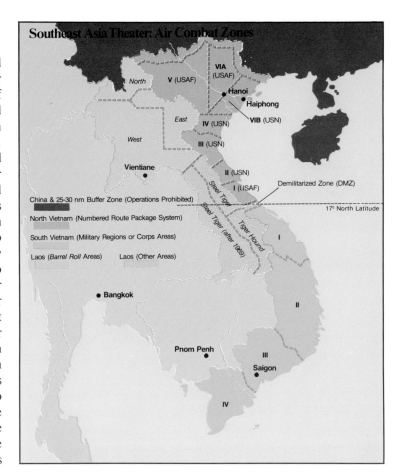

Southeast Asia Theater: Air Combat Zones

China & 25-30 nm Buffer Zone (Operations Prohibited)

North Vietnam (Numbered Route Package System)

South Vietnam (Military Regions or Corps Areas)

Laos (*Barrel Roll* Areas) Laos (Other Areas)

To complicate the situation, President Johnson and Secretary of Defense McNamara were taking a personal interest in the tactical air war in Southeast Asia. Split-second communications kept them abreast of the situation on the distant battlefront in a way no predecessor could have dreamed of. An unfortunate result was that administration time and energy became engrossed in making tactical decisions that better-trained field commanders should have been making. Instead of being able to get timely approval for strikes against elusive targets, Second Air Division commanders had to route their requests through MACV in Saigon to CINCPAC in Hawaii, who in turn had to pass the target 'nomination' back to the JCS in Washington, thence to the Secretary of Defense and the White House.

Left: An unarmed USAF 0-1 Bird Dog parked along with Army helicopters at a Forward Air Control base in the jungles of South Vietnam, July 1966.

Above: The F-100 Super Sabre was first introduced to Southeast Asia in a fighter-bomber role but was later used as an FAC under the code name *Misty*.

Approval or disapproval then made its way back down the chain of command. This time-lag factor was one of the heaviest burdens of the *Rolling Thunder* operation.

Rolling Thunder was the centerpiece of the interdiction campaign, but operations in Laos were an integral part of the effort to keep men and materiel in North Vietnam from reaching the South. The ongoing *Barrel Roll* operations were concentrated in route packages in north and northeast Laos, directed principally at interdicting supply lines feeding the communist Pathet Lao. On 3 April 1965 a new interdiction zone, code-named *Steel Tiger*, was established on the eastern Laotian panhandle stretching from the 17th parallel to the southernmost tip of Laos. The area was directly opposite the southern third of North Vietnam and the northern third of South Vietnam, composed of rugged jungle and mountain country bisected by the infiltration route known as the Ho Chi Minh Trail. In December 1965 the *Steel Tiger* area was divided in two, the southern half being redesignated *Tiger Hound* with interdiction operations assigned to a PACAF *Tiger Hound Task Force*.

With the rapid buildup of American aircraft in the skies over Southeast Asia during 1965 came the need for some kind of immediate on-sight command and control. Since *Farm Gate*, the basic building block of the on-sight or 'in-country' command was the Forward Air Controller (FAC), hovering over the battlefield in a single-engine light aircraft. Initially the FACs flew the tiny O-1 Bird Dog; later they graduated to the larger Cessna O-2. The FAC role was that of liaison between Army ground forces and USAF strike aircraft. Because of his relatively slow speed, the FAC had a much better view of the battlefield than faster, higher-flying jets, and could direct them to target by radio or smoke markers. In many cases the bomber pilots never saw the targets and relied entirely on the FACs. In the early years of the war the FACs were also an important tool for gathering intelligence about the enemy.

Until 1965 most air-strike command and control was located on the ground at air bases. With the ever-growing numbers of strike aircraft spreading their spider web of contrails across the Southeast Asian sky came the need for a more immediate control center to co-ordinate FACs and bombers. The answer was the Airborne Command and Control Center (ABCCC) which was located in a C-130 Hercules transport that positioned itself in a central location above the battlefield, and through which information about potential enemy targets was funneled from FACs and other sources to strike aircraft. The C-130 ABCCCs were used throughout South Vietnam and in Laos as well, where they operated under the code name *Hillsboro*.

Over North Vietnam, where there were no FACs, and where target authorization originated in Washington, command and

Above: TAC's *Big Eye* EC-121Qs were sent to Southeast Asia to fly airborne radar surveillance missions for PACAF.

control was more complex. Central control was at the Second Air Division (later Seventh Air Force) headquarters at Tan Son Nhut AB near Saigon, which relied on an advanced command/control center in the Laotian panhandle code-named *Motel*. The Navy equivalent, code-named *Red Crown*, was on a ship in the Gulf of Tonkin. A series of other radar installations was located throughout Thailand and South Vietnam, known as Control and Reporting Centers (CRC) and Posts (CRP). The northernmost, and among the busiest of the CRPs, was at Dong Ha AB north of Danang, code-named *Waterbag*. Because of its location *Waterbag* controlled all missions going into North Vietnam from bases in the south and rendezvous with refueling aircraft over the Gulf of Tonkin. *Waterbag* was also tied into the Navy Seventh Fleet radar net in the Gulf of Tonkin. The next link in the command-and-control chain was the EC-121 ABCCCs, code-named *Big Eye*. These ABCCCs, modified Lockheed Constellations, were the first AWACS (Airborne Warning and Control Systems). The EC-121 had been developed for the Air Defense Command (ADC) in the 1950s under the code name *Big Eye* to provide an airborne warning and control platform for interceptors defending North American airspace; they were first deployed to Vietnam in April 1965 as *Rolling Thunder* got underway. The *Big Eye* EC-121 ABCCCs, redesignated *College Eye* in March 1967, were initially based at Tan Son Nhut AB in South Vietnam, but transferred to Thailand in early 1967. Their stations included

the areas over north central Laos and off the coast of North Vietnam, north of *Red Crown* and Task Force 77 and southeast of the port of Haiphong. The EC-121's radar was inferior to that of the later Boeing E-3 AWACS in its ability to 'see' activities close to the ground where hills and other 'ground clutter' obscured its view. Nonetheless, the airborne positioning of the *College Eye* radar so far north made it much superior to land-based radar, and an invaluable final link in the chain of command and control that guided USAF strike aircraft to their targets.

THE SEVENTH AIR FORCE

On Christmas Eve 1965, the first phase of *Rolling Thunder* closed as the US announced the first of many temporary halts to bombing raids into North Vietnam (designed to give North Vietnam a chance to reconsider, and hopefully to end their supplying of arms and materiel – and recently of regular troops – to the Viet Cong). This bombing halt, like others to follow, was used instead as an opportunity to bolster North Vietnamese air defenses. When *Rolling Thunder* resumed 37 days later (30 January 1966) it was only the beginning of an increase in the US commitment to the war. On the political front, President Johnson met a week later in Honolulu with South Vietnamese President Thieu and his Premier, the flamboyant RVNAF Marshal Ky, to discuss the war and increased American economic aid. This was one of a series of high-level contacts during 1966 that included visits to South Vietnam by both

Chain of Command, Southeast Asia

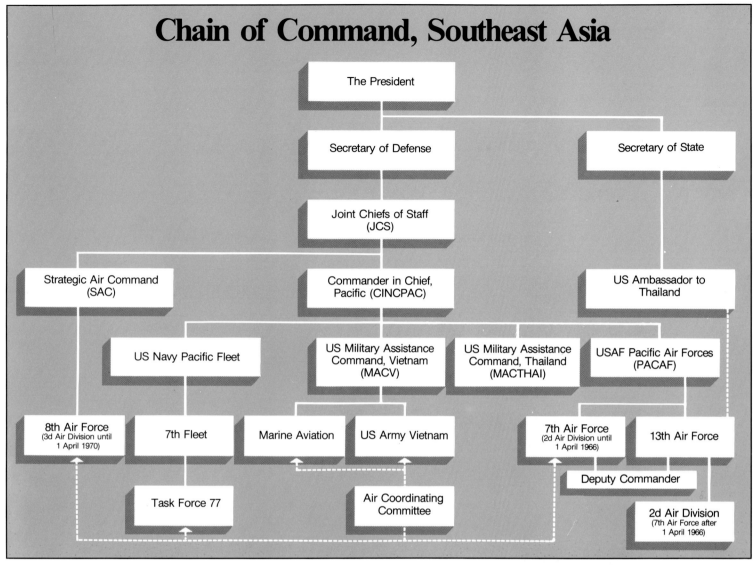

```
                              ┌──────────────┐
                              │ The President │
                              └──────────────┘
                     ┌──────────────┐              ┌──────────────┐
                     │ Secretary of │              │ Secretary of │
                     │   Defense    │              │    State     │
                     └──────────────┘              └──────────────┘
                     ┌──────────────┐
                     │ Joint Chiefs │
                     │ of Staff (JCS)│
                     └──────────────┘
  ┌──────────────┐   ┌──────────────┐              ┌──────────────┐
  │ Strategic Air│   │ Commander in │              │ US Ambassador│
  │ Command (SAC)│   │ Chief,       │              │  to Thailand │
  └──────────────┘   │ Pacific      │              └──────────────┘
                     │ (CINCPAC)    │
                     └──────────────┘
```

US Navy Pacific Fleet — US Military Assistance Command, Vietnam (MACV) — US Military Assistance Command, Thailand (MACTHAI) — USAF Pacific Air Forces (PACAF)

8th Air Force (3d Air Division until 1 April 1970) — 7th Fleet — Marine Aviation — US Army Vietnam — 7th Air Force (2d Air Division until 1 April 1966) — 13th Air Force

Task Force 77 — Air Coordinating Committee — Deputy Commander

2d Air Division (7th Air Force after 1 April 1966)

Secretary of Defense McNamara and Secretary of State Dean Rusk.

For the US Air Force, the increased commitment came with the upgrading of the Second Air Division, part of the Thirteenth Air Force, to full numbered status as the Seventh Air Force on 1 April 1966. The Seventh had been deactivated after World War II, having served with distinction in the USAAF effort, Pacific Theater. Now it was back.

In November 1965 Chief of Staff General McConnell had decided that the Second Air Division should report directly to PACAF rather than the Thirteenth Air Force. With the influx of men and aircraft, it was growing equal to a numbered air force almost the size of the Fifth during the Korean War. Meanwhile, the Thai Government had become uneasy about an arrangement that placed American forces in their country under the same command structure as those in South Vietnam. In April 1965, in the same spirit that led to creation of a MACTHAI alongside MACV, USAF forces in Thailand were put *directly* under command of the Thirteenth Air Force, while those in South Vietnam were under the Thirteenth Air Force via its Second Air Division to facilitate practical day-to-day operations, General McConnell established the simultaneous position of Deputy Commander over the Second Air Division and the Thirteenth Air Force (Thailand). With reactivation of the Seventh Air Force to assume the Second Air Division's role, the Commander changed as well, becoming Deputy Commander of both the Seventh Air Force and the Thirteenth Air Force (Thailand). Thus, US Air Force operations originating in both Thailand and South Viet-

Above: Seventh Air Force commander General Moore and an F-100 pilot confer with Air Force Secretary Harold Brown at Tan Son Nhut in January 1966. Brown later served as Defense Secretary under President Jimmy Carter.

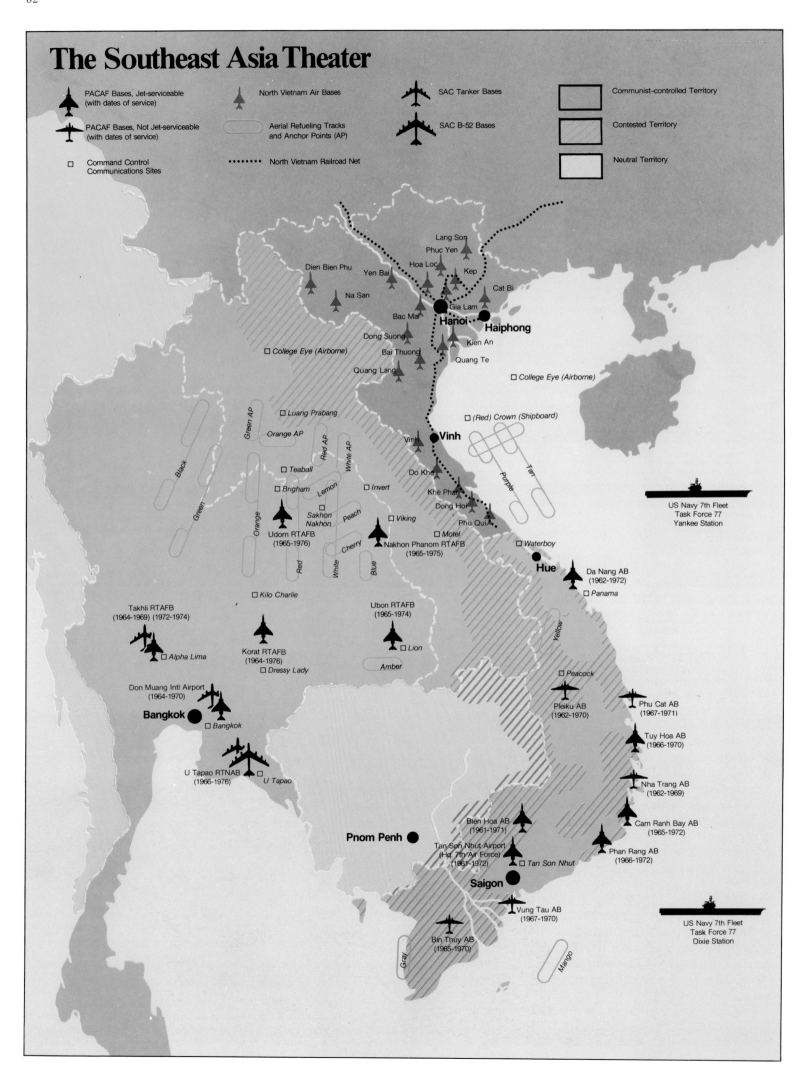

The Southeast Asia Theater

PACAF Bases, Jet-serviceable (with dates of service)

PACAF Bases, Not Jet-serviceable (with dates of service)

Command Control Communications Sites

North Vietnam Air Bases

Aerial Refueling Tracks and Anchor Points (AP)

North Vietnam Railroad Net

SAC Tanker Bases

SAC B-52 Bases

Communist-controlled Territory

Contested Territory

Neutral Territory

Lang Son

Phuc Yen

Hoa Loc

Kep

Dien Bien Phu

Yen Bai

Cat Bi

Na San

Gia Lam

Bac Mai

Hanoi

Haiphong

Dong Suong

Kien An

College Eye (Airborne)

Bai Thuong

Quang Te

Quang Lang

College Eye (Airborne)

Luang Prabang

(Red) Crown (Shipboard)

Green AP

Orange AP

Vinh

Vinh

Black

Red AP

White AP

Do Khe

Green

Teaball

Khe Phat

Tan

Brigham

Lemon

Invert

Dong Hoi

Purple

Orange

Sakhon Nakhon

Peach

Viking

Phu Qui

Motel

Udorn RTAFB (1965-1976)

Cherry

Nakhon Phanom RTAFB (1965-1975)

Waterboy

Red

White

Blue

Hue

Da Nang AB (1962-1972)

Kilo Charlie

Panama

Takhli RTAFB (1964-1969) (1972-1974)

Ubon RTAFB (1965-1974)

Yellow

Alpha Lima

Korat RTAFB (1964-1976)

Lion

Dressy Lady

Amber

Peacock

Pleiku AB (1962-1970)

Phu Cat AB (1967-1971)

Don Muang Intl Airport (1964-1970)

Bangkok

Tuy Hoa AB (1966-1970)

Bangkok

Nha Trang AB (1962-1969)

U Tapao RTNAB (1966-1976)

U Tapao

Cam Ranh Bay AB (1965-1972)

Bien Hoa AB (1961-1971)

Pnom Penh

Phan Rang AB (1966-1972)

Tan Son Nhut Airport (Hq. 7th Air Force) (1961-1972)

Tan Son Nhut

Saigon

Vung Tau AB (1967-1970)

Bin Thuy AB (1965-1970)

Gray

Mango

US Navy 7th Fleet Task Force 77 Yankee Station

US Navy 7th Fleet Task Force 77 Dixie Station

nam could be co-ordinated through the same office, although the US Ambassador to Thailand, as the senior American official, retained control of US forces based there. As part of the separation agreement, aircraft based in Thailand could be used against targets in Laos and North Vietnam, (although their use against targets in the latter would not be revealed until March 1967). South Vietnam was exempt, except in an emergency. South Vietnam-based aircraft could be used against targets in all three countries.

Because of an arrangement similar to the one in Thailand, all Seventh and Thirteenth Air Force aircraft engaged in *Barrel Roll, Steel Tiger* and *Tiger Hound* interdiction operations in Laos were nominally under direction of the US Ambassador to that country, who consulted with the Laotian Government whose ground forces, under General Vang Pao, were operating in these route packages. By extension, the US Air Attaché to the US Embassy in Laos, a USAF officer, became the US air commander for Laos, as he had the practical task of selecting targets and working with Seventh and Thirteenth Air Force commanders. Meanwhile, the Strategic Air Command's Third Air Division based on Guam maintained control of the *Arc Light* B-52 strikes in South Vietnam that had begun in June 1965. SAC did, however, continue its liaison office at Seventh Air Force Headquarters.

With reactivation of the Seventh Air Force and concomitant buildup, the USAF increased the number of bases from which jet fighters and fighter bombers could operate. When the US intervention commenced, the only jet-serviceable air bases available were Danang, Bien Hoa and Tan Son Nhut, the latter also serving as Saigon's international airport. In 1965, the big Navy facility at Cam Ranh Bay opened with its jet-serviceable field to which were assigned three squadrons of USAF F-4Cs, totaling 54 aircraft, or over half of the F-4Cs in Vietnam during the first year of their deployment. The next base to open was Phan Rang AB, which opened three days after the Seventh took over from the Second. During 1966 work began on Phu Cat AB; Tuy Hoa AB opened in November as a turnkey project whereby contractors designed and constructed a complete ready-to-use base.

THE DOGFIGHT SEASON RESUMES

On 23 April 1966 the USAF fought its first MiG battle since the victories scored the previous June. The northeast monsoon had subsided and the MiGs were back in force. Four F-4Cs of the 555th TFS were flying cover for air strikes against the Bac Giang bridge 25 miles northeast of Hanoi when a like number of MiG-17s made a head-on pass. The eight aircraft turned for another try, each attempting to outmaneuver his opposite number. When the fight ended, a pair of the MiGs had fallen victim to American air-to-air missiles.

Three days later, the first enemy MiG-21 was downed by Major Paul Gilmore and Lieutenant William Smith in an F-4C riding herd on an RB-66 reconnaissance plane over the Red River northeast of Hanoi. A second MiG-21 was encountered, but escaped when the Americans had to break off the chase because of low fuel reserves. The Soviet-built MiG-21 was, in the mid-sixties, the Russians' top fighter, as the MiG-15 had been during the Korean War. A light and highly maneuverable aircraft, the MiG-21 weighed in at 18,740 pounds versus 58,000 pounds for the F-4C. Designed as a direct result of lessons learned in the Korean War, the MiG-21 first flew in 1955 and went on to be produced in greater numbers than any combat aircraft since, serving with 33 air forces around the world. A potent adversary, the MiG-21 (NATO code-name *Fishbed*) was armed with a 23 mm twin-barrel cannon and up to four air-to-air missiles. Though 66 North Vietnamese Fishbeds would be shot down by American F-4s during the war, they took their toll on the Americans, who would not equal the ten-to-one kill superiority they achieved in the Korean War.

The first F-4 claimed by the enemy was lost to a troika of the older MiG-17s on 21 September 1966. The renewed *Rolling Thunder* Operations of 1966 (under auspices of the reactivated Seventh Air Force) saw many more sorties over the North and much higher USAF casualties. While downing 17 MiGs, five of them -21s, PACAF lost 379 aircraft during the year. Of these, the greatest number, 126, were F-105s. All but fifteen of the Thuds went down over North Vietnam or Laos, all to ground fire except for three lost to MiGs and four downed by surface-to-air missiles

Below: Air Force C-130s disgorge troops and supplies at Cam Ranh Bay AB as an F-4 makes its final approach in the distance. The sprawling complex at Cam Ranh is today a major Russian base.

Right: A shark-mouthed F-4E Phantom out of Korat RTAFB with drop tanks and bombs mounted on its external weapons pylons. The Phantom proved during Operation *Bolo* that it was the top dogfighter in Southeast Asia.

Below: Wolfpack commander Colonel Robin Olds returns from his 100th mission over North Vietnam. Olds shot down 14 Germans during World War II and four North Vietnamese MiGs.

Below right: A North Vietnamese MiG-21 photographed by USAF gun cameras during Operation *Bolo*.

85

(SAMs). Fifty-six F-4s went down during the year, 42 of them in combat. PACAF also lost 41 A-1 Skyraiders, 26 F-100 Super Sabres, 17 RF-101 reconnaissance aircraft, 13 B-57s and 37 of the little O-1 Bird Dogs used by FACs. Over North Vietnam, the SAMs were the most ominous threat. Even though only 18 aircraft were lost to an estimated 1219 SAM launches in 1966, the North Vietnamese were deploying more and using them more effectively. Thanks to the restricted zones placed around Hanoi and Haiphong, the North Vietnamese had been able to increase their antiaircraft artillery (AAA) defenses eightfold. They introduced up to 25 SAM battalions between the Gulf of Tonkin incident and the end of 1966.

OPERATION BOLO AND AIR SUPERIORITY

As 1967 began PACAF had nearly 1700 aircraft, up from 1100 a year before: it was the second largest Major Command in the US Air Force. Against this backdrop of ever-escalating American presence in the Theater, the Seventh Air Force was planning for what would be the biggest air-to-air battle of the entire war. Dubbed Operation *Bolo*, the mission was responding to increased MiG harassment of F-105s. Because North Vietnamese fighter bases were still restricted from attack by American aircraft, it was determined that the next best way to destroy the maximum number of MiGs was to lure them into combat in a fighter sweep similar to those used in World War II and in MiG Alley over Korea. The man selected to lead *Bolo* was Colonel Robin Olds, commander of the 8th TFW, the 'Wolf Pack,' and a combat veteran with 10 aerial victories in World War II. The force would be drawn from four tactical Fighter Wings and consist of 14 flights of F-4Cs, 6 flights of F-105s flying *Iron Hand* missions suppressing SAM and AAA sites, and 4 flights of F-104s with support electronic-radar-jamming aircraft (EB-66s) and tankers. The *Bolo* strike force would approach North Vietnam from both east and west, creating a pincer to prevent the MiGs from breaking off and running for China where they could not be pursued.

On the morning of 2 January, the *Bolo* aircraft went north, following the usual flight and call-signs patterns of a typical *Rolling Thunder* fighter bomber mission. Because of the weather, the MiGs were slow to respond – when they did, a surprise was in store. Instead of the lumbering Thuds, they found a sky full of F-4s, armed to the teeth and ready to fight. In the massive aerial battle that ensued, seven MiG-21s (half the North Vietnamese inventory) were brought down, all of them by F-4Cs of the 8th TFW using AIM-7 Sidewinder air-to-air missiles. Not a single American aircraft was lost. The superiority of the Phantom, like the Sabre Jet in the previous war, was established. As Colonel Olds, who got his first of four MiG kills that day put it, 'We outflew, outshot and outfought them.'

Four days later a pair of F-4s from the 8th TFW was supposed to fly *MiG CAP* (escort, MiG Combat Air Patrol) for a strike force of F-105s when the mission was canceled due to weather. With the F-4s ready to go, it was decided to put on another *Bolo* type charade for the enemy. The two F-4s would go north pretending to be RF-4s on a weather-reconnaissance mission. Northwest of Hanoi, four MiGs out of Phuc Yen appeared on radar and the two Phantoms went into action. The MiGs were unprepared and outmaneuvered; what remained of North Vietnam's store of MiG-21s after *Bolo* was reduced by two. It was to be the last encounter with MiGs until April, after the monsoon season.

April 1967 was a good month for PACAF, with four MiG-17s brought down on a single day, and by F-105s to boot. April also

Below: A SAC B-52F drops a string of 750 lb general-purpose bombs during Operation *Arc Light*. The black bellies first applied to these bombers in 1965 were a forerunner to the overall camouflage scheme that was adopted when the B-52Ds entered the fray.

Above: A camouflaged B-52D during an *Arc Light* strike on Vietcong positions near Bien Hoa AB in December 1966.

Right and above right: Armorers load general-purpose bombs onto the external weapons pylons of B-52Ds at U Tapao RTAFB in Thailand. Both U Tapao and Andersen AFB on Guam were used as B-52 bases during the war, but U Tapao was much closer to targets in Southeast Asia.

Below: Perched high above the cumulus, a B-52D out of Andersen AFB on Guam releases its deadly bomb load over the target.

saw the first lifting of restrictions on attacking MiG bases. A raid was quickly launched on 24 April against the enemy base at Hoa Lac, resulting in the destruction of at least 14 MiGs. If April was a good month for the MiG hunters, May was even better. During the month 21 MiGs were destroyed in aerial combat in the North, five of them MiG-21s. The tally was more than double that of April and surpassed that for all of 1966. Particularly unlucky for the North Vietnamese was 13 May, when an unprecedented seven MiG-17s were shot down by F-4s and F-105s.

The following day marked the first aerial victory achieved by an F-4 using the newly installed SUU-16 20mm rotary-barrel 'Gatling gun' cannon mounted in a pod under the center fuselage. In Korea it had been noted that a major flaw in the otherwise superior Sabre Jet had been its light armament of .50-caliber machine guns *vis à vis* the cannons on enemy MiGs. During the years immediately following the Korean War, 20mm cannons were installed in American fighters. However, by the later fifties advances in guided air-to-air missiles caused aircraft designers to conclude that American fighters no longer needed guns. With the onset of aerial combat in Vietnam, an old lesson was being relearned. The technologically sophisticated Sidewinder and Sparrow missiles were often failing to detonate when they should have destroyed an enemy aircraft. It was back to the drawing board. While the new F-4E was being redesigned with an internally mounted cannon, the SUU-16 gun pod was produced and retrofitted on the older F-4Cs. The pilots were delighted and Captain James Craig, one of the F-4C pilots to score on 14 May 1967 with the new gun pod, was swift to point out that 'The kills with the gun mode could not have been made with a missile.'

In 1967 USAF pilots shot down 59 MiGs, including 17 MiG-21s – the greatest number of any year of the war – while losing nine F-4s and 11 F-105s in aerial combat. Colonel Olds, the 8th TFW commander, became the top-scoring pilot with four kills, three of them during May and two in one day. While Olds would not score a fifth victory to become the first USAF ace of the Vietnam War, he did become the first and only American ace to score victories in both World War II and Vietnam, retiring with a total score of 14.

Total US Air Force losses in Southeast Asia for 1967 came to 421, as against 379 for the year before; 334 of them were due to hostile action. Of the total 113 were F-105s, 95 were F-4s, and 23 were RF-4s. There were 878,771 combat sorties flown (up 69% over 1966) dropping 681,700 tons of ordnance, 87% more than the previous year.

THE TET OFFENSIVE AND THE BOMBING HALT

By the beginning of 1968, the North Vietnam People's Air Force had been virtually defeated. Constant pressure from the superior USAF forces against both aircraft and bases had sent it largely to safe bases in China. On the ground in South Vietnam, however, the situation was entirely different. On 30 January the North Vietnamese and Viet Cong launched a massive offensive designed to coincide with Tet, the lunar new year. The northern city of Hue was captured and parts of Saigon were overrun; a concerted effort was made to overrun both the Seventh Air Force bases in the Saigon area, Tan Son Nhut and Bien Hoa. While the Tet Offensive was eventually beaten back, it was done only at great cost to American and South Vietnamese forces. The price would be paid in Washington, where the Johnson Administration had a severe jolt. Tet showed an increasingly disgruntled American electorate that administration policy of the past four years had not worked. There was an enormous groundswell of public outcry for withdrawal from Southeast

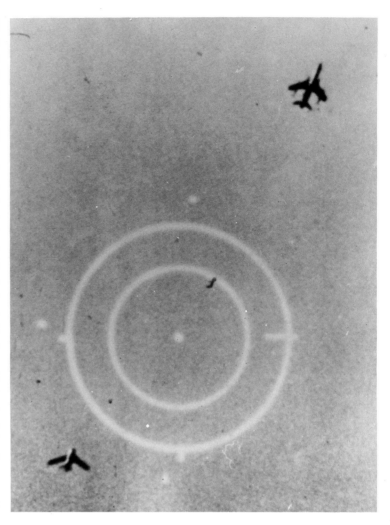

Above: Caught in a gunsight, a North Vietnamese MiG-17 closes on an F-105 during a raid on the Paul Doumer Bridge in Hanoi, December 1967.

Right: Rolling Thunder raiders blast the runway at Phuc Yen airfield in December 1967.

Asia. In a dramatic televised address, President Johnson told the American people that he would not be a candidate for re-election in 1968 and that, effective 1 April, *Rolling Thunder* bombing raids would not be made in North Vietnam above the 20th parallel. Three days later the restriction would move south to the 19th parallel. Johnson also announced that he would gradually reduce American strength in South Vietnam, and that he hoped North Vietnam would show good faith and do the same. It was announced that high-level talks would be convened to negotiate an end to the war: they began in Paris on 10 May 1968.

Air combat over North Vietnam continued for the first six weeks of the year, with eight MiGs downed by F-4Ds during that time. With the bombing halt, it would be four years before US Air Force fighters would fly against MiGs again.

On 1 November 1968, four days before the presidential election, President Johnson further de-escalated the war by announcing a halt to all bombing missions of any kind over North Vietnam – the end of *Rolling Thunder*. Armed reconnaissance flights would continue, and ultimately reveal massive rebuilding of the supply network that fed enemy forces in the South as well as a strengthening of antiaircraft defenses. It was not the good-faith de-escalation that Johnson had hoped for, but his administration was passing from the scene and the newly elected Richard M Nixon would maintain the bombing halt.

The end of *Rolling Thunder* was also that of USAF activities in the North, but the war in South Vietnam raged with renewed fury. In 90 attacks on American bases, 35 aircraft were destroyed

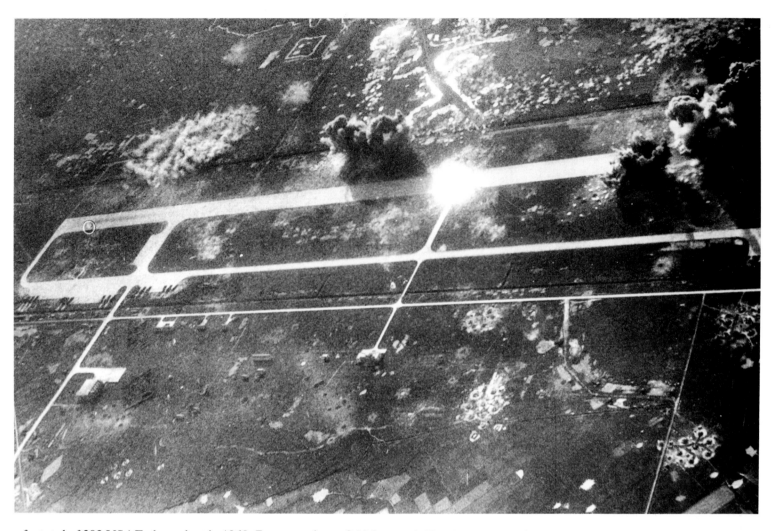

of a total of 392 USAF planes lost in 1968. Between them, SAMs and MiGs accounted for twelve USAF aircraft compared to 40 in 1967. Despite the end of *Rolling Thunder*, the total number of combat sorties was up to 18% over 1967 (1,034,839) with 1,092,200 tons of ordnance dropped.

NEW TACTICS OF INTERDICTION

With all hope of achieving interdiction at the source in North Vietnam dashed by the end of *Rolling Thunder*, US Air Force commanders had to turn to other means to stem enemy aggression. In November 1968 aircraft that had been part of *Rolling Thunder* turned their immense firepower to South Vietnam, where F-100s were now used as FACs under the code name *Misty*, and to Laos where a new series of interdiction operations designated *Commando Hunt* began. In *Commando Hunt I*, between November 1968 and April 1969, 67,094 PACAF and 3811 B-52 *Arc Light* sorties were flown against enemy positions and lines of communication in the *Steel Tiger* area of Laos. *Commando Hunt I* was immediately followed by a second series, then by *Commando Hunt III* on the first anniversary of Johnson's bombing halt. By that time Cessna A-37B Dragonflys, the attack version of the T-37 trainer, were being introduced to two newly activated Attack Squadrons in South Vietnam. Meanwhile, the last of an older bird, the B-57 light bomber, departed Vietnam after five years in the war zone.

Even as there was a continued emphasis on interdiction via bombing and strafing, other tactics were brought into play. The *Ranch Hand* defoliation program continued: despite the failure of *Sherwood Forest* in 1965, wishful thinking led to several more attempts to burn the forests to expose the enemy. At the beginning of 1966 two operations in January and March *Hot Tip I*

and *Hot Tip II* – sought to destroy the vegetation on Cu Pong Mountain in South Vietnam. The weather, humidity, ordnance and method of delivery were described as 'satisfactory,' but the results were not. In the words of one MACV officer, 'The damn trees simply won't burn.'

Despite a record of costly failure, it would take another two years later to fully discredit the forest-fire approach. Between January and April 1968, under the code name *Pink Rose*, B-52s flew three separate offensives against a single seven-square-kilometer area of South Vietnam armed with huge quantities of incendiaries. The results were predictably poor.

Meanwhile, another unconventional weapon was being tested in the counterinsurgency war that would make bombing and forest fires appear Stone-Age-like by comparison. In late 1966 Defense Secretary McNamara, who viewed the war as something of a proving ground for high-tech theories, developed a system that came to be called *Practice Nine*. It was a surveillance system that employed seismic and acoustic sensors to be dropped into the dense jungles along the Ho Chi Minh Trail infiltration routes. The theory was that since they were hidden in the thick jungle, you could use the sensors to see and hear the enemy as he moved down the trail. The top-secret *Practice Nine* sensors, redesignated *Dye Marker* in July 1967 (after having been known briefly under the code name *Illinois City*), were sown across the area of South Vietnam just below the Demilitarized Zone (DMZ) that constituted the border with North Vietnam. In September 1967, as *Dye Marker* was being revealed to the public, the line of sensors was extending westward into Laos under the code name *Muscle Shoals*. There would be two distinct subsystems included in *Muscle Shoals*, an antivehicle system called *Mud River* and an antipersonnel system designated *Dump Truck*. The *Mud River* sensors were first positioned by air drop in December in an operation involving both Air Force and Navy aircraft, with Thailand based USAF EC-121R 'Batcats' acting as relay platforms. With the sensors in place, problems immediately arose around interpretation of the data they were picking up. As the 'bugs' were being worked out of this bugging system, the still-classified operations were renamed again (May 1968), *Dye Marker* becoming *Duel Blade* and *Muscle Shoals* becoming *Igloo White*. *Igloo White* would quickly become an integral part of the Tactical Air Control System controlling the *Commando Hunt* combat operations. As of October 1967 all the EC-121 operations, including *College Eye*, and now *Igloo White*, had been consolidated into Korat RTAFB, with the Infiltration Surveillance Center (designated *Dutch Mill* because of the shape of its antenna) located at Nakhon Phanom RTAFB to co-ordinate *Commando Hunt* and *Igloo White* under the code name *Task Force Alpha*.

By early 1969 the EC-121s flying *Igloo White* relay missions were increasingly threatened from North Vietnamese antiaircraft defenses; the proposal was to replace them with Beechcraft TQU-22A drones. This was tried between March and July under the code name *Pave Eagle I*: results left much to be desired and the TQU-22As were withdrawn for further study. Five QU-22Bs would return as *Pave Eagle II* in October 1970, but would augment *Igloo White* for only a few months before engine problems grounded them again. By the end of 1970, the two squadrons of 12 *Igloo White* EC-121Rs that had made up the 553d Reconnaissance Wing at Korat RTAFB were merged into the 553d RS; the wing was dissolved and assigned to the 388th TFW with the QU-22Bs that were now the 554th RS. In August 1971 the QU-22Bs were grounded again and the reliable C-130 ABCCCs were assigned to augment the now-obsolescent EC-121s as the *Igloo White* airborne command and control center and sensor relay system for the air war over Laos.

The next 41 month-phase saw a gradual and continuous reduction in the number of USAF sorties flown and aircraft lost in Southeast Asia. In 1969 the USAF flew 966,949 combat sorties, down from over a million in 1968. In 1970 711,440 missions were flown; in 1971 the tally was down to 450,031, less than half the number flown in 1969. In 1969 294 USAF aircraft were lost, nearly a hundred fewer than the previous year. In 1970 the number was down to 171; in 1971 it was further reduced to 87, though the total aircraft loss now stood at 1599, at a cost approaching three billion dollars.

One fact behind the figures was the termination of *Rolling Thunder*. Another was that in July 1969 the new Nixon Administration had announced the 'Nixon Doctrine,' a policy that

Above: A US Air Force EC-121R Batcat of the 553d Reconnaissance Wing taxis down the runway at Korat RTAFB in January 1969. A Thai Air Force T-6 can be seen in the background.

Top: The venerable C-47 served a variety of functions for both the USAF and the RVNAF throughout the war. The 'Delta' referred to is that of the Mekong.

Right: This RF-4C cracked up on landing at Danang AB in April 1969. The unit cost for each of the 499 RF-4Cs delivered to the USAF was $2.3 million.

called for 'Vietnamization' of the war. The plan included gradual reduction of US forces with more and more of the operation to be taken over by Vietnamese forces which had theoretically become stronger over the years. On 15 August Defense Secretary Melvin Laird gave American forces the mission of helping the Vietnamese take over the war. Under the Improvement and Modernization Program that was part of Vietnamization, the RVNAF would double in size by 1972. It would be supplied with more sophisticated aircraft, including the versatile F-5 Tiger jet fighter/fighter-bomber developed by Northrop for the export trade, which was then serving with a number of smaller air forces worldwide. By the end of 1970, the RVNAF had 728 aircraft and over 700 crews organized into 30 squadrons. During the year they flew 292,523 sorties, about 41% of the number flown by the USAF.

By the end of 1972, under Projects *Enhance* and *Enhance Plus*, the RVNAF had a strength of 1817 aircraft including 135 F-5s, 245 A-37s, 540 UH-1 Huey helicopters and a variety of other, piston-engined, aircraft. Air crew strength was up to 1297 and an average of 60,000 sorties were being flown per month; 277 aircraft had been lost in 1972.

THE GUNSHIPS

Considering the abundance of weapons and tactics being supplied by the authorities in Washington, it is ironic that the most unique weapons system developed and deployed in Southeast Asia evolved by improvisation. This was the gunship, and the first platform to become one was not the latest top-secret jet but the venerable old C-47 Skytrain that had first seen service with the USAAC back in 1938.

The need from which the gunship grew was that to deliver a concentrated barrage of gunfire on a specific target. The time

Top: An AC-47 Spooky gunship banks slightly for a low, slow pass.

Above: Multi-barreled Gatling guns bark firey death from SUU-8 gun pods aboard a 'Spooky,' November 1966.

Below: A detailed sideview of an AC-47 at Bien Hoa in December 1965 showing machine guns that were used before the advent of gun pods.

frame in which even the slowest aircraft could deliver firepower to a stationary target was only a few seconds. What was needed was an aerial gun platform that could concentrate gunfire for several, or even many, minutes on such targets as enemy troop concentrations and strong points, particularly in the dead of night. It was determined that this could be achieved by mounting the guns so as to fire at a 90-degree angle to the side of the aircraft rather than straight ahead or behind. The plane would first circle, with guns aimed toward the circle's center. The circle would then become the base of an inverted cone, with the line of fire forming the cone itself; at the point of the cone where all the lines of fire converged would be the target. A transport aircraft would be the ideal platform, as it was relatively slow and had a large open fuselage in which to mount guns and ammunition. The gunships would become the most heavily armed aircraft in Southeast Asia. Most carried a sizable number of fixed-mounted guns, including several 20mm, 40mm and in some cases 75mm cannons.

The first gunships were 20 C-47 Skytrains redesignated AC-47 and deployed at the end of 1965 with the 4th Air Commando Squadron. They were initially nicknamed 'Spooky' (all gunships would have nicknames beginning with S), but came to be known as 'Puff the Magic Dragon' or 'Dragon Ship' from the fire and smoke they emitted. Puff was an immediate success: no enemy hideout could withstand the firestorm it created. With the success of a weapons system mounted in an aircraft almost thirty years in service, it was natural that the Air Force should decide to use its top-of-the-line tactical transport as a gunship. In September 1967 four AC-130 Gunship II's (later Spectre), with even greater firepower, were deployed to Laos where they achieved 'good results.' By February 1968 the 16th Special Operations Squadron at Ubon RTAFB was to join the 4th ACS, which became the 4th SOS. Because C-130s were still a first-line transport, the Air Force decided to utilize some of the fleet of Korean

Above: Airmen Ronald Snyder, James Schmisser and Allen Sims load an AC-47 minigun.

Below: The Cholon area of Saigon was raked by 'Spooky' when it was overrun by the Viet Cong during the Tet Offensive in February 1968.

Above: An AC-119G Shadow gunship off the coast of South Vietnam in July 1970. The Shadows were converted from the old C-119 Flying Boxcar transports of Korean War-era fame and were first introduced at Nha Trang AB in December 1968.

Facing page: A time exposure taken by USAF Captain Ralph Jones from a Saigon rooftop showing a pair of 'Spooky' gunships at work on Vietcong positions in Saigon during the 1968 Tet Offensive. (*See preceding page, bottom.*)

War-era C-119G transports (on the verge of retirement) as gunship platforms. The conversion was made, with the AC-119Gs modified to handle the increased weight. As part of Operation *Combat Hornet*, four AC-119G Shadows arrived at Nhu Trang AB in December 1968.

In October 1969 the first of 13 jet-augmented AC-119K Stingers of the 18th SOS arrived at Phan Rang AB in South Vietnam. By year's end there would be 29 AC-119 gunships of both types in service, with all but three of the original AC-47s being phased out. Those retained were for defense of the base at Udorn RTAFB in Thailand. The AC-130 gunships, most powerful of the lot, were modernized: 11 were returned to service by the end of 1970. A year later, as part of the Vietnamization program, the AC-119G Shadows were turned over to the RVNAF, with the USAF retaining the jet-assisted AC-119Ks, of which it now had 16 in addition to 18 AC-130s.

The gunships became one of the most-feared weapons of the war and one of its most successful tactical air weapons. A decade later the AC-130 Spectre gunships were still an important part of the Air Force, attached to the First Special Operations Wing based at Hurlburt Field, Florida.

LINEBACKER

At the beginning of 1972, American troop levels in Southeast Asia were down to 117,000, their lowest level since 1964; and President Nixon had just announced that another 70,000 would be withdrawn by May. USAF air combat had been restricted from North Vietnam for over three years, and the RNVAF was receiving a steady stream of new aircraft under *Enhance*, with an eye toward the day when they could assume the entire burden of the air war themselves. With the

American commitment dwindling and the South Vietnamese forces still building up, North Vietnamese military planners saw a window of opportunity which they decided to exploit. On 29 March 1972 North Vietnam launched a massive conventional invasion of the South, with 12 divisions of regular troops supported by artillery and tanks. It was by far the biggest conventional offensive they had ever fielded. The bombing halt had given them the respite needed to rebuild their road and rail systems, which made the present invasion possible.

The North Vietnamese air force was becoming aggressive as well. A MiG-21 had shot down a USAF HH-53 rescue helicopter over Laos with an air-to-air missile in January 1970, but they had been largely absent from combat for several years. Early in 1972 they had started to conduct combat air patrols of their own in the *Barrel Roll* areas of Laos. On the night of 21 February 1972, four years and one week since the last jet-to-jet engagement in the

skies over Southeast Asia, Major Robert Lodge and Lieutenant Roger Locher of the 555th TFS were flying a *MiG CAP* mission in an F-4D over *Barrel Roll* when *Red Crown* warned them of nearby MiGs. They watched on radar as three MiGs closed on them. The F-4 crew fired three Sidewinders and watched as the missiles exploded one by one in the night sky, the last accompanied by a huge fireball. The remaining MiGs gave chase to the Phantom, but aborted the pursuit after about four minutes, sensing a trap and/or not wanting to be drawn too deep into American-controlled air space. A week later another MiG-21 attempted to intercept American aircraft over northern Laos; *MiG CAP* went into action again. Another F-4D from the 555th TFS, this time manned by Lt Col Joseph Kittenger and Lieutenant Leigh Hodgdon, closed on the MiG. Both of the aircraft fired their air-to-air missiles, but the MiG was a little too late. Kittenger watched his Sidewinder collide with the MiG and took evasive action to avoid the incoming missiles. A few days later, within days of his scheduled departure from Southeast Asia, Kittinger was the loser in another MiG encounter and became the first American POW of the renewed air-to-air war.

On the first full day of the big North Vietnamese invasion, as if to underscore the intention to renew the war on all fronts, the enemy launched another MiG sweep into Laos. The ensuing air battle sent one fewer MiG back to North Vietnam, but enemy forces were making rapid progress on the ground in the South. On 16 April 1972 the bombing halt officially ended; US Navy and Air Force fighter-bombers went North against lines of communication, rail heads and supply facilities in and around Hanoi and Haiphong. This time the antiaircraft defenses were stronger, and the MiGs more prevalent than at any time during *Rolling Thunder*. Three MiG-21s were shot down by Sidewinder-armed Phantoms on the 16th.

On 8 May the President announced the mining of Haiphong and other harbors and a new – this time largely unrestricted – air offensive against North Vietnam to be called *Linebacker*. North Vietnamese defences had been strengthened since *Rolling Thunder*, but American pilots were ready to meet the challenge. Besides the lifting of restrictions, US airmen had an arsenal of new weapons to aid them. Among these were the improved radar-guided 'smart' bombs that were used to destroy the Thanh Hoa railway and highway bridge five days after the beginning of *Linebacker*. The bridge, because of its difficult location, had withstood repeated attacks during *Rolling Thunder* and had become something of a symbol to the North Vietnamese.

A PAIR OF ACES IN THE TRIPLE NICKEL

As air-to-air combat proliferated with the onset of *Linebacker*, one squadron began to stand out. The Thailand-based 555th Tactical Fighter Squadron, called 'Triple Nickel' because of the three fives, was already almost a household word around the fighter fields of Southeast Asia because it had achieved many more MiG kills than any other USAF squadron in the theater. The 555th had been part of Colonel Robin Old's Eighth Tactical Fighter Wing (the 'Wolf Pack') at the time of operation *Bolo*; its pilots, including Colonel Olds, had accounted for four of the seven MiGs shot down during *Bolo* and both the MiGs downed four days later.

The Triple Nickel was now flying combat air patrols out of Udorn RTAFB as part of the 432nd Tactical Reconnaissance Wing, and had scored one of two victories chalked up by PACAF over Hanoi on the opening day of *Linebacker*. Two days later (10 May) the 555th was northwest of Hanoi on combat air patrol when the F-4 team of Major Robert Lodge and Captain Roger Locher, who had scored the first victory of the year and their second on 8 May, picked up two MiGs on radar. They closed on the enemy, engaged one of the MiG-21s and blew his wing off with an AIM-7 Sparrow just as they were themselves struck by an air-to-air missile. The Phantom rolled out of control, with flames beginning to melt the cockpit canopy. Locher managed to eject from the aircraft, landing in a remote jungle valley in North Vietnam where he lived off the land until he was rescued three weeks later. Moments after Locher and Lodge were hit their

Below: Claws for the MiG hunters. Sidewinder (foreground) and Sparrow air-to-air missiles are readied for loading aboard a Phantom.

Statistical Analysis of the 137 Enemy Aircraft Downed in Combat in Southeast Asia by the US Air Force

Type of USAF Aircraft Scoring Victory		Type of Weapon Credited with Each Kill				Type of Enemy Aircraft Downed	
F-4:	107½	AIM-7 Sparrow:	50	AIM-4 Falcon:	5	MiG-21:	68
F-105:	27½	Gunfire, 20mm:	41	Maneuvering Tactics:	5	MiG-17:	61
B-52:	2	AIM-9 Sidewinder:	34	Gunfire, .50 cal (B-52):	2	MiG-19:	8

Enemy Aircraft Downed in Combat by year

1965:	2	1967:	59	1969:	0	1971:	0	1973:	1
1966:	17	1968:	8	1970:	0	1972:	50		

The Final Score of Aircraft Downed in Air-to-Air Combat
137 North Vietnamese Aircraft
63 US Air Force Aircraft

Top: Captains Steve Ritchie (*left*) and Chuck DeBellevue (*right*) of the 555th Tactical Fighter Squadron, the 'Triple Nickel,' were the first USAF aces of the war and scored most of their victories while crewing together in the same F-4 Phantom.

Above: DeBellevue and Ritchie (foreground) with Lt Col Griff Baily and Captain Jeff Feinstein at Udorn RTAFB. The slogan of the 432nd Tactical Recon Wing (which contained the 555th) was: 'Protect the Force, Get the Pictures . . . and Kill MiGs.'

Below: Captain Jeff Feinstein killed five MiG-21s to become the last USAF ace of the war.

Above: A SAC tanker gasses up two 388th TFW F-4Es while three 354th TFW A-7s wait their turn.

wingmen, Lieutenant John Markle and Captain Stephen Eaves, engaged what may well have been the same MiG. They fired a pair of Sparrows and a second MiG went down. Meanwhile a third MIG was trying to get into firing position when he fell into the sights of another F-4 manned by Captains Steve Ritchie and Chuck De Bellevue. The 555th had lost a flight leader that day, but they had also sent three MiGs into the jungle below.

In the next two days the Triple Nickel scored twice more, giving it six victories in five days and 26 for the year to date. The victory on 12 May was particularly notable because the two crewmen involved, Wayne Frye and James Cooney, were both Lieutenant Colonels. As Cooney remarked later, they had 'probably set a world's record for the total age of an air crew in an F-4 for a MiG kill.' He was right: their combined age was 85.

The four MiGs destroyed during the remainder of May included the second for Captain Ritchie and a second for Captain Jeffrey Feinstein of the 13th Tactical Fighter Squadron. On 8 July Ritchie was teamed with De Bellevue again to make a formidable team that shot down two of the three MiGs to fall to the Air Force that day. On the 18th and 29th of July Feinstein scored his third and fourth kills, making him the third USAF pilot in the war (after Olds in 1967 and Ritchie earlier in the month) to score four confirmed victories. Both Ritchie of the 555th and Feinstein of the 13th had a probable fifth kill disallowed during June by the Seventh Air Force Enemy Aircraft Claims Evaluation Board, so competition was developing over

Above: Four 388th TFW F-4E Phantoms return to Korat RTAFB after a mission over North Vietnam.

Below: Major Ralph Kuster in a 388th TFW F-105 drills a MiG-17 with 20 mm cannon fire, 3 June 1967.

which would be first to achieve the coveted fifth confirmed kill, making him the first USAF ace of the war.

On 28 August Ritchie and De Bellevue were in the lead Phantom of a four-plane flight providing MiGCAP for a *Linebacker* strike mission over North Vietnam when a MiG-21 was picked up on radar. They rolled the big F-4 into firing position and fired two Sparrows to entice the MiG into a turn. As the enemy took evasive action, the Phantom fell into his six o'clock position and fired two more air-to-air missiles – Steve Richie became the first fighter pilot in Southeast Asia to join the ranks of USAF aces.

The victory also gave De Bellevue his fourth score and further enhanced the 555th's position as the top-scoring squadron in the war. On 9 September De Bellevue, now teamed with Captain John Madden, was part of a flight of 555th TFS Phantoms flying MiGCAP west of Hanoi. A MiG-21 was sighted visually and the pair made a pass, firing two Sparrows that failed to guide properly and missed. Captain Calvin Tibbett and Lieutenant William Hargrove were observing and promptly jumped into the fray. They fired two Sidewinders which, like the Sparrows before them, failed to guide, so they opened fire with their 20mm cannon. A stream of tracers cut into the MiG, the pilot ejecting just as the plane turned nose down. The flight was beginning to re-form when several MiG-19s jumped them. Madden and De Bellevue went into a low-speed 'yo-yo' maneuver behind the MiGs as they tried to evade the Phantom. As the three aircraft

Below: The F-111 had disastrous teething troubles when first introduced in 1968 but was a potent fighting machine when reintroduced in 1972.

Right: Letting Saigons be bygones: an aerial view of Tan Son Nhut a couple of weeks before the final collapse.

rolled across the muggy late-summer sky, the F-4 crew fired two Sidewinders, both of which found their mark. The Americans came out of the maneuver at 1500 feet as one of the MiG-19s exploded into the runway at the Phuc Yen air base. The encounter not only made De Bellevue the second USAF ace of the war, it gave him a sixth kill that made him the highest-scoring American ace of the war. There would also be two US Navy aces, with five kills each. On 13 October Captain Feinstein was flying with 13th TFS Commander Lt Col Curtis Westphal over Hanoi when they encountered a MiG-21 out of Kep. If the Triple Nickel was lucky for Ritchie and De Bellevue, the 'Double 13s' were unlucky for the MiG pilot when an AIM-7 Sparrow made Jeffrey Feinstein the third and final USAF ace in the skies over Southeast Asia.

THE ELEVEN-DAY WAR

While their MiGCAPs duelled in the clouds, the *Linebacker* fighter bombers pummeled North Vietnam with fewer and fewer of the target restrictions that had hamstrung the *Rolling Thunder* campaign. While the smart bombs represented a technological advance over their predecessors, aircraft technology was advancing too. The F-111 had been deployed to Takhli RTAFB in 1967 under the code name *Combat Lancer* as an experimental fighter bomber, but had been recalled to the drawing board, so to speak, when several crashed. The problem was not so much in the aircraft but in one of its systems – terrain-avoidance radar. When perfected and reintroduced in September 1972 as part of *Linebacker*, it made the F-111 a highly feared and potent weapon. They called it 'Whispering Death,' because the terrain-avoidance radar permitted the plane to fly very close to the ground, far below enemy radar coverage; thus it arrived over the target before it could be seen, heard or detected in any way.

The venerable Thuds were joined by the F-111s and the MiGCAPs swept the skies. By October the exhausted North Vietnamese let it be known that they would be willing to allow the stalled Paris Peace Talks to go forward. With some hope for a negotiated settlement in the air, *Linebacker* was terminated on 23 October.

By December, however, it seemed that North Vietnam saw *Linebacker*'s termination as a repeat of the bombing halt of 1968; it began to drag its feet again in peace talks. The United States was prepared. After eight inconclusive years of limited air warfare, it was decided to launch the unrestrained air offensive against North Vietnam that had been proposed again and again since 1964. Beginning on 18 December, the B-52s, which had been used only occasionally in southernmost North Vietnam, would be used against Hanoi and Haiphong, the targets once restricted even for fighter bomber operations. Over a hundred of the enormous strategic bombers were available for the campaign, which would be designated *Linebacker II*. Original strategy called for a three-night maximum effort, with the huge bombers of SAC's Eighth Air Force flying from U Tapao RTNAFB, Thailand and Andersen AFB on Guam. Their vast firepower would be augmented by both PACAF and Seventh-Fleet fighter bombers who would hit the same targets by day. All strike aircraft would be supported by *MiG CAP* provided again by both PACAF and Seventh Fleet. It would be the largest air operation of the war.

For three nights the vast armada had thundered over the most important strategic targets in North Vietnam, when the decision came down to continue the maximum effort indefinitely. With a standdown on Christmas Day, *Linebacker II* ran for eleven punishing days, during which time no target of importance was spared – railyard, airfield or petroleum-storage complex. At the end North Vietnam was, for the first time, a beaten nation: by 29 December 1972 their means of waging war had been virtually

DAO COMPOUND
TAN SON NHUT AIRFIELD

15 April 1975

DAO BUILDING

TENNIS COURTS

BASEBALL FIELD

destroyed. The SAM missiles that had knocked down 15 B-52s early in the campaign had been used up, and most of the MiGs were either destroyed on the ground or sitting on inoperable runways. The North Vietnamese had little choice but to return to the peace talks and to bargain in good faith. In less than a month, a cease-fire had been signed and that phase of the long and bloody conflict which had involved the United States so deeply was over.

THE LAST FLIGHT OUT

The war in Southeast Asia did not end with *Linebacker II*. Limited tactical operations would continue against parts of North Vietnam until 15 January 1973, and in South Vietnam until the 27th; B-52 *Arc Light* raids continued until the following day, officially ending as the peace accords were being signed in Paris.

Under operation *Countdown*, USAF personnel were withdrawn from South Vietnam, reaching a manpower ceiling of 12 military and 28 civilians by 29 March. All PACAF/Seventh Air Force aircraft had been flown out or turned over to the RVNAF a month earlier. The first American prisoners of war in North Vietnam, mostly USAF and Navy pilots, were released on 12 February with the USAF given the task of flying C-141 transports to Hanoi to bring the men out to Clark AB in the Philippines.

USAF air operations continued from the bases in Thailand against communist insurgents in Laos and Cambodia until 15 August when Congress passed a resolution banning the bombing. On 7 November the Senate and the House of Representatives overrode a presidential veto and passed the War Powers Resolution, which made it impossible to commit American forces to combat for more than sixty days without Congressional approval. The US had not only gotten out of the war in Vietnam, it had closed the door on going back.

During the dozen years it spent fighting the war in Southeast Asia, the US Air Force had flown 5,226,701 combat sorties and suffered casualties of 2118 killed, 3460 wounded and 599 still missing in action. Aircraft lost to combat and other factors totaled 2257, including 445 F-4s, 397 F-105s, 243 F-100s and 30 B-52s, at an estimated cost of $3,129,948,000. During their missions the USAF dropped 6,162,000,000 tons or ordnance, twelve times the total dropped in Korea and nearly three times that expended in World War II. In aerial combat the USAF shot down 137 MiGs with the last, a MiG-21, downed on 8 January 1973. In turn the USAF lost 67 aircraft to the MiGs for a loss rate of 2 to 1.

The United States was now out of Vietnam, the Seventh Air Force relocated to the Philippines; forces in Thailand were gradually being phased out. Against this backdrop, North Vietnamese and Viet Cong went back to business as usual throughout 1974, with South Vietnam fighting back. On 28 February 1975 they launched an offensive like that which had precipitated *Linebacker I* three years earlier, but this time there was no American response. One by one, South Vietnamese units crumbled as province after province fell to the tank- and artillery-supported North Vietnamese offensive. USAF transports, meanwhile, were operating a continuous evacuation airlift of Americans and South Vietnamese from Tan Son Nhut and Bien Hoa.

On 21 April South Vietnamese President Thieu resigned and fled the country. Eight days later a joint US military operation involving PACAF units and designated *Frequent Wind* evacuated 395 Americans and 5205 others from a surrounded Saigon, the last flight out being made by a helicopter from the roof of the US Embassy. Next day, 30 April 1975, North Vietnamese armored units occupied Saigon. Both South Vietnam and the NLF ceased to exist, Hanoi now controlled all of Vietnam and the war was over at last.

TACTICAL AIR POWER IN THE US AIR FORCE

TACTICAL AIR POWER

Tactical air power is the basic building block of every air force and indeed the reason for their existence. Of more than 140 air forces in the world, barely half a dozen have a strategic air-power capability, while all have some form of tactical capability.

Tactical air power, by definition, involves the use of aerial combat and support in warfare toward an immediate tactical goal, either defensively or offensively. Tactical airpower includes support of land or sea forces in battle, interception of enemy aircraft attacking one's homeland or one's forces behind the lines, interdiction of enemy forces and supply routes behind *his* lines and achieving air superiority over a battlefield or theater. Tactical air power also includes reconnaissance, which can be defined as intelligence gathering (from the air) to support land, sea or air combat operations. Tactical air power has been used by hundreds of air forces in wars and skirmishes all over the world since the early 20th century. In our own troubled times, hardly a month goes by without some news of tactical air operations somewhere in the world.

If tactical air power is the basic building block of an air force, the fighter aircraft is the keystone of such air power. Fighters, generally known as pursuit planes up to World War II, are relatively small, fast and highly maneuverable compared to bombers, the other major type of combat aircraft. The fighter's primary mission is to fight other aircraft, whether in duelling for air superiority or intercepting enemy bombers. The interceptor is a fighter designed primarily to attack intruding enemy aircraft. The fighter's secondary mission of ground support is to attack enemy ground positions with bombs, rockets or guns. Fighters engaged in this type of mission are called fighter bombers and are distinguished from the other principal tactical aircraft (light bombers or attack planes, including such subtypes as dive bombers and torpedo bombers) by the fact that they could convert themselves to fighters at any time by jettisoning their bombs.

Attack aircraft, or light bombers, are usually in the same size and weight class as fighters, but often trade the speed and maneuverability required of a fighter in air-to-air combat for the ability to carry a heavier load of air-to-ground ordnance. Tactical ground support is the primary mission of attack aircraft or light bombers. Of the basic aircraft in the tactical arsenal, fighters, interceptors and fighter bombers may be different versions of the same basic aircraft, while attack aircraft or light bombers are designed specifically for ground support or interdiction.

Right: An F-15 pilot climbs into his bird on the flight line at Holloman AFB, New Mexico.

THE TACTICAL AIR COMMAND

Tactical air power has been an important part of the US Air Force and its predecessors since World War I. Today the Tactical Air Command (TAC) and the Strategic Air Command (SAC) are roughly equal in personnel strength as the two largest USAF Major Commands, each with just over 100,000. While SAC is the only strategic air command, TAC has more aircraft and is the centerpiece of USAF tactical air power, which also includes three major regional Commands, with additional personnel and aircraft: the Alaskan Air Command (AAC), The Pacific Air Forces (PACAF) and The United States Air Forces in Europe (USAFE). TAC is responsible for training the pilots and developing the weapons and tactics that are rotated into the front-line regional Commands. TAC's importance is seen in the fact that two Major Commands with tactical missions were integrated into it in the late 1970s. The United States Air Forces Southern Command (USAFSO), headquartered at Albrook AFB in the Panama Canal Zone, became the USAF Southern Air Division under TAC control, with Division headquarters relocated to Howard AFB, Canal Zone. In June 1979 the Aerospace Defense Command (ADCOM or ADC), responsible for the nation's air defense and the major American component in the joint US-Canadian North American Air Defense Command (NORAD), became part of TAC; its commander became TAC Deputy Commander for Air Defense. In the trend of that era toward absorbing USAF tactical air power into TAC, PACAF was scheduled to be disbanded and its assets incorporated into TAC by 1 July 1975, but the order was postponed and, 11 months later, rescinded. It would not, however, be improbable to envision all tactical Commands being ultimately incorporated into TAC.

The Tactical Air Command and the Aerospace Defense Command (known as the Air Defense Command until 1 January 1968), the core of today's TAC, were both founded as Major Commands on 21 March 1946 along with the Strategic Air Command. These three Major Commands were designed to incorporate the heart of USAAF combat air power and become the basic structure of the new USAF, which would come into being 18 months later. TAC basic organization consisted of the major tactical numbered Air Forces from the European Theater of World War II – the Ninth and Twelfth – being brought stateside and stretched over the installations, training and organization framework of the Third Air Force (in the Southeast quadrant of the continental US). In May 1946 TAC headquarters was established at Langley Field, Virginia (Langley AFB after 1947), where it has remained ever since.

Because of the precipitous drop in both personnel and first-line aircraft strength in the late forties, as well as a drop in funding, both ADC and TAC were cut back drastically in December 1948, losing their Major Command status. They became components of a newly created umbrella Command, the Continental Air Command (CONAC). Two years later, in December 1950, with Chinese intervention in the Korean War and the obvious need to build up American air power, both TAC and ADC were restored to Major Command status, retaining it until they merged into a single Major Command in 1979.

The USAF Southern Command (USAFSO), which was to become TAC's Southern Air Division, originally became a Major Command – the Caribbean Air Command – in November 1947, redesignated USAFSO in July 1963. Created from the World War II-era Sixth Air Force, the Caribbean (like the Joint US-Brazil Air Command) indicated US emphasis on the South Atlantic during that period because of the southern route's

The Commanders of the Tactical Air Command

Lt Gen E R Quesada 21 Mar 1946-23 Nov 1948
Maj Gen Robert Lee 24 Dec 1948-20 June 1950
Maj Gen Glenn Barcus 17 July 1950-25 Jan 1951
Gen John Cannon 25 Jan 1951-31 Mar 1954
Gen O P Wayland 1 Apr 1954-31 July 1959
Gen Frank Everest 1 Aug 1959-30 Sept 1961
Gen Walter Sweeney, Jr 1 Oct 1961-31 July 1965
Gen Gabriel Disosway 1 Aug 1965-31 July 1968
Gen William Momyer 1 Aug 1968-30 Sept 1973
Gen Robert Dixon 1 Oct 1973-30 Apr 1978
Gen W L Creech 1 May 1978-

The Commanders of the Air Defense Command

Lt Gen George Stratemeyer	21 Mar 1946–30 Nov 1948
Maj Gen Gordon Saville	1 Dec 1948–31 Dec 1950
Lt Gen Ennis Whitehead	1 Jan 1951–25 Aug 1951
Gen Benjamin Chidlaw	25 Aug 1951–31 May 1955
Maj Gen Frederick Smith, Jr (acting)	31 May 1955–19 July 1955
Gen Earle Partridge	20 July 1955–17 Sept 1956
Lt Gen Joseph Atkinson	17 Sept 1956–15 Aug 1961
Lt Gen Robert Lee	15 Aug 1961–31 July 1963
Lt Gen Herbert Thatcher	1 Aug 1963–31 July 1967
Lt Gen Arthur Agan	1 Aug 1967–31 Dec 1967

The Commanders of the Aerospace Defense Command

Lt Gen Arthur Agan	1 Jan 1968–28 Feb 1970
Lt Gen Thomas McGehee	1 Mar 1970–1 July 1973
Gen Seth McKee	1 July 1973–1 Oct 1973
Gen Lucius Clay, Jr	1 Oct 1973–31 Aug 1975
Gen Daniel James, Jr	1 Sept 1975–5 Dec 1977
Gen James Hill	6 Dec 1977–30 Nov 1979

The Commanders of the Aerospace Defense Center, Tactical Air Command

Gen James Hill	1 Dec 1979–1 Jan 1980
Gen James Hartinger	1 Jan 1980–31 Aug 1980

(With creation of the Space Command on 1 Sept 1982, the functions of the Aerospace Defense Center were absorbed by Space Command, and the ADC Commander became SPACECOM Commander)

importance during the war. With the June 1979 merger, TAC had control not only of all the USAF tactical air assets in the continental United States but those as far south as the Panama Canal and as far east as Iceland (where US Air Forces, Iceland, had been part of ADC).

TAC's mission is to organize, train, equip and maintain a highly mobile tactical air force capable of deployment anywhere in the world either on its own, through one of the three major regional Commands (as through PACAF in Southeast Asia), or through the Rapid Deployment Force (RDF). The mission includes all the classic elements of tactical air power: air superiority; interdiction; close air support; reconnaissance; electronic combat countermeasures (jamming etc) and tactical air control (control of tactical combat aircraft). To quote directly, 'TAC is the US Air Force's mobile strike force . . . able to deploy US general purpose air forces anywhere in the world on a moment's

The Tactical Air Command (TAC)

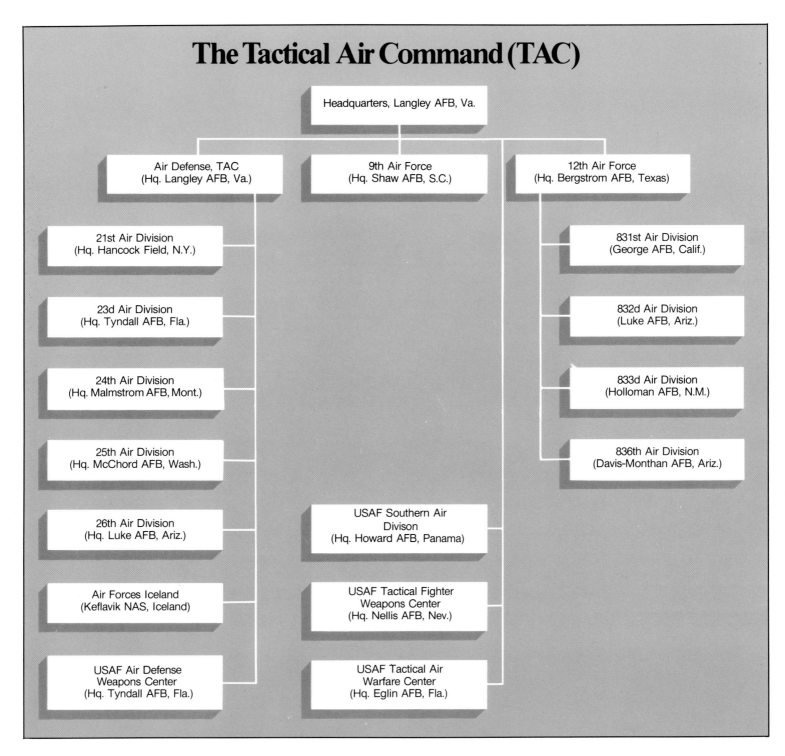

Headquarters, Langley AFB, Va.

Air Defense, TAC
(Hq. Langley AFB, Va.)

9th Air Force
(Hq. Shaw AFB, S.C.)

12th Air Force
(Hq. Bergstrom AFB, Texas)

21st Air Division
(Hq. Hancock Field, N.Y.)

23d Air Division
(Hq. Tyndall AFB, Fla.)

24th Air Division
(Hq. Malmstrom AFB, Mont.)

25th Air Division
(Hq. McChord AFB, Wash.)

26th Air Division
(Hq. Luke AFB, Ariz.)

Air Forces Iceland
(Keflavik NAS, Iceland)

USAF Air Defense
Weapons Center
(Hq. Tyndall AFB, Fla.)

831st Air Division
(George AFB, Calif.)

832d Air Division
(Luke AFB, Ariz.)

833d Air Division
(Holloman AFB, N.M.)

836th Air Division
(Davis-Monthan AFB, Ariz.)

USAF Southern Air
Divison
(Hq. Howard AFB, Panama)

USAF Tactical Fighter
Weapons Center
(Hq. Nellis AFB, Nev.)

USAF Tactical Air
Warfare Center
(Hq. Eglin AFB, Fla.)

notice for tactical air operations in support of national security, and to provide combat ready forces to defend North America against aerospace attack.'

TAC is also a component of several joint multiservice military commands like the US Readiness, US Atlantic and US Southern Commands. Through the TAC Deputy Commander for Air Defense (ADTAC), TAC replaced ADC as the US component in NORAD until creation of the Space Command (SPACE-COM) in 1982.

As part of its mission, TAC is involved in dozens of realistic tactical air exercises in the United States annually (including the joint US-Canada air defense exercise code-named *William Tell*); Canada, Egypt (*Bright Star*), Germany, Italy and Korea are other sites for such exercises. A vital part of TAC training is a series of exercises designed by General Robert Dixon (TAC Commander 1973-78). Known as 'Flags', these were developed in the late seventies to give USAF personnel practical, highly realistic training to prevent repetition of the mistakes that had

plagued Air Force operations during the war in Southeast Asia. *Red Flag*, the best-known, occurs several times a year for six-week periods at the huge Air Force Bombing and Gunnery Range north of Nellis AFB in the tip of Nevada. Its objective is to provide fighter pilots with realistic air-to-air combat missions. War in the skies over Vietnam had proved that despite training prior to actual combat, fighter pilots still had a lot to learn, and that most of their mistakes occurred during their first ten missions. If a pilot survived his tenth mission the odds improved vastly, showing that he had mastered the necessary skills. But what of the airman who didn't survive ten missions? Air Force training had produced great *pilots*, but it seemed to take experience to produce great *combat pilots*. General Dixon conceived *Red Flag* as a way of giving pilots ten combat missions under controlled conditions. TAC created an 'enemy' in its 4440th Tactical Fighter Training Group formed at Nellis AFB, against which pilots flying in *Red Flag* do mock battle. Calling themselves Aggressors, the pilots of 4440th fly the Northrop F-5,

Above: AFRES C-130s on the line at TAC's Howard AFB, Panama.

Below: Keflavik NAS; Iceland-based TAC Phantoms intercept a Russian Tu95 over the North Atlantic.
Right: A flight of 49th TFW F-15 Eagles out of Holloman AFB. The Eagle is TAC's top fighter.

similar in size, appearance and radar signature to the MiG-21, the commonest Soviet-bloc tactical aircraft. The F-5s are even painted with Soviet and Warsaw Pact camouflage schemes. The name *Red Flag* implies the nature of the 'enemy.' Opposing aircraft are shot down by computers rather than guns, but in other respects *Red Flag* is realistic, with the Aggressors flying Soviet and Warsaw-Pact tactics as well as markings. *Red Flag* also involves units from the US Navy, Canada and various NATO air forces.

Black Flag is the maintenance counterpart of the more visible *Red Flag*. Its maintenance crews practice keeping aircraft flying under frantic wartime conditions.

Blue Flag trains command-control and communications (C^3) personnel to ply their vital trade under wartime conditions. Training is tailored to simulate theaters in which the C crews might have to operate – Europe, Korea or the Persian Gulf.

Checkered Flag is the exercise under which TAC units from stateside deploy to overseas bases, usually of other tactical Commands, from which they would have to operate in an emergency. Crews learn the peculiarities of a given base, runways, local weather, facilities available, etc.

Copper Flag is the TAC Air Defense (ADTAC) equivalent of Red Flag in which air-defense crews, both air and ground-based, practice defending against enemy tactical or strategic air attack.

Green Flag trains tactical air forces in the use of Electronic Warfare (EW) and Electronic Countermeasures (ECM). It is the Electronic Warfare counterpart of the other *Flags* and a *Green Flag* exercise is held annually at Nellis AFB in co-ordination with a *Red Flag*.

Silver Flag was designed to prepare TAC ground personnel in such fields as civil engineering, air-base ground defense, law enforcement and medical services to function under wartime conditions. *Silver Flag* has three principal elements. WARSKIL trains noncombat TAC personnel to do their jobs under a wartime scenario. WARFIL trains selected personnel from bases in the United States whose skills or specialties would require their deployment to the front in wartime. The Base Augmentation Programs of *Silver Flag* have the task of providing smooth and efficient transportation of TAC personnel under emergency conditions.

TACTICAL AIR COMMAND BASES

Langley AFB (TAC Headquarters)
Location: 3 miles north of Hampton, Virginia
Area: 3500 acres
Altitude: 10ft
Personnel: 9258 Military
          1710 Civilian
The base was activated 30 December 1916 as Langley Field, and is the oldest continually active AFB in the country. It was named for aviation pioneer and scientist Samuel Pierpont Langley, who died in 1906. The host unit is the 1st Tactical Fighter Wing flying F-15s. Tenants include 5th Weather Wing (MAC), 2d Aircraft Delivery Group (TAC), 480th Reconnaissance Technical Group (TAC), 48th Fighter Interceptor Sqdn (TAC) and the US Army TRADOC Flight Detachment. The NASA Langley Research Center is located across base.

Bergstrom AFB
Location: 7 miles SE of downtown Austin, Texas
Area: 3998 acres
Altitude: 541ft
Personnel: 5050 Military
          915 Civilian
The base was activated on 22 September 1942, named for Captain John Bergstrom, the first Austin serviceman to die in World War II (8 December 1941 in the attack on Clark Field in the Philippines). The base is headquarters for both the 12th Air Force (TAC) and the 10th Air Force (AFRES), and is the site of the TAC NCO Academy West. Also located on base are the 67th Tactical Recon Wing with RF-4Cs and the 924th Tactical Fighter Gp (AFRES) flying F-4Ds.

Cannon AFB
Location: 7 miles west of Clovis, New Mexico
Area: 25.663 acres
Altitude: 4295ft
Personnel: 3900 Military
          418 Civilian
The base was activated in August 1942 and was named for General John K Cannon, commander of Allied Air Forces in the Mediterranean area in World War II. It is the home of the 27th Tactical Fighter Wing flying F-111s.

Davis-Monthan AFB
Location: Outskirts of Tucson, Arizona
Area: 11,000 acres
Altitude: 2620ft
Personnel: 6489 Military
          1327 Civilian
The base was activated in 1927 and named for 1st Lt Samuel Davis, and 2nd Lt Oscar Monthan (died 1921 and 1924 respectively). The base is the headquarters of the 836th Air Div and home to the 355th Tactical Training Wing (A-10 combat training), 602d Tactical Control Wing, 41st Electronic Combat Sqdn, 868th Tactical Missile Training Sqdn, and SAC's 390th Strategic Missile Wing responsible for Tital IIs based in Arizona. The base is also the site of AFLC's Military Aircraft Storage and Disposition Center, where several thousand aircraft are mothballed in the dry desert air for possible future use (see page 208).

England AFB
Location: 5 miles west of Alexandria, Louisiana
Area: 2282 acres
Altitude: 89ft
Personnel: 3173 Military
          540 Civilian
The base was activated in October 1942 and later named for Lt Col John England, a World War II ace (17.5 victories) who was killed in an F-86 crash on 17 November 1954. The base is home to the 23d Tactical Fighter Wing flying A-10s.

George AFB
Location: 6 miles NW of Victorville, California
Area: 5347 acres
Altitude: 2875ft
Personnel: 5842 Military
          450 Civilian
The base was activated in 1941, and renamed for World War I ace Brig Gen Harold George, who was killed on 29 April 1942. Headquarters of the 831st Air Div, the base is the home of 37th Tactical Fighter Wing (the Wild Weasel F-4Gs), 35th Tactical

Above: The base headquarters building at Langley AFB in Virginia.

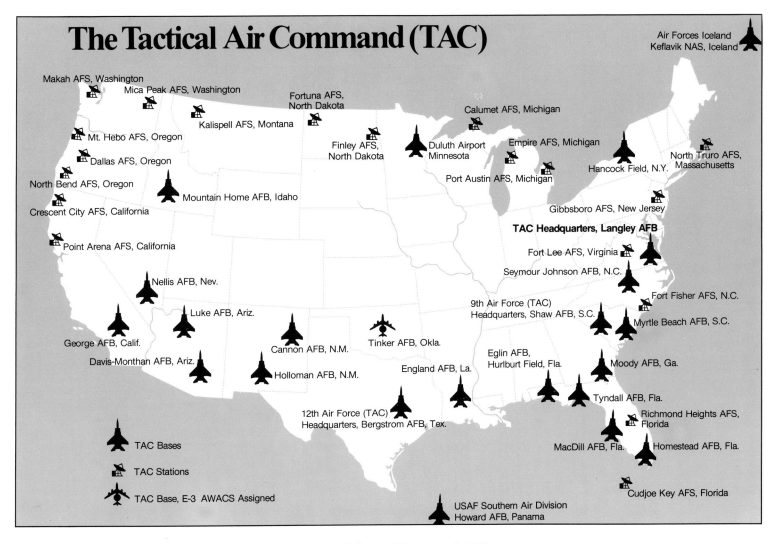

The Tactical Air Command (TAC)

Air Forces Iceland
Keflavik NAS, Iceland

Makah AFS, Washington
Mica Peak AFS, Washington
Fortuna AFS, North Dakota
Calumet AFS, Michigan
Kalispell AFS, Montana
Mt. Hebo AFS, Oregon
Finley AFS, North Dakota
Duluth Airport Minnesota
Empire AFS, Michigan
North Truro AFS, Massachusetts
Dallas AFS, Oregon
North Bend AFS, Oregon
Port Austin AFS, Michigan
Hancock Field, N.Y.
Crescent City AFS, California
Mountain Home AFB, Idaho
Gibbsboro AFS, New Jersey
Point Arena AFS, California
TAC Headquarters, Langley AFB
Fort Lee AFS, Virginia
Seymour Johnson AFB, N.C.
Nellis AFB, Nev.
9th Air Force (TAC) Headquarters, Shaw AFB, S.C.
Fort Fisher AFS, N.C.
Luke AFB, Ariz.
Myrtle Beach AFB, S.C.
George AFB, Calif.
Cannon AFB, N.M.
Tinker AFB, Okla.
Eglin AFB, Hurlburt Field, Fla.
Moody AFB, Ga.
Davis-Monthan AFB, Ariz.
Holloman AFB, N.M.
England AFB, La.
Tyndall AFB, Fla.
12th Air Force (TAC) Headquarters, Bergstrom AFB, Tex.
Richmond Heights AFS, Florida
MacDill AFB, Fla.
Homestead AFB, Fla.
TAC Bases
TAC Stations
TAC Base, E-3 AWACS Assigned
Cudjoe Key AFS, Florida
USAF Southern Air Division Howard AFB, Panama

Fighter Wing (Pave Spike F-4Es), F-4 transitional training, German Luftwaffe F-4 training and a TAC F-106 group.

Hancock Field
Location: Ten miles NNE of Syracuse, New York
Area: 765 acres
Altitude: 421ft
Personnel: 818 Military
          315 Civilian
Activated in 1942 as Syracuse Army Air Base, it was renamed in 1952 for US Congressman Clarence Hancock (1885-1949) of Syracuse. The 4789th Air Base Group is host to the 21st NORAD Region, 21st TAC Air Div, 3513th USAF Recruiting Sqdn, 174th Tactical Fighter Wing (ANG).

Holloman AFB
Location: 6 miles SW of Alamogordo, New Mexico
Area: 50,697 acres
Altitude: 4093ft
Personnel: 5934 Military
          1104 Civilian
The base was activated in 1942 and renamed for missile pioneer Col George Holloman, who was killed on 19th March 1946. The base is the headquarters of the 833d Air Div, playing host to 49th Tactical Fighter Wing (F-15), 479th Tactical Training Wing (AT-38), 4449th Mobility Support Sqdn (*Harvest Bare*), 82nd Tactical Control Flight and 40th Aerospace Rescue and Recovery Sqdn among others. The AFSC 6585th Test Group conducts aircraft and missile-system tests and evaluation, and operates the Central Inertial Guidance Test Facility, High Speed Test Track Facility and the Radar Target Scatter (RATSCAT) site.

Homestead AFB
Location: 5 miles NNE of Homestead, Florida
Area: 3491 acres
Altitude: 7ft
Personnel: 5814 Military
          1150 Civilian
Activated in April 1955, the base is home to TAC's 31st Tactical Training Wing (F-4D), 726th Tac Control Sqdn (TAC), 482d Tactical Fighter Wing (AFRES), and the 301st Aerospace Rescue and Recovery Sqdn (AFRES).

Hurlburt Field, Eglin AFB
Location: 5 miles west of Fort Walton Beach, Florida
Area: 464,980 acres (entire Eglin AFB)
Altitude: 35ft
Personnel: 3602 Military
          315 Civilian
Located on AFSC's Eglin AFB reservation, Hurlburt Field was activated in 1943 and is a TAC base named for Lt Donald Hurlburt who was killed in a crash here on 2 October 1943. The field is the headquarters of the 2nd Air Division, the focal point of all Air Force Special Operations. Under the 2nd Air Division are the 1st Special Operations Wing equipped with MC-130E Combat Talon, AC-130H Spectre Gunship, HH-53 Pave Low III and the UH-1N; the USAF Special Operations School; Special Operations Combat Control Team; and Special Operations Weather Team. The 2nd Air Div also has units based at Clark AB, Philippines; Rhein-Main AB, Germany and Howard AFB in Panama. Assigned as tenant units at Hurlburt Field are the 4442d Tac Fighter Control Group (USAF Ground Operations School) and the 823d Civil Engineering Sqdn (*Red Horse*).

Luke AFB
Location: 20 miles WNW of Phoenix, Arizona
Area: 5631 acres
Altitude: 6ft
Personnel: 6242 Military
1350 Civilian
Activated in 1941, the base was named for Lt Frank Luke, the 'Arizona Balloon Buster' who was the first airman to receive the Medal of Honor in World War I. He was killed in action near Murvaux, France, on 29 September 1918. Luke AFB, the largest fighter-training base in the world, is headquarters for both the 26th and 832d TAC Air Divisions as well as the 405th and 58th Tactical Training Wings, conducting training in both F-16 and F-15. The headquarters of the 26th NORAD Region is also at Luke AFB.

MacDill AFB
Location: Tampa, Florida
Area: 5631 acres
Altitude: 6ft
Personnel: 6242 Military
1350 Civilian
Activated on 15 April 1941, the base was named for Col Leslie MacDill who had been killed in a plane crash on 8 November 1938. The base is headquarters for the US Readiness Command and the US Central Command, as well as the 56th Tactical Training Wing, conducting F-16 replacement training.

Moody AFB
Location: 10 miles NNE of Valdosta, Georgia
Area: 6050 acres
Altitude: 233ft
Personnel: 3470 Military
             629 Civilian
The base was activated in June 1941 and named for Major George Moody, who had been killed on 5 May while test-piloting a Beech AT-10. Moody is home to the 347th Tactical Fighter Wing flying F-4Es.

Mountain Home AFB
Location 56 miles SE of Boise, Idaho
Area: 6639 acres
Altitude: 3000ft
Personnel: 4175 Military
             699 Civilian
Activated in April 1942, the base is home to the 366th Tactical Fighter Wing flying the F-111 fighter and EF-111 Electronic Countermeasures variant.

Below: An F-4E Phantom of the 347th Tactical Fighter Wing based at Moody AFB, Georgia. TAC and the other tactical commands use the two-letter tailcode first introduced in Southeast Asia to identify aircraft with their bases.

Above: A group of fighter pilots sip diet cola and recap the day's activities in a Nellis AFB locker room after a gruelling *Red Flag* exercise over the parched Nevada desert.

Myrtle Beach AFB
Location: Just south of Myrtle Beach, South Carolina
Area: 3793 acres
Altitude: 25ft
Personnel: 3270 Military
       455 Civilian
Sharing a runway with the Myrtle Beach Airport, the base was an Army Air Field between 1941 and 1947. It was reactivated by the USAF in 1956. Current operations are by the 354th Tactical Fighter Wing flying A-10s.

Nellis AFB
Location: 8 miles NE of Las Vegas, Nevada
Area: 11,274 acres (base alone)
     3,012,770 acres (with attached USAF ranges)
Altitude: 2171ft
Personnel: 9266 Military
      1083 Civilian
With its attached USAF gunnery and bombing ranges, Nellis is the largest USAF base, in fact, larger than some of the foreign countries whose pilots sometimes attend exercises here. Activated in July 1941, the base is named for Lt William Nellis, a fighter pilot killed on 27 December 1944 over Europe. The host unit is the Tactical Fighter Weapons Center, which conducts advanced tactical fighter training and realistic combat training (such as Operation *Red Flag*) for the USAF and US Navy as well as NATO and other allied countries. Units include the 57th Fighter Weapons Squadron, 4440th Tactical Fighter Training Group (*Red Flag*), 474th Tactical Fighter Wing and the USAF Thunderbirds Air Demonstration Squadron.

Indian Springs AF Auxiliary Field (Nellis AFB)
Location: 45 miles NW of Las Vegas
Area: 1652 acres
Altitude: 3124ft
Personnel: 343 Military
      13 Civilian
Activated in 1942 the base is now home to the 554th Combat Support Squadron of the 554th Range Group who provide bombing and gunnery range support for tactical operations out of Nellis AFB, as well as US Department of Energy nuclear-weapons testing.

Seymour Johnson AFB
Location: Goldsboro, North Carolina
Area: 4281 acres
Altitude: 109ft
Personnel: 5155 Military
      837 Civilian
The base was activated on 12 June 1941 and named for Navy Lt Seymour A Johnson of Goldsboro, who had been killed in a crash on 4 March. The base is one of several for the 4th Tactical Fighter Wing F-4Es with a dual-based commitment to NATO. It is also home to SAC's 68th Air Refuelling Group and AFCC's 2012th Communications Squadron.

Shaw AFB
Location: 10 miles WNW of Sumter, South Carolina
Area: 11,645 acres
Altitude: 244ft
Personnel: 5408 Military
      709 Civilian
Activated on 30 August 1941, the base is named for 2nd Lt Ervin Shaw, killed in action with the Air Service on 9 July 1918. It is the headquarters of the 9th Fighter Wing (flying F-16s and RF-4Cs) as well as the 507th Tactical Air Control Wing.

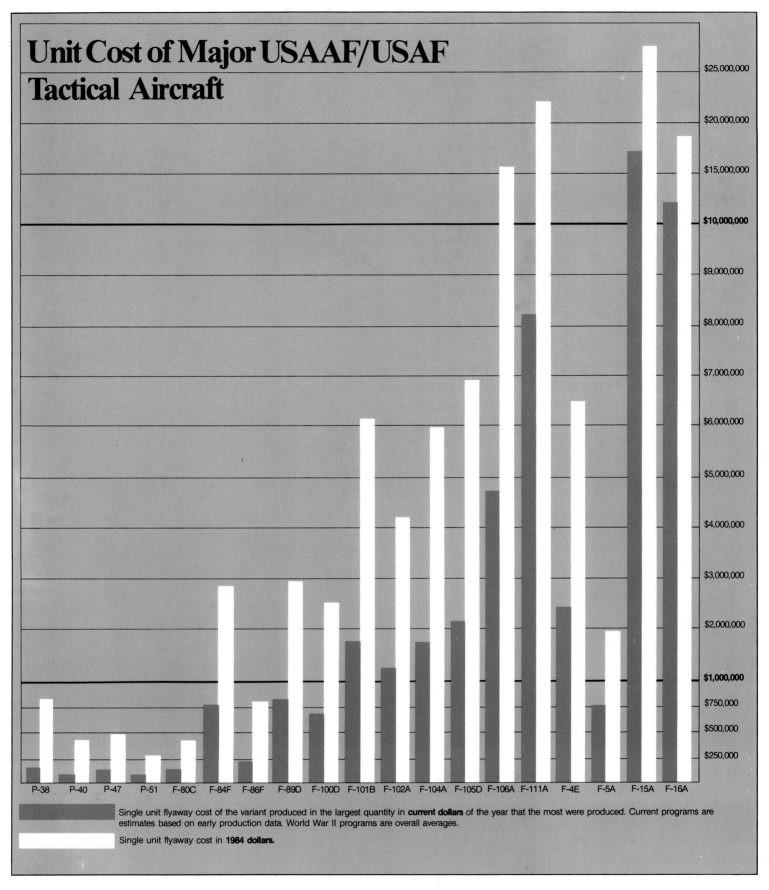

Unit Cost of Major USAAF/USAF Tactical Aircraft

Single unit flyaway cost of the variant produced in the largest quantity in **current dollars** of the year that the most were produced. Current programs are estimates based on early production data. World War II programs are overall averages.

Single unit flyaway cost in **1984 dollars.**

Tyndall AFB
Location: 13 miles east of Panama City, Florida
Area: 28,000 acres
Altitude: 18ft
Personnel: 4250 Military
          1198 Civilian
The base was activated on 7 December 1941, the day Pearl Harbor was attacked, and named for Lt Frank Tyndall, a World War I fighter pilot killed on 15 July 1930. The base is the home of the USAF Air Defense Weapons Center and the focal point of operational and technical expertise in the area of air defense for all services. The center conducts testing and evaluation of pilots, tactics and weapons, including the biennial Project *William Tell* interceptor meet to test the skills of the best Air Defense interceptor units from the US and Canada. The base is also home to the TAC/NCO Academy East, the 23d NORAD Region headquarters, ATC's 3625th Technical Training Squadron and AFCC's 2021st Communications Squadron.

US AIR FORCES IN EUROPE

Since the end of World War II Europe has been seen as the likeliest locale for a major power confrontation that could lead to World War III. To meet this threat, the US Air Forces in Europe (USAFE) were organized as a Major Command of the new USAF in 1947. USAFE was formed from the tactical air assets left in Europe after postwar demobilization and is today the second largest (after TAC) tactical Command. USAFE operates nearly 800 tactical aircraft and has over 1500 TAC aircraft in the United States preassigned to it – these could be in place in Europe within 30 days. The aircraft are assigned to bases on both continents through the Co-located Operating Base (COB) program. USAFE is the largest regional Command, with over 50,000 uniformed personnel. Headquartered at **Ramstein AB** in Germany, it is the American contribution to the Allied Air Forces Central Europe (AAFCE), the tactical air component of the North Atlantic Treaty Organization (NATO). USAFE is composed of three numbered Air Forces, the Third, Sixteenth and Seventeenth.

The USAFE Seventeenth Air Force, based at **Sembach AB** along with the Luftwaffe of the German Federal Republic (Bundesrepublik Deutschland, BRD), is the major air element in NATO defense of Central Europe. The area is critical because it faces the largest concentrations of Soviet and Warsaw Pact land and air power. All bases of the Seventeenth are located in the BRD with the exception of the 32d Tactical Fighter Squadron, based at **Camp New Amsterdam** near Soesterberg in the Netherlands. Flying F-15s, the 32d TPS is under joint operational control of the Seventeenth Air Force and the Netherlands Air Defense Center, as its primary role is to work with the Royal Netherlands Air Force (Koninklijk Luchtmacht Nederland, KLN) to maintain allied air superiority over the Netherlands in the event of war. There are six fighter wings assigned to the Seventeenth Air Force, all headquartered in the BRD and flying A-10s, F-4s, F-15s, F-16s and RF-4s. Also in Germany, historic **Tempelhof Central Airport** in Berlin is maintained as an American support base, and the Military Airlift Command (MAC) has its 435th Tactical Airlift Wing at **Rhein-Main AB** across the runway from Frankfurt's Rhein-Main Airport, Ger-

many's major international air hub. Rhein-Main AB is also the MAC air-cargo hub for supplies being delivered to American forces in Germany, but much of the traffic is now going into Ramstein AB because of growing civilian operations at Rhein-Main airport.

The Third Air Force, headquartered at **RAF Mildenhall** in England, is USAFE's largest in terms of personnel and facilities. While the Seventeenth has the bulk of USAFE's tactical combat aircraft, the Third provides support facilities through nine RAF bases in southern England. Besides supporting rotational MAC airlift operations and SAC strategic reconnaissance and air refueling operations, the Third has two Tactical Fighter Wings flying F-111 fighter bombers, one with A-10 attack aircraft and a Tactical Recon Wing with RF-4s. The latter has an 'Aggressor' Squadron, the 527th TFTS flying F-5s in *Red Flag*-type exercises. The Third Air Force also has a civil engineer and heavy-repair squadron at **RAF Wethersfield**; its 501st Tactical Missile Wing at **RAF Greenham Common** supports the deployment of the BGM-109G Ground Launched Cruise Missile (GLCM).

USAFE units across southern Europe and into Asia Minor are under the Sixteenth Air Force Command headquartered at **Torrejon AB** in Spain. The Sixteenth has a Tactical Fighter Training Wing (the 406th) at Zaragoza AB, Spain, and a Tactical Fighter Wing (the 401st), flying F-16s at its home base of Torrejon. In addition there are three bases in Italy: **San Vito AS**, a support and communications station; **Comiso AS**, where the 487th Tactical Missile Wing supports the Ground Launched Cruise Missile; and **Aviano AB** in northern Italy, a major support and refueling base. Aviano AB's refueling function is important for USAFE and other NATO aircraft, because combat aircraft are not permitted to ròutinely overfly neutral Austria and Switzerland and routing them over France eats up a lot more fuel than would a direct Germany-to-Italy flight. Bases in Greece and Turkey support both USAFE tactical operations and electronic surveillance of military activities in the southwestern Soviet Union and the southern flank of the Warsaw Pact. The bases in Turkey are administered by TUSLOG (The Turkey/United States Logistics Group) headquartered at **Ankara AB** and provide support services for a wide range of USAFE, NATO and MAC aircraft operating in the area on a rotational basis. MAC

Above: Two F-15 Eagles over Germany during the 1982 *Reforger/Crested Cap* exercise.
Below: A 52d TFW USAFE F-4G out of Spangdahlem AB, Germany, armed with AGM-45 Shrike missiles (*see pages 148-9*).

Above: USAFE ground crewmen in chemical warfare gear prepare to land Mk82 bombs onto an A-10 attack plane at Sembach AB. A crucial element of USAFE training is preparation for doing one's job in an environment contaminated by enemy chemical weapons.

units providing airlift for TUSLOG operate out of **Incirlik AB** to nine sites around the country in an ongoing operation code-named *Turkey Trot*.

NATO operations in the eastern Mediterranean have always been complicated by tension between NATO members Greece and Turkey over Cyprus. Turkey's 1974 invasion of Cyprus resulted in a US arms embargo (since lifted) aimed at Turkey.

Recently, there was the threatened withdrawal of Greece from NATO and the cancellation of USAFE base rights there.

Prior to 1966, another major concentration of USAFE air power was located in northern France with USAFE units based at Chaumont AB, Dreux AB, Evreux Fauville AB, Laon AB, Etain AB, Chambley AB, Toul Rosieres AB, Phalsbourg AB and Chateauroux AS; rotational units operated through bases in

The United States Air Force in Europe (USAFE)

French Morocco, such as Nouasseur AB, until 1956. In 1966 French President Charles de Gaulle ended USAFE's nearly two-decade presence in France by withdrawing his country from the NATO military command structure and expelling all NATO units from the country, including NATO headquarters and USAFE units. Shortly thereafter, the United States lost another major base in the theater – Wheelus AFB in Libya – when King Idrus was overthrown by the sinister but charismatic Muammar Quaddafi.

USAFE's mission today is to work with other NATO air forces to provide for air defense of Western Europe and to support NATO ground forces defending Western Europe in the event of a Soviet and/or Warsaw-Pact invasion. USAFE also monitors Soviet and Warsaw-Pact activities during peacetime and provides support for MAC and SAC units operating in Europe. In

1977 USAFE was the first regional Major Command to receive the F-15 Eagle air superiority fighter and the A-10 'Warthog' tactical air-support attack aircraft, both the top of their respective lines. In 1980 the first of the G-model F-4 Phantom, the 'Wild Weasel' or SAM suppressor version, made its appearance with USAFE units. Two years later the F-16 fighting Falcon, a fighter/fighter-bomber with the advanced capabilities of the F-15, made its debut with USAFE.

USAFE participates with other NATO air forces as well as US Army units in a number of training exercises such as *Reforger* and *Crested Cap* from Norway to the Mediterranean every year. USAFE is, of course, also a participant in the *Flag* exercises. In recent years these exercises have included training personnel to perform ground operations in chemical warfare protection suits and the development of procedures for Rapid Runway Repair.

THE PACIFIC AIR FORCES

The Pacific Air Forces (PACAF), the air component of the US Pacific Command, were originally called the Far East Air Forces (FEAF), the name being changed in July 1957. The FEAF was created during World War II by a merger of the Fifth and Thirteenth Air Forces (the Seventh being added later in the war). The FEAF became the air component of General MacArthur's Far East Command; at the end of the war it was joined by the previously independent Twentieth Air Force. With the defeat of Japan FEAF headquarters was moved to Tokyo. The onset of the Korean War in 1950 made FEAF the principal air element of the United Nations Command, with the front-line Fifth and Twentieth Air Forces augmented by a FEAF Bomber Command composed largely of SAC B-29s on temporary assignment.

On 1 July 1957 FEAF officially became the Pacific Air Forces (PACAF), the single USAF Command for the Pacific Theater, with two numbered Air Forces – the Fifth in Japan and the Thirteenth in the Philippines. Both the other numbered Air Forces, the Seventh in Hawaii and the Twentieth on Okinawa, had been dissolved since 1955. Command headquarters was moved to Hickam AFB adjacent to the Navy's base at Pearl Harbor, Hawaii, while the Fifth Air Force moved from its headquarters at Moriyama near Nagoya, Japan, to the plush former FEAF headquarters at Fuchu AS near Tokyo. Fuchu AS was also close to Tachikawa AB and Yokota AB, two of the major Fifth Air Force bases in Japan. PACAF began with 89,679 personnel and 959 aircraft (including 152 F-100s and 249 F-86s), but by the time PACAF was called upon for sustained operations in Southeast Asia in 1964, personnel strength had been reduced to 65,155 with 582 aircraft (including 110 F-102s and 153 F-105s) in the inventory. The rapid escalation of the war in Southeast Asia, and PACAF's new responsibility for USAF air operations there, sent Command strength to a peak of nearly 170,000 personnel and 2100 aircraft prior to the bombing halt in 1968. The Seventh Air Force was reactivated at Tan Son Nhut AB in South Vietnam and PACAF found itself operating from 18 bases in Southeast Asia, including ten in South Vietnam, seven in Thailand and Ching Chuan Kang AB (Republic of China) on Taiwan. As more and more responsibility for the conduct of the air war was turned over to the South Vietnamese, and tactical aircraft assigned to PACAF were gradually returned to TAC and reserve units, PACAF sank back to its prewar strength. By 1975 the Seventh Air Force had ceased to exist. In May PACAF flew

The Commanders of the US Air Forces in Europe

Brig Gen John McBain	15 Aug 1947–20 Oct 1947
Lt Gen Curtis LeMay	20 Oct 1947–15 Oct 1948
Lt Gen John Cannon	16 Oct 1948–20 Jan 1951
Gen Lauris Norstad	21 Jan 1951–26 July 1953
Lt Gen William Tunner	27 July 1953–30 June 1957
Gen Frank Everest	1 July 1957–31 July 1959
Gen Frederic Smith, Jr	1 Aug 1959–30 June 1961
Gen Truman Landon	1 July 1961–31 July 1963
Gen Gabriel Disosway	1 Aug 1963–31 July 1965
Gen Bruce Holloway	1 Aug 1965–31 July 1966
Gen Maurice Preson	1 Aug 1966–31 July 1968
Gen Horace Wade	1 Aug 1968–31 Jan 1969
Gen Joseph Holzapple	1 Feb 1969–31 Aug 1971
Gen David Jones	1 Sept 1971–30 June 1974
Gen John Vogt	1 July 1974–31 Aug 1975
Gen Richard Ellis	1 Sept 1975–31 July 1977
Gen William Evans	1 Aug 1977–1 Aug 1978
Gen John Pauly	1 Aug 1978–1 Aug 1980
Gen Charles Gabriel	1 Aug 1980–30 June 1982
Gen Billy Minter	1 July 1982

The Commanders of the Far East Air Forces

Lt Gen George Kenney	15 June 1944–30 Dec 1945
Lt Gen Ennis Whitehead	30 Dec 1945–25 Apr 1949
Lt Gen George Stratemeyer	26 Apr 1949–20 May 1951
Lt Gen Earle Patrtridge (acting)	21 May 1951–9 June 1951
Gen O P Weyland	10 June 1951–25 Mar 1954
Gen Earle Partridge	26 Mar 1954–31 May 1955
Gen Laurence Kuter	1 June 1955–see below

The Commanders of the Pacific Air Forces

Gen Laurence Kuter	1 June 1955–31 July 1959
Gen Emmett O'Donnell, Jr	1 Aug 1959–31 July 1963
Gen Jacob Smart	1 Aug 1963–31 July 1964
Gen Hunter Harris	1 Aug 1964–31 Jan 1967
Gen John Ryan	1 Feb 1967–31 July 1968
Gen Joseph Nazzaro	1 Aug 1968–31 July 1971
Gen Lucius Clay, Jr	1 Aug 1971–30 Sept 1973
Gen John Vogt	1 Oct 1973–30 June 1974
Gen Louis Wilson, Jr	1 July 1974–31 May 1977
Lt Gen James Hill	1 June 1977–14 June 1978
Lt Gen James Hughes	15 June 1978–1 July 1981
Lt Gen Arnold Braswell	1 July 1981–

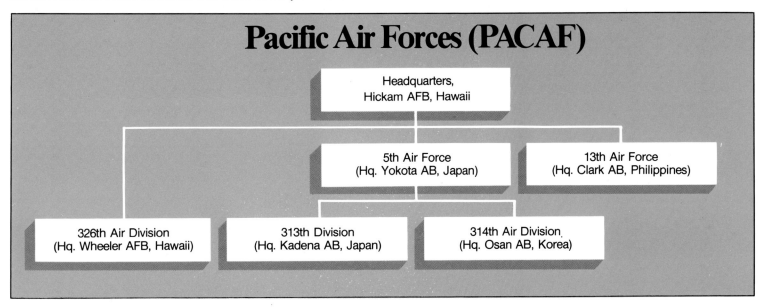

Pacific Air Forces (PACAF)

Headquarters,
Hickam AFB, Hawaii

5th Air Force
(Hq. Yokota AB, Japan)

13th Air Force
(Hq. Clark AB, Philippines)

326th Air Division
(Hq. Wheeler AFB, Hawaii)

313th Division
(Hq. Kadena AB, Japan)

314th Air Division
(Hq. Osan AB, Korea)

its last missions in Southeast Asia, evacuating personnel from Saigon under operation *Frequent Wind* and helping to rescue the crew of the American merchant vessel SS *Mayaguez*, which had been hijacked by Cambodian revolutionaries in international waters. In 1976 PACAF strength declined to 34,111 personnel and 255 aircraft, as the last bases in Thailand were returned to the Thai Government.

Today PACAF strength has stabilized slightly above the 1976 level, with qualitative improvements in aircraft strength in the form of F-15 aircraft now assigned to the 313th Air Division on Okinawa and F-16s to the 314th Air Division in Korea. While its numbers have stabilized, PACAF's area of responsibility has increased beyond the Pacific The Pacific Command and PACAF now have responsibility for the Indian Ocean region as well, an area that stretches from the east coast of Africa to the west coast of the Americas, covering more than a hundred million square miles or half the surface of the earth.

PACIFIC AIR FORCES BASES

Hickam AFB, Hawaii
Location: West of Honolulu, adjacent to Honolulu Airport
Area: 2731 acres
Altitude: 3ft
Personnel: 5116 Military
           1957 Civilian

PACAF headquarters is still at Hickam, a stone's throw from the Pacific Command Headquarters at Pearl Harbor. The base was activated in September 1937 and named for Lt Col Horace Hickam, killed in a crash at Fort Crockett, Texas, on 5 November 1934. The base is home to the 154th Tactical Fighter Group of the Hawaii Air National Guard as well as MAC's 834th Airlift Division and First Weather Wing. The base also serves as headquarter site for Air Force Communications Command and Electronic Security Command activities in the Pacific.

Pacific Air Forces (PACAF)

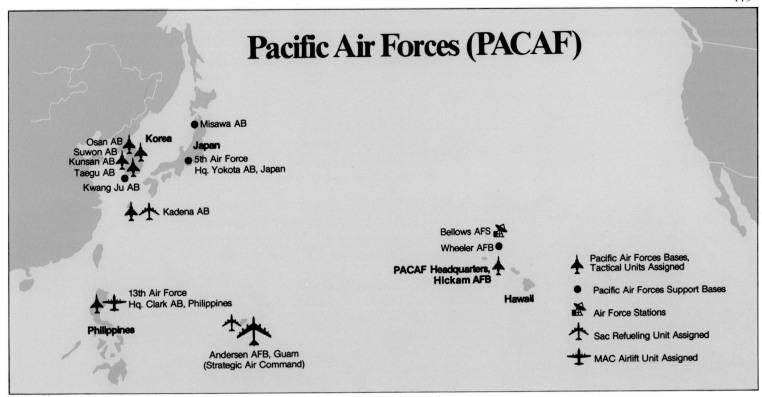

Misawa AB

Korea

Osan AB
Suwon AB
Kunsan AB
Taegu AB
Kwang Ju AB

Japan

5th Air Force
Hq. Yokota AB, Japan

Kadena AB

Bellows AFS
Wheeler AFB

PACAF Headquarters, Hickam AFB

13th Air Force
Hq. Clark AB, Philippines

Philippines

Hawaii

Andersen AFB, Guam
(Strategic Air Command)

Pacific Air Forces Bases, Tactical Units Assigned

Pacific Air Forces Support Bases

Air Force Stations

Sac Refueling Unit Assigned

MAC Airlift Unit Assigned

Above: An F-16 'Commando' Falcon prepares for refueling over the Pacific enroute to Hickam AFB for a *Cope Elite* exercise.

Left: PACAF Eagles from Kadena AB with Royal Singapore Air Force and Royal Australian Air Force aircraft during the *Kangaroo 81* exercise.

Wheeler AFB, Hawaii

Location: At the center of Oahu, north of Hickam AFB
Area: 1369 acres
Altitude: 845ft
Personnel: 720 Military
          112 Civilian

The oldest active air base in Hawaii, Wheeler was activated in February 1922 and named for Major Sheldon Wheeler, Commanding Officer of Luke Field, Hawaii, killed in a crash there on 13 July 1921. Wheeler AFB is the headquarters of PACAF's 326th Air Division, which operates the Air Defense Control Center, the operational control facility for the interceptors of the Hawaii Air National Guard that provide the air defense umbrella for Hawaii.

Clark AB in the Philippines, two hours north of Manila (now technically a Philippine air force base), the oldest and largest American air base outside the United States, continues to be home to the Thirteenth Air Force and its Third Tactical Fighter Wing. The largest concentration of PACAF air power is under the Fifth Air Force, with the Fifth's air power focused in Korea with the 314th Air Division at **Osan AB. Yokota AB**, Fifth Air

Force headquarters, serves as a support base. Meanwhile, the combat aircraft assigned by Fifth Air Force to augment the air defense capabilities of the Japanese Air Self-Defense Force (JASDF), are located with the 313th Air Division at **Kadena AB** on the Japanese Island of Okinawa. In the Indian Ocean, Air Force activites center on the large secret Navy base on the British island of Diego Garcia.

PACAF READINESS EXERCISES

To prepare for its role in defending the vast region under its charge, PACAF, like USAFE and TAC, engages in numerous annual and semiannual training exercises. The largest is *Team Spirit*, held in Korea and not only PACAF but the US Army, US Navy, US Marine Corps and Republic of Korea forces. *Cope Thunder* is the PACAF equivalent of TAC's *Red Flag*, a series of realistic tactical warfare exercises held seven times a year on the Crow Valley Gunnery Range near Clark AB in the Philippines, with the 26th Tactical Fighter Training Squadron's F-5s in the role of Aggressors. *Cope Thunder* involves units from all the American services throughout the Pacific as well as Philippine Royal Australian and Royal New Zealand Air Force units. In 1982 Royal Thai Air Force units participated in *Cope Thunder* for the first time. A corollary exercise, *Combat Sage*, uses realistic combat scenarios to evaluate the effectiveness of air-to-air weapons systems.

The northern counterpart of *Cope Thunder*, code-named *Cope North*, is flown out of Misawa AB in northern Japan as a joint exercise with Japan's JASDF. *Cope North* provides integrated training for the two forges in air defense, including airborne command and control, as well as air-to-ground missions. The need to tighten up Japanese air defense was clearly demonstrated in 1976, when Russian pilot Lt Viktor Belenko successfully penetrated Japanese air space in a MiG-25 Foxbat interceptor. Belenko's objective was to land and defect, but had he been on an attack mission he would not have been intercepted. *Cope North* is designed to train PACAF and JASDF pilots to prevent such penetrations. PACAF exercises include joint maneuvers with other Asian allies such as the joint Royal Australian Air Force (RAAF/USAF *Pacific Consort* and *Kangaroo*.

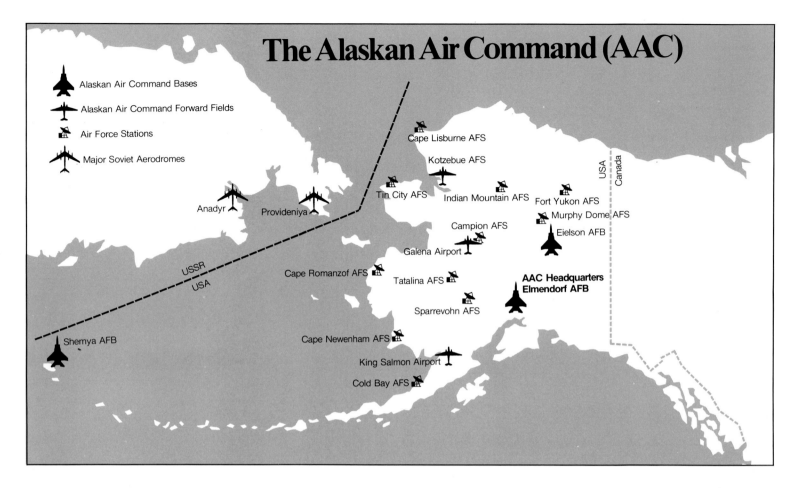

The Alaskan Air Command (AAC)

Alaskan Air Command Bases

Alaskan Air Command Forward Fields

Air Force Stations

Major Soviet Aerodromes

Cape Lisburne AFS

Kotzebue AFS

Tin City AFS

Indian Mountain AFS

Fort Yukon AFS

Murphy Dome AFS

Anadyr

Provideniya

Campion AFS

Eielson AFB

Galena Airport

USSR

USA

Cape Romanzof AFS

Tatalina AFS

AAC Headquarters
Elmendorf AFB

Sparrevohn AFS

Shemya AFB

Cape Newenham AFS

King Salmon Airport

Cold Bay AFS

USA
Canada

THE ALASKAN AIR COMMAND

Just below the Arctic Circle in the Bering Strait, there is a place where one can stand in one of the fifty United States and see Soviet Union territory only two miles away. This site is on Little Diomede Island, Alaska, where only a thin strip of water (in winter, passable ice) separates the world's two super-powers. This proximity of Alaska to the Soviet Union under-scores the importance of the Alaskan Air Command to overall security of the United States. Cold and loneliness make Alaska's remote corners a cruel and forbidding place, but also one of stark and awesome beauty. As the prophet of air power, Billy Mitchell, said in 1935, 'Alaska is the most strategic place in the world.'

The Alaskan Air Command (AAC) was created on 18 December 1945 by redesignation of the World War II-era Eleventh Air Force. AAC headquarters was moved from Adak Island to Elmendorf Field (Elmendorf AFB since 1947) near Anchorage on 1 October 1946 where it has remained since. With the onset of the cold war, the AAC's primary mission was to provide early warning of possible Russian air attack over the Polar route and to shoot down Russian bombers. With the mission of flying Combat Air patrol over the roof of the North American continent, AAC has taken the motto 'Top Cover for America.' The AAC interceptor units were initially equipped with P-51s, replaced in succession by F-80s, F-94s, F-89s, F-102s F-4s (1970) and in 1983, F-15s. AAC reached peak aircraft strength (200) in 1957 (when F-89s were the first-line inter-ceptor); it has declined steadily ever since.

In 1947 the Navy's Hoge Board, studying national defense, and an AAC study, independently recommended establishment of radar stations in Alaska to answer the need for early warning of possible Russian attack. Plans called for between 22 and 58 Aircraft Control and Warning System (AC&W) sites, but because of the same budget restrictions that were plaguing the

entire Defense Department, only ten sites and two control centers were funded in the 1949 budget. AAC began a design for a permanent system with five coastal sites at Cape Lisburne, Cape Newenham, Cape Romanzof, Tin City (closest to Little Diomede Island) and Northeast Cape (St Lawrence Island). In addition to the coastal sites, there would be five Ground Control Intercept (GCI) radar sites in the interior of Alaska at Campion, Tatalina, King Salmon Airport, Fire Island and Murphy Dome. They would be divided into two sectors, with the Southern Sector Control Center at Elmendorf AFB and the Northern at Ladd AFB (now the Army's Fort Wainwright) near Fairbanks. When the latter was turned over to the Army in 1960, both control centers were consolidated at Elmendorf.

Construction began on the AC&W system in 1950, but with the outbreak of the Korean War five temporary sites were quickly established at Elmendorf AFB, Ladd AFB, King Salmon Airport, Nome and Gambell on St Lawrence Island. The emer-gency sites went on-line on 27 June 1950, marking 24-hour-a-day operation of the Alaskan air defense system, which has been continuous ever since. Meanwhile, construction continued on the permanent sites, with Murphy Dome, Fire Island and King Salmon opening in 1951. Tatalina and Campion opened the following year, Cape Lisburne, Cape Romanzof, Northeast Cape and Tin City in 1953. As a result of the Korean War, two additional sites were funded: the first, at Indian Mountain, opened in 1935; the other, at Sparrevohn, became operational in 1954 along with the site at Cape Newenham. The following year construction began on six additional GCI sites at Middleton Island, Ohlson Mountain, Bethel, Fort Yukon, Kotzebue and Unalakleet, all of which were completed in 1958.

On 12 September 1957 the joint US-Canada North American Air Defense Command (NORAD) was established (and the Alaskan NORAD region a year later). Campion and King Salmon became NORAD Control Centers, each with responsi-bility for the GCI sites in its area. In 1957 JCS approved extend-

ing the Distant Early Warning (DEW) Line of radar stations out from Alaska into the Aleutian Islands. Six such sites were authorized at Cold Bay (the main site), Nikolski, Port Heiden, Port Moller, Cape Saridref and Driftwood Bay, all of which went into service under AAC control in 1959.

The final system of 18 AC&W/GCI and six DEW Line Stations was in place for only four years when AAC closed the sites at Middleton Island, Ohlson Mountain and Bethel for reasons of economy. In 1969 the Joint Chiefs of Staff ordered a cutback in air defense forces, which resulted in closing the NORAD sites at Northeast Cape, Fire Island and Unalakleet as well as the DEW Line sites in the Aleutians. Of the latter, Cold Bay remained open and was converted to a NORAD Surveillance Station. In 1973 Campion was downgraded from a NORAD Control Center to a GCI site and Kotzebue from a GCI site to a surveillance station.

In 1970 further cutbacks were made in the fabric of Alaskan air defense. The Nike Hercules surface-to-air missiles batteries around the city of Fairbanks and Eielson AFB were deactivated, and rotational assignments of Aerospace Defense Command F-106s to AAC from bases in the 'lower 48' states under the code name *College Shoes* were terminated. In 1979 the Nike Hercules system was deactivated in the Anchorage-Elmendorf AFB area, marking the first time since 1940 that the area had not ground-to-air artillery or missile air defense.

In 1971 the traditional air defense role of AAC gradually began to give way to tactical air support with activation of the 25th Tactical Air Support Squadron and establishment of the Yukon and Blair Lakes Electronic Warfare Ranges. In 1973 USAF Chief of Staff John Ryan commissioned a study code-named *Saber Yukon* to verify the need for the now-outdated Alaskan AC&W system. The following year, the need verified, AAC began the *Seek Igloo* program, the first major modernization of the system. In 1979 General Electric received the contract to build the first *Seek Igloo* AN/FPS-117 Minimally Attended

Above: Two squadrons of Elmondorf-based all-weather F-102s were AAC's only interceptors from 1960 to 1969.

Radar system at King Salmon. By 'minimally attended' was meant that the sites would be automated, requiring fewer operating personnel in these often isolated regions. The *Seek Igloo* program was completed in 1984 with the Air Stations at Tin City, Tatalina, Sparrevohn, Murphy Dome, Indian Mountain, Fort Yukon, Cold Bay, Cape Romanzof, Cape Newenham and Cape Lisburne as well as King Salmon coming on-line as Minimally Attended Radar sites. The former radar has been replaced by state-of-the-art, three-dimensional (range, azimuth,

The Commanders of the Alaskan Air Command

Brig Gen Joseph Atkinson	1 Oct 1946–25 Feb 1949
Brig Gen Frank Armstrong, Jr	26 Feb 1949–27 Dec 1950
Maj Gen William Old	27 Dec 1950–14 Oct 1952
Brig Gen W R Agee	27 Oct 1952–26 Feb 1953
Maj Gen George Acheson	26 Feb 1953–1 Feb 1956
Lt Gen Joseph Atkinson	24 Feb 1956–16 July 1956
Maj Gen Frank Armstrong, Jr	17 July 1956–23 Oct 1956
Maj Gen James Davis	24 Oct 1956–27 June 1957
Lt Gen Frank Armstrong, Jr	28 June 1957–18 Aug 1957
Brig Gen Kenneth Gibson	19 Aug 1957–13 Aug 1958
Maj Gen C F Necrason	14 Aug 1958–19 July 1961
Maj Gen Wendell Bowman	26 July 1961–8 Aug 1963
Maj Gen James Jensen	15 Aug 1963–14 Nov 1966
Maj Gen Thomas Moore	15 Nov 1966–24 July 1969
Maj Gen Joseph Cunningham	25 July 1969–31 July 1972
Maj Gen Donavon Smith	1 Aug 1972–5 June 1973
Maj Gen Charles Carson, Jr	18 June 1973–2 Mar 1974
Maj Gen Jack Gamble	19 Mar 1974–30 June 1975
Lt Gen James Hill	1 July 1975–14 Oct 1976
Lt Gen M. L. Boswell	15 Oct 1976–30 June 1978
Lt Gen Winfield Scott, Jr	1 July 1978–1 Apr 1981
Lt Gen Lynwood Clark	1 Apr 1981–

height) radar which will remote-track data to the Elmendorf Region Operations Center at Elmendorf AFB. The highly automated nature of the equipment has reduced staffing requirements at the sites by up to 80% or more.

As an indication of the Alaskan Air Command's renewed importance, its commander, since 1975, has been designated senior military officer for Alaska, Commander of the Joint Task Force, Alaska, in time of war and Commander of the Alaska NORAD Region.

ALASKAN AIR COMMAND BASES

Elmendorf AFB (AAC Headquarters)
Location: Adjacent to Anchorage, Alaska
Area: 13,400 acres
Altitude: 118ft
Personnel: 6120 Military
             1483 Civilian

Activated in 1940 as Elmendorf Army Air Field at Fort Richardson, the base is named for Captain Hugh Elmendorf, who was killed on 13 January 1933 at Wright Field, Ohio. The 18th Pursuit Squadron arrived in February 1941. In early 1942, shortly after the American entry into World War II, the Eleventh Air Force was established here. Elmendorf and the Eleventh played an important part in the Aleutian Campaign during the war and in later air operations against the Kurile Islands north of Japan. Always the principal fighter base in Alaska, Elmendorf used the slogan 'Top Cover for America' before it was adopted in 1969 as the AAC motto. Beyond being a fighter base, Elmendorf has been an important stop for MAC flights between the United States and the Far East.

The Elmendorf AFB host unit is the 21st TFW with its 43d TFS and 5021st Tactical Operations Squadron. The base is also home to the NORAD Alaska Region Control Center, the 1931st Communications Group (AFCC), the 6981st Electronic Security Squadron (ESC), the 616th Military Airlift Group and such MAC units as the 17th Tactical Airlift Squadron, the 11th Weather Squadron, the 71st Aerospace Rescue and Recovery Squadron and the AAC Rescue Coordination Center that has accounted for more than 3600 rescues since it was established in 1961.

Eielson AFB
Location: 26 miles SE of Fairbanks, Alaska
Area: 35,000 acres
Altitude: 534ft
Personnel: 3233 Military
             343 Civilian

Activated in October 1944, the base is named for the Arctic aviation pioneer Carl Ben Eielson, first man to fly across the Arctic Basin (Point Barrow to Spitzbergen) and the first to fly airmail in Alaska. He was killed in a crash near Siberia on 9 November 1929. The field was originally planned and built as a satellite to nearby Ladd Field (later Ladd AFB), which was a way station for Lend-Lease delivery flights to Russia during World War II. In 1947 Eielson became full-fledged AAC base and has since survived the deactivation of Ladd AFB as an Air Force installation. In the late 1950s and early 1960s Eielson, now with one of the longest runways in North America, became a forward base for SAC B-36s and B-52s as well as SAC tankers. Eielson is still an important base for SAC tankers and for SAC RC-135 electronic reconnaissance aircraft that fly regular missions to the periphery of Russian air space near the Kamchatka Peninsula, the site of several top-secret Soviet military installations. It was an Eielson-based SAC RC-135 that crossed paths with the Korean Air Lines 747 shot down by Soviet interceptors on 1 September 1983 (and which the Russians later claimed they had confused with the 747).

The Eielson host unit is the 343d Composite Wing incorporating the 343d Combat Support Group, the 25th Tactical Air Support Squadron and the 18th TFS. The units conduct Air Support training on the nearby Blair Lakes conventional bombing and gunnery range and Yukon Electronic Warfare Range. SAC tanker operations at Eielson are under control of SAC's Sixth Strategic Wing. The Air Training Command has also located its Arctic Survival School at Eielson.

Shemya AFB
Location: On the western tip of the Aleutian Island chain.
Area: 11.25 sq miles
Altitude: 270ft
Personnel 570 Military
             0 Civilian

Above: A group of Alaskan Air Command A-10 Thunderbolts of the 18th Tactical Fighter Squadron out of Eilson AFB, May 1982.

Shemya is the westernmost part of the United States, so located that the International Date Line had to be routed around it so it would be in the same day as the rest of the United States. Known as 'The Black Pearl,' the 4.5-mile-long island was captured by the Japanese early in World War II and wrested from their control on 28 May 1943, in the final days of the battle to retake the larger nearby island of Attu. A 10,000-foot runway, still the center-piece of the base, and birchwood hangers were built at Shemya to accommodate B-29 strategic bomber attacks against Japan (which were ultimately flown from the Marianas south of Japan and not from Shemya). The base was kept busy during the war as an Eleventh Air Force B-24 and B-25 base. After the war it became an air refueling site on the Great Circle Route between Anchorage and the Far East, playing an important part in airlift operations during the Korean War. In July 1954 Shemya was declared surplus, deactivated and turned over to the Civil Aeronautics Authority (forerunner of the Federal Aviation Administration – FAA) who in turn leased it to Northwest Orient Airlines, which maintained its presence there until 1961. The Air Force resumed operations on Shemya in 1958, in support of various strategic intelligence activities as well as aircraft refueling. Shemya recovered importance steadily until 21 June 1968, when it was redesignated from an Air Force Station to an Air Force Base.

In August 1977 the new *Cobra Dane* AN/FPS-108 Phased Array Radar facility became operational at Shemya, replacing the older AN/FPS-17 Detection and AN/FPS-80 Tracking Radars monitoring space and missile activity in eastern Siberia and Kamchatka. The *Cobra Dane* facility is now under SPACECOM control, having been operated successively by ADC and SAC. AAC Tactical aircraft, now including F-15s based at the other AAC bases, are regularly rotated through the 10,000-foot runway on the Black Pearl of the frigid North Pacific – 1600 miles from Anchorage but only 600 miles from Petro-pavlovsk.

Left: An AAC ground crew chief refuels an F-111A at Elmendorf AFB during Operation *Brim Frost 81.*

Above: Three AAC F-89 Scorpions in flight over Alaska's Mt McKinley in July 1954. Scorpions were the premier US Air Force all-weather interceptor throughout the mid-fifties. The last F-89 left AAC service in July 1960, leaving F-102s providing 'Top Cover for America'. Standard Air Force markings during this era included insignia red wingtip and tail surfaces, which show as a neutral grey in this photo. By 1959 the insignia red was giving way to vivid fluorescent orange. The purpose of the high-visibility markings was the need to locate the aircraft should it be downed in some trackless wilderness, such as this one presided over by AAC.

TACTICAL AIRCRAFT

The tactical fighter aircraft in service with the US Air Force fall into three eras or generations. The first generation were those early jets in operational service during the first decade following World War II, 1945-1955. These included the F-80, the F-84 and the F-86 Sabre Jet. In the second generation were the larger, more sophisticated jets of the Century Series, so named because they began with the F-100 and were numbered sequentially through F-106. They were followed by the F-110, which became the famous F-4 Phantom, the premier American fighter from 1965 to 1975. The third generation incorporated lessons learned by the Air Force in Southeast Asia and the best of the microelectronics, high-technology boom of the seventies. Third-generation aircraft include the Air Force's F-15 and F-16 and the Navy's F-14 and F-18.

THE FIRST GENERATION

The fighters of the Korean War era began with much of the same technology that had marked World War II fighters and culminated in North American's F-86. The swept-wing F-86 was the superior fighter over Korea and the most successful jet fighter produced until that time. The **F-86** (A, E, & F models) **Sabre Jet** was really the ultimate USAF air superiority fighter of the period and would remain so long after the cease-fire in Korea.

The three most important USAF tactical aircraft to follow the F-86 were of a new type, predicated on improved technology and necessitated by a growing threat of Russian bomber attack. The type was the all-weather air defense interceptor, the most important of which would be the Northrop F-89 Scorpion. In the late 1940s the only all-weather interceptors in the USAF inventory were the propellor-driven (now out-moded) F-82 and F-61. Early in 1949, because of delays in the F-89 program, two other types were procured to supplement the F-89. In March 1949, with their F-86A going into active service, North American proposed an all-weather interceptor version of the F-86. The new interceptor would be based on the F-86 airframe and would have a single crewman. The single-seat configuration was a radical departure for an all-weather interceptor – it was customary in such aircraft to have a second crewman to back up the pilot in navigation and weapons-system operation. North American believed the sophisticated electronics it was developing would compensate for the absence of the second crewman and the Air Force went along, ordering 124 aircraft. The converted F-86A, incorporating a Hughes Fire-Control System, was designated XF-95 and first flew in September 1949. When the Russians were known to possess the atomic bomb, the Air Force ordered an additional 31 of the new aircraft (7 October) which was redesignated YF-86D.

The first YF-86D, with a J47-GE-17 turbo jet engine developing 6650lb of thrust with afterburner, flew on 22 December 1949 less than a year after the program got underway.

Procurement of the **F-86D** became, despite early program slippage, a high-priority Air Force program. In April 1953 (nearly two years behind schedule) the F-86D finally entered service with active Air Defense Command squadrons. By the end of the year ADC had 600 of them; by June 1955 1026 (or 73%) of the Command's 1405 interceptors were F-86Ds, the remainder being F-94Cs and F-89Ds. Few F-86Ds served overseas. The FEAF in Korea received a few but they were withdrawn as unsuitable for the short fields available there. Six years later, in 1959, two squadrons (the 431st and 437th FIS) went to

Spain in support of SAC bombers at Torrejon and Zaragoza. In all there were 2504 F-86Ds built for service with the USAF and the Air National Guard: they would serve until June 1961. Some F-86Ds were converted to F-86L standard with advanced electronics, and 120 of an advanced F-86D, redesignated F-86K, were also built.

Above: The all-weather interceptor version of the Sabre Jet, designated F-86D, with its distinctive nose radome.

Above right: The F-84F, carrying fuel tanks in its role as a SAC escort fighter, was a swept-wing development of the F-84 Thunderjet. *Below:* A lineup of F-84Fs at Elmendorf AFB, Alaska.

F-86D Sabre Jet
Manufacturer: North American Aviation
First year of service: 1951
Aircraft type: Single-seat interceptor
Wingspan: 37ft 1in
Length: 40ft 4in
Weight: 17,000lb (gross)
Range: 836 miles
Service ceiling: 54,600 feet
Top/Cruising speed: 707mph
Powerplant: (1) 5700lb thrust (7630lb with afterburner) General
    Electric J47-GE-17 turbojet
Armanent/Capacity: (24) 2.75 inch FFAR rockets

F-84F Thunderstreak (RF-84F called Thunderflash)
Manufacturer: Republic Aviation
First year of service: 1954
Aircraft type: Single-seat fighter, fighter-bomber, tactical
    reconnaissance aircraft (RF-84F)
Wingspan: 33ft 7in
Length: 43ft 5in
Weight: 13,800lb (gross)
Range: 2200 miles (with drop tanks)
Service ceiling: 46,000 feet
Top speed: 695mph
Powerplant: (1) 7200lb thrust Wright J65-W-3 turbojet
Armament/Capacity: Six .50 caliber machine guns

The second of the postwar interceptors was **Lockheed's F-94 Starfire**, which was based on their earlier F-80 Shooting Star. A lot of hopes were being pinned on the F-89 Scorpion, but it was an all-new design and the F-94, like the F-86D, would work from existing technology and give the Air Force interim all-weather interceptors. The first of the two-man F-94s, 14% longer than the one-man F-80s, entered service in May 1950 and served in Korea beginning late the following year. The Starfires were based at Suwon AB to provide fighter interceptor cover (replacing the old F-82s) for the American bases in South Korea and escort for B-29 strikes against the North. Although not too successful against low-flying aircraft, few planes proved as reliable as the F-94 against the enemy in the Korean War, especially in nasty weather and darkness, for which the F-94 was designed. The F-94s flew when most other aircraft were grounded by bad weather. Most Korean veterans praised the plane: it was rugged and could rack up a lot of flying hours without maintenance. The Air Force received a total of 854 Starfires, including 356 F-94Bs and 387 F-94Cs, with the latter serving USAF units until 1959 and ANG units until 1960.

Throughout this time, the interceptor the USAF had been waiting for was **Northrop's F-89 Scorpion**, so named because the upsweep of its tail resembled that of an angry scorpion ready to strike. During World War II Northrop had built the P-61 Black Widow (also named for a poisonous invertebrate) which resembled the Scorpion in being a multi-seat, twin-engine night fighter that was the largest American fighter to see service during its time.

The F-89, like the F-80, F-84 and F-94, was of straight-winged design, lacking the swept-wing characteristic that made the F-86 such a radical design. The XF-89 first flew in August 1948, with the first F-89A going into service in September 1950. Only 48 F-89A and B models were delivered due to problems with airframe and engine design. The C version of this long-awaited interceptor was also plagued with structural deficiencies that resulted in a series of disastrous crashes during flight-testing in 1952, which in turn resulted in the grounding of the whole program for several months.

Eventually 163 F-89Cs were delivered, but the bugs were finally worked out of the system with the F-89D, of which 682 were delivered. Entering operational service with ADC in January 1954, the F-89D was the first USAF fighter to abandon guns in favor of missiles. The F-89D was also the first to have permanently mounted wing-tip pods from which missiles would be fired. The missiles were the Hughes GAR-1 (originally designated XF-98, later designated AIM-4) Falcon supersonic (Mach 3) radar-guided, air-to-air, solid-fuel rockets with a range of about four miles. Beginning in November 1956, 350 F-89Ds were redesignated F-89J, having been modified to carry the Douglas MB-1 (later designated AIR-2) Genie unguided rockets, the first air-to-air rocket to carry a nuclear warhead. The first firing of a live-armed Genie took place on 19 July 1957, when an ADC F-89J fired the rocket over the northern part of the range at Yucca Flat, Nevada, detonating the nuclear warhead at 15,000 feet. The F-89J was an important part of the ADC arsenal in the late fifties, reaching a peak inventory of 286 in June 1958. With the advent of the Genie-capable F-101 and F-106, ADC began turning its F-89s over to the Air Guard, with whom nuclear armed F-89Js served until 1968.

Below: The Lockheed F-94 Starfire, a supersonic outgrowth of the F-80 program, carried 24 rockets in a firing ring around the nose, operated above 45,000 feet, had nose radar, and provided ejection seats for both crewmen. It was 41 feet 4 inches long and had a span of 37 feet 6 inches.

Above: An F-89J in flight with its full armament of two MB-1 Genie nuclear-armed rockets and four Hughes GAR-2 (later AIM-4) Falcon guided missiles. (Tactical missiles are discussed on pages 148-9).

Below: Early model Scorpions carried six nose-mounted machine guns. F-89 landing gear consisted of very thin large-diameter wing wheels, so designed to retract into the Scorpion's thin wing.

F-89D Scorpion
Manufacturer: Northrop Aircraft
First year of service: 1954 (F-89A, 1950)
Aircraft type: Single-seat interceptor
Wingspan: 59ft 8in
Length: 53ft 7in
Weight: 45,575lb
Range: 1000 miles
Service ceiling: 43,500 feet
Top speed: 610mph
Powerplant: (2) 5600lb thrust Allison J35-A-35 turbojets
Armament: (104) 2.75 inch folding fin aerial rockets (FFAR) in wing pods. Earlier models were armed with 20mm cannons. The F-89J was an F-89D modified to carry two Genie nuclear air-to-air missiles.

Major USAAF/USAF Fighters
and their Periods of Service

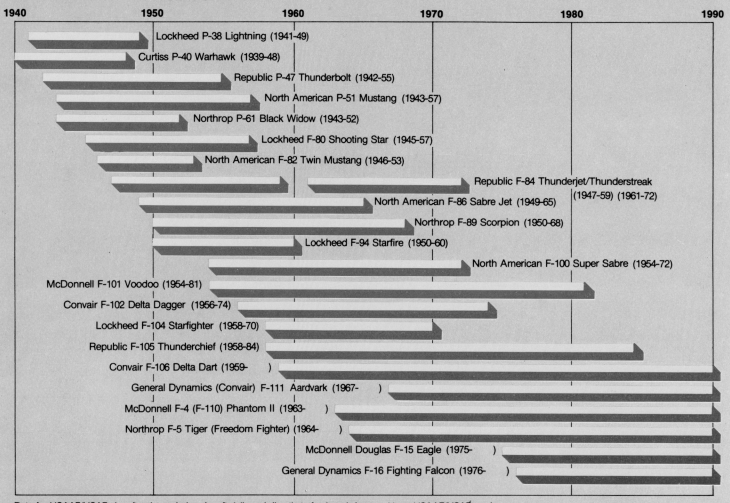

| 1940 | 1950 | 1960 | 1970 | 1980 | 1990 |

Lockheed P-38 Lightning (1941-49)

Curtiss P-40 Warhawk (1939-48)

Republic P-47 Thunderbolt (1942-55)

North American P-51 Mustang (1943-57)

Northrop P-61 Black Widow (1943-52)

Lockheed F-80 Shooting Star (1945-57)

North American F-82 Twin Mustang (1946-53)

Republic F-84 Thunderjet/Thunderstreak (1947-59) (1961-72)

North American F-86 Sabre Jet (1949-65)

Northrop F-89 Scorpion (1950-68)

Lockheed F-94 Starfire (1950-60)

North American F-100 Super Sabre (1954-72)

McDonnell F-101 Voodoo (1954-81)

Convair F-102 Delta Dagger (1956-74)

Lockheed F-104 Starfighter (1958-70)

Republic F-105 Thunderchief (1958-84)

Convair F-106 Delta Dart (1959-   )

General Dynamics (Convair) F-111 Aardvark (1967-   )

McDonnell F-4 (F-110) Phantom II (1963-   )

Northrop F-5 Tiger (Freedom Fighter) (1964-   )

McDonnell Douglas F-15 Eagle (1975-   )

General Dynamics F-16 Fighting Falcon (1976-   )

Data for USAAF/USAF aircraft only, excludes aircraft delivered directly to foreign air forces without USAAF/USAF service.

Periods begin with operational service, not first recorded flight. Periods include service with Air National Guard, but do not include mothballed aircraft.

Major USAAF/USAF Attack Aircraft
and their Periods of Service

| 1940 | 1950 | 1960 | 1970 | 1980 | 1990 |

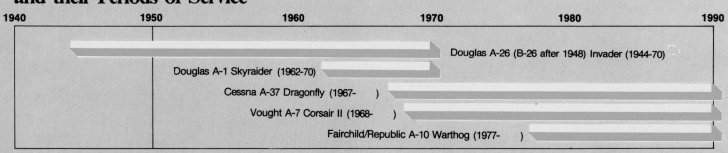

Douglas A-26 (B-26 after 1948) Invader (1944-70)

Douglas A-1 Skyraider (1962-70)

Cessna A-37 Dragonfly (1967-   )

Vought A-7 Corsair II (1968-   )

Fairchild/Republic A-10 Warthog (1977-   )

Data for USAAF/USAF aircraft only, excludes aircraft delivered directly to foreign air forces without USAAF/USAF service.

Periods begin with operational service, not first recorded flight. Periods include service with Air National Guard, but do not include mothballed aircraft.

Major USAAF/USAF Fighters
Total Number Delivered

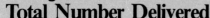

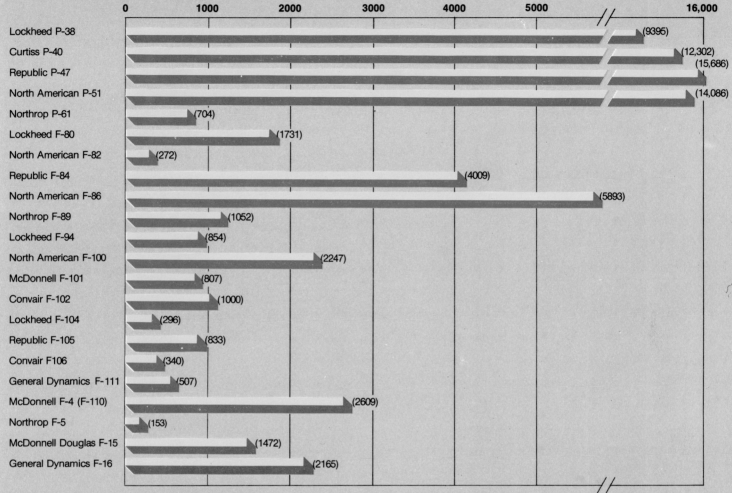

Data for USAAF/USAF aircraft only, excludes aircraft delivered directly to foreign air forces without USAAF/USAF service.

Major USAAF/USAF Attack Aircraft
Total Number Delivered

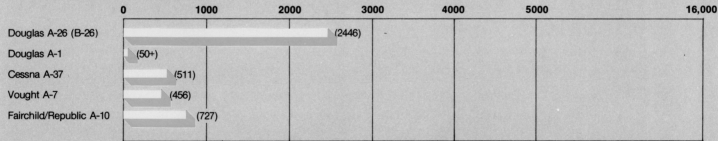

Data for USAAF/USAF aircraft only, excludes aircraft delivered directly to foreign air forces without USAAF/USAF service.

THE CENTURY SERIES

The first of the Century Series was, of course, the **F-100**. It was North American Aviations' attempt to provide a successor to its very successful F-86 Sabre Jet. Called Super Sabre (what else?), the F-100 was also a swept-wing, single-seat, all-purpose fighter. The prototype first flew in May 1953, with the first operational F-100As going into service in September 1954. The F-100C became operational in July 1955,

the F-100B becoming the prototype for the third Sabre, the F-107, which would never get past the prototype stage. The F-100C differed from the F-100A in that it had underwing pylons for ordnance and fuel tanks, and that it was aerial refuelable.

While the 205 F-100As and 476 F-100Cs were designed as fighters, the 1274 F-100Ds were built to function primarily as fighter-bombers, a role that was secondary with the earlier Super Sabres. The F-100D was first delivered to operational units in June 1956; these were rapidly deployed to overseas bases to

A Century series family portrait. Clockwise from below: Lockheed's F-104 Starfighter, North American's F-100 Super Sabre, Convair's F-102 Delta Dagger, McDonnell's F-101 Voodoo and the Republic F-105 Thunderchief. Of those not pictured, the Republic F-103 and North American F-108 were Mach 3 interceptor designs that were never built. Two examples of the needle-nosed North American F-107 Super Super Sabre (with top-mounted intake that started life as F-100B) were built and the VTOL (Vertical Take-off and Landing) Ryan F-109 never made it past the experimental stage. The Convair F-106 arrived later, serving the Air Force for 30 years, and the F-110 and F-111 belonged to another era.

replace F-84s. FEAF received 46 at Itazuke AB in Japan, while USAFE received 70 at Etain AB and Chaumont AB in France and Boulihaut AB and Sidi Slimange AB in Morocco. F-100s were introduced into combat operations over Laos in May 1962. F-100 operations over North Vietnam began in 1965; two years later most had been deployed to Southeast Asia, with only five F-100 squadrons remaining in the United States.

The F-100F was a two-seat development of the F-100C originally intended as a trainer. It was armed with only two of the 20mm M-39 cannons of which the F-100D carried four. It first entered TAC inventory in January 1958 and was quickly deployed to PACAF and USAFE squadrons. In Southeast Asia F-100Fs were modified as 'Wild Weasel' aircraft, assigned to destroying North Vietnamese SAM sites. A total of 294 F-100Fs served with the USAF, the last ones being phased out along with the last F-100D in 1972.

McDonnell's F-101 Voodoo began on the drawing board as a long-range bomber escort with the designation F-88. The Air Force cancelled the F-88 program in 1950 shortly after the first flight of the second prototype because of budget constraints. The F-88, however, turned out to be a good plane despite the cancellation and the enormous success of the parallel North American F-86 Sabre Jet. In January 1952 the Air Force contracted with McDonnell to build an updated version of the F-88, now designated F-101. Flight testing began in 1954 and the first F-101A entered operational service with TAC in July 1957. The Air Force also contracted for a reconnaissance version, designated RF-10A, which became operational in May 1957. The RF-101A initially incorporated the long focal-length Fairchild KA-1 and KA-2 framing cameras and the Fairchild CAI KA-18 strip camera. An updated recon version, the RF-101C, entered operational service the same year and became the reconnaissance workhorse of the Air Force. Refitted with newer high-resolution cameras by 1962, RF-101Cs were used for surveillance over Cuba and provided irrefutable evidence that the Russians were installing offensive missiles there. The RF-101 was also the only Voodoo to see action in Southeast Asia, being used for reconnaissance and strike evaluation from 1961 through 1970 when they were replaced by RF-4Cs. The Voodoo is also remembered for its interceptor version, the two-place F-101B which entered ADC service in January 1959. Later interceptors built after 1961 were designated F-101F and there were a total of 480 F-101B/F interceptors in a total of 887 Voodoos of all types.

Above: The first flight of Kelly Johnson's F-104 Starfighter over Edwards AFB in February 1956.

F-100D Super Sabre
Manufacturer: North American Aviation
First year of service: 1954 (F-100A)
Aircraft type: Air superiority fighter and fighter-bomber
Wingspan: 38ft 9in
Length: 47ft 0in
Weight: 34,832lb (gross)
Range: 1500 miles (with external tanks)
Service ceiling: 35,000 feet
Top speed: Mach 1.3
Powerplant: (1) 17,000lb thrust Pratt & Whitney J57-P-21A turbojet
Armament: Four 20mm guns and underwing pylons for six 1000lb bombs, 2 Sidewinder or 2 Bullpup air-to-air missiles

F-101B Voodoo
Manufacturer: McDonnell Aircraft Corp (now McDonnell Douglas)
First year of service: 1957
Aircraft type: Fighter-bomber and all-weather interceptor
Wingspan: 39ft 8in
Length: 67ft 4¾in
Weight: 46,500lb (gross)
Range: 1550 miles
Service ceiling: 51,000 feet
Top speed: Mach 1.85
Powerplant: (2) 14,990lb thrust Pratt & Whitney J57-P-55 turbojets
Armament: Three AIM-4D Falcon air-to-air missiles carried internally, and two AIR-2A Genie nuclear-warhead unguided rockets under the fuselage

F-104A Starfighter
Manufacturer: Lockheed Aircraft
First year of service: 1958
Aircraft type: Single-seat fighter, interceptor
Wingspan: 21ft 11in (without tip tanks)
Length: 54ft 9in
Weight: 28,779lb (gross)
Range: 1300 miles with external fuel tanks
Service ceiling: 55,200 feet
Top/Cruising speed: Mach 2
Powerplant: (1) 14,800lb thrust General Electric J79-GE-3 turbojet
Armament/Capacity: (1) 20mm cannon plus various combinations of FFAR rockets, AIM-9 Sidwinder missiles and gravity bombs.

The **Lockheed F-104 Starfighter**, known familiarly as the 'missile with a man in it,' was designed by Kelly Johnson and submitted to the Air Force by Lockheed on its own initiative. Based on Korean War experience, Lockheed knew the Air Force might be looking for a high-speed light-weight fighter capable of operating from forward fields. The Air Force hesitantly issued a contract to Lockheed in 1953 and XF-104 flight testing began the following year. The first F-104A entered operational service with ADC (not TAC as originally intended) in January 1958. The two-seat F-104B was similar, with the addition of a 20mm Vulcan cannon to the Sidewinder missiles provided for earlier. Incorporating aerial refueling capabilities, the F-104C and D were designed for tactical air support, and several served in Southeast Asia. The US Air Force accepted a total of 663 F-104s but retained only 296 for its own use, the rest being transferred to allied countries under the Military Assistance Program. In addition, many were produced under Lockheed license in Canada, Japan and Germany.

The **F-105 Thunderchief** was Republic Aviation's Mach 1.5 successor to the F-84 Thunderstreak. The Thunderchief, or 'Thud' as it came to be known during the Vietnam War, began life as a nuclear-capable tactical bomber and became the most commonly used fighter-bomber of the war. The first flight of the YF-105A prototype occurred in October 1955, with the first operational Thud, an F-105B, entering TAC service in August 1958. Only 80 F-105As and Bs were delivered, the principal production model being the F-105D. There were 610 F-105Ds built, followed by 143 F-105Fs, some of which were modified as F-105Gs. A total of 833 F-105s were delivered, 355 fewer than authorized by Congress.

Convair's F-102 Delta Dagger and F-106 Delta Dart both had their roots in the theories of the German scientist Dr Alexander Lippisch. During World War II Lippisch had developed several aircraft designs with delta-configuration wing types, among them the Messerschmitt Me-163. After the war, while the Messerschmitt-designed swept wing was being used by Boeing and North American, Consolidated Vultee (later Convair) enlisted the assistance of Dr Lippisch in the design of its tailless, pure-delta-winged research aircraft, the Model 7002 – the first of this type. First flown in 1948, the 7002 (later designated XF-92) led to an Air Force requirement for a supersonic delta-winged interceptor that came to be known as the '1954 Ultimate Interceptor.' The contract was won by Corvair and was designated F-102. The first YF-102 flew in October 1953, but design changes and changes in requirements delayed delivery of the first production

Left: Notable Century-birds, a 351st TFW F-105 (*top*) and a sleek ADC F-102.

F-102A Delta Dart ('Deuce')
Manufacturer: Convair Division of General Dynamics
First year of service: 1956
Aircraft type: Single-seat all-weather interceptor
Wingspan: 38ft 4½in
Length: 68ft 4½in
Weight: 28,000lb gross
Range: 1350 miles
Service ceiling: 54,000 feet
Top/Cruising speed: Mach 1.3
Powerplant: (1) 17,000lb thrust Pratt & Whitney J57-P-23/25 turbojet
Armament/Capacity: Three AIM-4 Falcon and one AIM-26 Nuclear Falcon missile carried internally. Earlier provision for unguided HVAR rockets had been deleted by the early 1970s. No guns.

F-102A until June 1955; the first did not enter operational service until the following April. The F-102 was delivered to AAC, PACAF and USAFE in 1958 and served for nearly a decade. The F-106 began as the F-102B, a much improved aircraft in which all the lessons learned the hard way in the F-102A program would be put to use. The designation of the new 'ultimate Interceptor' was changed to F-106 in April 1956, and the prototype flew in December 1956, only three years after the first F-102. The first F-106As entered ADC service in May 1959 and have continued in USAF and Air Guard service for well over a quarter of a century – longer than any other US Air Force fighter. Given this longevity of service, the F-106, with its continual modernization programs, may be the closest the Air Force could have come in the mid-1950s to developing the 'Ultimate Interceptor.' The F-106 was the last production aircraft in the Century Series, and with the retirement of the F-105 in 1984 it remains the only one still in active service.

Above: College Shoes F-106s with ADC insignia on their tails over Alaska's Mt McKinley.

Below: TAC F-104s, one equipped with an air refueling probe.

F-105D Thunderchief ('Thud')
Manufacturer: Fairchild Industries, Fairchild Republic Division
First year of service: 1961 (F-105B, 1958)
Aircraft type: Single-seat all-weather fighter-bomber
Wingspan: 34ft 11¼in
Length: 67ft ¼in
Weight: 52,546lb (gross); 27,500lb (empty)
Range: 1842 miles
Service ceiling: 52,000 feet
Top speed: Mach 2.1
Powerplant: (1) 26,500lb thrust Pratt & Whitney J75-P-19W turbojet
Armament: One 20mm multibarrel rotary cannon plus more than 14,000lb of stores underwing and underfuselage.

F-106A Delta Dart
Manufacturer: Convair Division of General Dynamics
First year of service: 1959
Aircraft type: Single-seat all-weather interceptor
Wingspan: 38ft 3½in
Length: 70ft 8¾in
Weight: 42,400lb (gross); 25,300lb (empty)
Range: 1200 miles
Service ceiling: 65,000 feet
Top speed: Mach 2
Powerplant: (1) 24,500lb thrust Pratt & Whitney J57-P-17 turbojet
Armament: One 20mm cannon on most F-106As plus one Genie missile and four AIM-4 Falcon missiles carried internally

F-111F ('Aardvark')
Manufacturer: General Dynamics
First year of service: 1967
Aircraft type: Two-seat variable-geometry fighter-bomber (see FB-111A)
Wingspan: 63ft 0in (spread); 31ft 11.4in (fully swept)
Length: 73ft 6in
Weight: 100,000lb (gross); 47,481lb (empty)
Range: 2925 miles without external fuel
Service ceiling: 59,000 feet
Top speed: Mach 2.5
Powerplant: (2) 25,100lb thrust Pratt & Whitney TF30-P-9 turbofans
Armament: One 20mm multibarrel cannon plus up to 25,000 pounds of bombs, missiles or fuel tanks

F-5E Tiger II
Manufacturer: Northrop
First year of service: 1972 (F-5A, 1964)
Aircraft type: Single-seat air superiority fighter
Wingspan: 26ft 8in
Length: 47ft 4¾in
Weight: 24,722lb (gross); 9723lb (empty)
Range: 1543 miles with external fuel tanks
Service ceiling: 51,800 feet
Top speed: Mach 1.64
Powerplant: (2) 5000lb thrust General Electric J85-GE-21B turbojets
Armament: Two 20mm cannons plus up to 7000lb of mixed ordnance on 4 underwing and one underfuselage pylons

THE TRANSITION YEARS

The **General Dynamics F-111 Aardvark** began with the controversial Defense Department Tactical Fighter Experimental (TFX) program in 1960. The desired plane was a tactical aircraft that could do everything and do it for both the Air Force and the Navy. The TFX was given the designation F-111 in 1961, with the F-111A destined for the Air Force and the F-111B for the Navy. The problems inherent in designing a plane that could be all things to all people were enormous, and serious difficulties arose. The Navy dropped out of the program but the Air Force continued. The first flight of the resulting variable-geometry F-111A took place on 21 December 1964, 22 months after the program began and 2 weeks ahead of schedule; it was not until 16 October 1967 that the F-111s entered operational service with TAC. They were rushed into service in Southeast Asia during the following March under the code name *Combat Lancer*. Problems with the plane's Terrain Following Radar resulted in several losses and it was returned to the drawing board and not redeployed until the fall of 1972. After the war the F-111D and E, and ultimately the F-111F, continued in production as fighter bombers. The original F-111 F had a range of 2925 miles without external fuel and a service ceiling of 59,000 feet: top speed, Mach 2.5. Meanwhile two other distinctive aircraft types have used the basic F-111 airframe. First, SAC has taken advantage of the inherent long-range and heavy-load-carrying capability of the airframe for its strategic medium bomber

version, the FB-111. Beginning in 1979 TAC began to deploy a Grumman-developed electronic warfare version, designated EF-111. The EF-111 is designed to provide barrier surveillance jamming, suppression of SAM threats during close air support operations and escort jamming for deep strike missions.

No single fighter aircraft epitomized the US Air Force during the war in Southeast Asia – and the following decade – better than **McDonnell's F-4 Phantom II.** More Phantoms have been produced for the Air Force than any other plane since the Sabre Jet. They provided the backbone of AAC, USAFE, PACAF and TAC from the late sixties until the early eighties when the F-15 began to come on-line in large numbers. The F-4s, however, will continue to serve as second- and even first-line fighters with Air Force units around the world well into the nineties. Since the war in Southeast Asia, the multirole F-4E has been continually updated with such hardware as Northrop's TISEO (Target Indentification System, Electro-Optical) and the Pave Tack system, which provides the F-4 with nighttime and all-weather capabilities to track and target ground targets for laser, infrared and electro-optically guided weapons. Some F-4Es have been modified as F-4G 'Wild Weasels' equipped to detect, locate and destroy enemy missile sites and tracking radar by means of programable electronic warfare software and antiradar missiles such as the new AGM-88 HARM.

The RF-4C, the high-speed reconnaissance version of the Phantom, was brought into service during the war in Southeast Asia to replace the RF-101 which could function only in daylight.

The basic RF-4 package includes standard optical cameras for daytime use and infrared sensors for nighttime operations. Seventeen of the 505 originally constructed have been retrofitted with Side-Looking Airborne Radar (SLAR) for all-weather standoff surveillance; 24 RF-4s are equipped with a Tactical Electronic Reconnaissance (TEREC) sensor for locating sources

F-4E Phantom II
Manufacturer: McDonnell Douglas
First year of service: 1967 (F-4C, 1963)
Aircraft type: Two-seat multi-role fighter, reconnaissance aircraft (RF-4C)
Wingspan: 38ft 7½in
Length: 63ft 0in
Weight: 61,795lb (gross); 30,328lb (empty)
Range: 1300 miles
Service ceiling: 40,000 feet
Top speed: Mach 2
Powerplant: (2) 17,900lb thrust General Electric J79-GE-17A turbojets
Armament: One 20mm rotary multibarrel cannon, up to 4 Sparrow, Shrike or Sidewinder missiles on 4 underwing and 4 underfuselage pylons (up to 16,000lb of external stores)

Transition-era fighters clockwise from upper left: A USAFE F-111 'Vark' out of RAF Lakenheath; the plucky and economical Northrop F-5 (see graph on page 113); and the McDonnell Phantom, as F-110A prototype in 1962 and as F-4C in Vietnam in 1965.

Above: Wild Weasel F-4Gs of the 35th Tactical fighter Wing out of George AFB on the Nellis AFB flight line during *Red Flag*. (Please note F-4G reference on page 212.)

Top right: An F-4E ready to roll. The multi-barrelled 20 mm cannon under the F-4E's chin made a difference in Vietnam and became an integral design element of both the F-15 and F-16.

of electronic emissions. Other modernization programs include the Pave Tack Infrared system for enhanced all-weather target locating.

Developed as a light, uncomplicated, low-cost fighter for the export trade in the 1950s, **Northrop's N-156 Freedom Fighter** found its way into Air Force inventory in 1964 under the designation F-5 Tiger. Over the years, the US Air Force has accepted delivery of over 1000 F-5s, nearly all of them transferred or sold to such countries as South Vietnam, South Korea, the Philippines, Turkey, Iran, Greece, Norway and Nationalist China under the Military Assistance Prógram or the Foreign Military Sales Program. Those few which are retained in USAF service are used principally by Aggressor squadrons in dissimilar air-to-air combat training exercises like TAC's *Red Flag* because their size and shape approximates that of the Eastern Bloc's MiG-21. By and large, when its performance is considered against its very economical cost, the F-5 is an excellent aircraft. It is, however, less sophisticated technologically than the larger and more expensive aircraft that the USAF has tended to purchase for its own first-line fighter squadrons. Northrop has sought to address this problem through the introduction (early 1980s) of a much-improved version designated F-20 (originally F-5G) Tigershark.

THE NEW GENERATION

The Century Series fighters were designed in the 1950s for supersonic combat high in the stratosphere in new kinds of dogfights. In the late 1960s and early 1970s the Air Force found itself in a shooting war in which real dogfights demonstrated that aircraft design had strayed from the practical lessons of earlier combat. The axiom that the more complicated the weapons system, the less likely it was to work, proved at least

F-15A Eagle
Manufacturer: McDonnell Douglas
First year of service: 1974
Aircraft type: Single-seat high-performance air superiority fighter
Wingspan: 42ft 9¾in
Length: 63ft 9in
Weight: 68,000lb (gross); 27,300lb (empty)
Range: 2878 miles without external fuel
Service ceiling: 65,000 feet
Top speed: mach 2.5
Powerplant: (2) 23,930lb thrust Pratt & Whitney F100-PW-100 turbofans
Armament: One 20mm multibarrel rotary cannon plus 4 Sparrow and 4 Sidewinder missiles on underside pylons (up to 16,000lb of external stores)

partially true. Sophisticated air-to-air missiles were seen to be no substitute for good old-fashioned guns, and the F-4 had to be retrofitted with 20mm cannons. Maneuverability (as had been proven in earlier air wars) was more important than speed, but the Century Series had generally traded maneuverability for ever-higher speeds. Most dogfights were waged at the same speeds as in the Korean War.

Discussion of an air superiority fighter to replace the F-4 began in the late 1960s. It culminated in a contract award to the McDonnell division of McDonnell Douglas to build this new experimental fighter designated FX. The contract was signed in January 1970, the first flight of the resulting **YF-15 Eagle** taking place in July 1972. Deliveries of operational aircraft followed in 1973. In early 1975 a specially prepared F-15 nicknamed 'Streak Eagle' set eight world time-to-height speed records, six of which remain unbroken, including *Climb to 20,000 meters* (65,616ft) in 2 minutes 2.94 seconds. The Eagle is armed with both guns and

Above left: Their missile racks empty after a training mission, two McDill AFB Eagles roll out to return to base.

Above: This Hill AFB F-16 is armed with AIM-9L and J Sidewinders, 2000-lb Mk 84 bombs, and an ALQ-110 ECM pod on its centerline (*see pages 148 and 212*).

F-16A Fighting Falcon ('Viper,' 'Electric Jet')
Manufacturer: General Dynamics
First year of service: 1979
Aircraft type: Single-seat air superiority and multirole fighter
Wingspan: 32ft 10in
Length: 49ft 6in
Weight: 35,400lb (gross); 15,586lb (empty)
Range: 2000 miles
Service ceiling: 50,000 feet
Top speed: Mach 2
Powerplant: (1) 25,000lb thrust Pratt & Whitney F100-PW-200 (3) turbofan
Armament: One 20mm multibarrel rotary cannon plus 2 wingtip mounted Sidewinder missiles and 7 other external pylons for fuel tanks, air-to-air or air-to-surface weapons

air-to-air missiles, whose effectiveness is enhanced by an IFF (Identification, Friend or Foe) system that distinguishes aircraft that can be seen visually but not identified. The lightweight Hughes radar system has 'look-down' capability, meaning that it can track small high-speed objects even at tree-top level. The Eagle cockpit is also enhanced by a 'head up' display (HUD) that projects all the data from the control panel onto the windshield – in a dogfight the pilot doesn't have to look down to read altitude, airspeed or other data. The first units to receive F-15s were TAC's 1st TFW at Langley AFB and USAFE's 36th TFW at Bitburg AB, followed by TAC's 49th TFW at Holloman AFB and PACAF's 18th TFW at Kadena AB in 1979. By 1982 the Eagle was flying with all four Major Tactical Commands as well as TAC's Air Defense interceptor squadrons.

In 1972 the Air Force began to test, under its Lightweight Fighter Prototype program, two prototype aircraft designed to incorporate such emerging technologies as decreased structural

weight through the use of composites to replace metal, blended body aerodynamics, fly-by-wire electronic controls and automatically variable wing leading edges to enhance the already outstanding maneuverability entailed by the lighter weight. The two planes selected to flight-test these new technologies were the YF-17 designed by Northrop Aviation, maker of the lightweight F-5, and the YF-16 by General Dynamics, which hadn't been involved with a USAF fighter program since Convair (whom General Dynamics had since acquired) had produced the highly successful F-106 over a decade earlier. Two prototypes of each design were built and flight-tested, with the production contract awarded to General Dynamics in April 1975. The first **F-16A Fighting Falcon** (the F-16B is the two-seat trainer version) flew in December 1976, with the first operational unit, the 388th TFW at Hill AFB, receiving their first Falcons in January 1979. Meanwhile, the F-16 was selected for co-production by four NATO countries in Europe: Belgium, Norway, Denmark and the Netherlands. The Belgian air force also accepted the first European-built F-16 in January 1979. USAFE's 50th TFW became the first overseas USAF Tactical Wing to receive the Falcon in 1982, with the 8th TFW at Kunsan AB, Korea, the first PACAF unit equipped with the F-16. In addition to the NATO countries producing it, the plane is also in service with Egypt, Pakistan, Venezuela, Korea, and Israel, which has used it in live combat since 1981. Like the F-15, the F-16 is equipped with both 'look down' radar and 'head up' display; built-in structural and

wiring provisions and systems allow its expansion to precision-strike, night-attack and long-range intercept missions as well as air superiority and combat air patrol. Beginning in 1984 the F-16C (the F-16D is its two-seat trainer version) added such improvements as provisions for the AMRAAM air-to-air missiles and the LANTIRN navigation and attack system.

General Dynamic's Convair Division was the first to design and build operational delta-winged aircraft for the Air Force, and General Dynamics is reviving that tradition with the **F-16XL.** The F-16XL is essentially a delta-winged 'cranked arrow' F-16 providing improved range, payload, speed and maneuverability. This version began flight testing in July 1982 as a possible candidate for the Air Force's next-generation air superiority/deep interdiction fighter.

THE WARTHOG

Since the Air Force was created in 1948, most of its attack planes had their start somewhere else. The A-1 and A-7 were both born as US Navy carrier-based attack bombers. The A-26/B-26 was a World War II light bomber. The A-37 Dragonfly was developed from a Cessna T-37 trainer and thrown into combat in Southeast Asia. It was not until the war in Vietnam that the Air Force began to think seriously about designing an entirely new aircraft specially for ground attack and close air support. The program was called AX for Attack, Experimental: like the two-plane competition in the Lightweight Fighter Prototype program, the AX would involve a two-plane fly-off. The competition was held from October through December 1972 between Northrop's A-9 and Fairchild Republic's A-10, with the latter winning the production contract.

The **Fairchild Republic A-10** is a unique aircraft to say the least. It was nicknamed by its maker Thunderbolt II, for Re-

Right: An F-16A escorts a delta-winged F-16XL through its paces at the 1982 Farnborough Air Show. For the demonstration both aircraft were equipped with the visible AIM-9 missiles as well as AIM-7s on the undercarriage. The F-16 is the first USAF aircraft to operate experimentally with voice-activated controls.

Below: A flock of F-16 Falcons on a training mission. The blue color coding on the wing-tip mounted Sidewinders indicates that their warheads are inert.

Above: Its engines mounted high and aft to confuse ground-launched heat-seeking missiles, the A-10 Thunderbolt II is equipped with underwing Multiple Ejection Racks (MER) and in this case an AGM-65 Maverick air-to-ground missile (*see pages 148-9*).

public's P-47 Thunderbolt, used in the ground-attack role in World War II (and because Republic tactical aircraft had always had the prefix 'Thunder'). Because of its unusual appearance – called ugly even by the pilots who know and love it – the A-10 is universally known in the Air Force as the 'Warthog.'

Fighters are easily the most glamorous aircraft in any air force. Their mission is to fly high and fast and to maneuver smoothly and gracefully. Attack planes are the other side of the tactical air-power coin. They are built to fly low, fly slow and carry a big load.

The Warthog was not designed for supersonic flight, and certainly not to win any beauty contest; it was designed to kill tanks. Its speed, barely 400mph, is entirely sufficient for its primary mission. There is a popular cartoon posted in A-10 squadron locker rooms that shows a Russian tank head-on with an A-10 looming up behind him, also head-on. The caption is the Russian tank commander urging his driver to 'Step on it, Ivan, I think he's gaining on us.'

The real beauty of the A-10 is in the way it is designed to fulfil its primary mission. It incorporates such modern technology as a

head up display, but it is primarily designed for survival and firepower. Its survivability is enhanced by heavy armor, particularly in the cockpit area, and by the redundancy of its systems – whole portions of the plane may be shot away without its becoming unflyable. The A-10's firepower begins with its huge GAU-8/A 30mm, seven-barrel rotary cannon. The gun is located in the bottom centerline of the forward fuselage, with the nose wheel offset for the sake of the gun. The GAU-8/A fires up to 4200 rounds per minute of armor-piercing ammunition designed with nonradioactive uranium slugs for heavier impact. While this ferocious cannon is itself enough to destroy a tank or similar target, the A-10's arsenal also includes various bombs and rockets as well as the Maverick air-to-ground missile. For target designation the A-10 carries a Pave Penny laser system pod.

The first A-10 squadron became operational with TAC at Myrtle Beach AFB in 1977; since then Warthog squadrons have joined USAFE, PACAF, AAC and the Air Force Reserve.

Below: A Maverick-armed 81st TFW (USAFE) Warthog lands at Sembach AB in Germany.

A-10 Thunderbolt II ('Warthog')
Manufacturer: Fairchild Industries, Fairchild Republic Div
First year of service: 1977
Aircraft type: Single-seat close air-support attack aircraft
Wingspan: 57ft 6in
Length: 53ft 4in
Weight: 50,000lb (gross); 24,959lb (empty)
Range: 288 miles (with 110 minute loiter over target and 20 min fuel reserve)
Cruising speed: 439mph without ordnance
Powerplant: (2) 9065lb thrust General Electric TF34-GE-100 turbofans
Armament: One 30mm multibarrel cannon plus 8 underwing and three underfuselage attachments for 16,000lb of bombs, missiles, gun pods and jammer pods

Below: Neither a fighter nor an attack plane, the E-3A with its skunk-striped radome is an essential part of the TAC fleet, providing Airborne Warning And Control Systems (AWACS) services for TAC in complex air-combat scenarios.

Above: The Vought A-7 Corsair II is based on a US Navy carrier-based attack plane and had its baptism of fire with the USAF in Southeast Asia in 1968, where it turned in an outstanding performance.

Above: Inside a TAC E-3A AWACS, controllers can manage a large number of combat aircraft on various operations over a wide geographic area. The AWACS would be essential in Central Europe if war broke out.

A-7D Corsair II
Manufacturer: LTV Vought
First year of service: 1968
Aircraft type: Single-seat subsonic attack aircraft
Wingspan: 38ft 9in
Length: 46ft 1½in
Weight: 42,00lb (gross); 19,781lb (empty)
Range: 2871 miles with external fuel tanks
Top speed: 698mph
Powerplant: (1) 14,500lb thrust Allison TF41-A-1 non-after-
    burning turbofan
Armament: One 20mm multibarrel cannon plus up to 15,000lb of
    air-to-air or air-to-surface missiles, bombs, or gun pods on six
    underwing and two underfuselage attachments

E-3 Sentry (former designation EC-137)
Manufacturer: Boeing Commercial Airplane Company/Boeing
    Aerospace Company
First year of service: 1977
Aircraft type: Airborne Warning And Control System (AWACS)
Wingspan: 145ft 9in
Length: 152ft 11in
Weight: 325,000lb
Endurance: 11 hours+ (unrefueled)
Service ceiling: 29,000 feet
Cruising speed: 600mph
Powerplant: (4) 21,000lb thrust Pratt & Whitney TF33 turbofans
Surveillance radar: AN/APV-1 with IFF and data link fighter-
    control (TADIL-C) antennae

Above: An F-15 Eagle and A-10 Warthog of TAC's Tactical Fighter Weapons School at Nellis AFB, Nevada. Air Force blue with yellow markings is standard color for all USAF ground vehicles (*upper left*) except flight-line emergency vehicles (*bottom center*). (*See photos pages 14 and 15.*)

TACTICAL MISSILES

The first tactical air-to-air missiles in USAF service were those that evolved from World War II technology, like the **High Velocity Aerial Rocket (HVAR)** and **Folding Fin Aerial Rocket (FFAR)** that were relatively inexpensive unguided rockets that armed the early jet fighters. The growing sophistication of aerial rockets in the 1950s led to the discontinuance of guns in fighter aircraft.

Many of the early tactical rockets are still in use, such as the **AIR-2 (Air Intercept Rocket) Genie** nuclear-armed unguided rocket that was first deployed aboard the F-89J in the late 1950s. Many thousands were produced through 1962, and Genies still remain in service aboard USAF F-106 and Canadian F-101 interceptors.

The Hughes **AIM-4 (Air Intercept Missile) Falcon** was the first air-to-air guided missile to be adopted by the Air Force, becoming the standard armament on all USAF all-weather interceptors. Original versions were the radar homing AIM-4A and infrared homing AIM-4C, of which around 21,500 were produced between 1956-9. The AIM-4D is a 'cross-bred' version combining the infrared homing system of the AIM-4G Super Falcon with the airframe of the AIM-4C. Thousands of early Falcons were converted to AIM-4 D standard. The AIM-4F and G Super Falcon, less susceptible to electronic countermeasures than the Falcon, were introduced beginning in 1960. Both also had increased performance, with the AIM-4F using a Hughes semi-active radar homing guidance system, and the AIM-4G using an infrared homing system. A nuclear-capable version, the AIM-26 Nuclear Falcon, was introduced in 1960 but is no longer in service.

The Raytheon **AIM-7 Sparrow** is a supersonic radar-homing, long-range, all-weather, all-altitude air-to-air missile. It became standard on the F-4 Phantom and was used extensively in Vietnam. About 34,000 first-generation AIM-7Cs through Es were produced. The AIM-7F was introduced in the 1970s, followed by the AIM-7M in 1980. About 5400 AIM-7Fs and 4300 AIM-7Ms have been produced incorporating larger motors, doppler guidance and improved electronic countermeasures. The mono-

Above: An F-86 unleashes a salvo of HVARs over Nellis AFB.

pulse seeker introduced on the AIM-7M provides an improved cost-performance ratio and adds a look-down capability.

The **AIM-9 Sidewinder**, with fewer than 24 moving parts, is one of the simplest and cheapest (less than half the cost of a Sparrow) air-to-air guided missile in the Air Force. The first AIM-9B was successfully fired in 1953; since then many thousands have been produced by General Electric and Philco for the Air Force as well as the US Navy and many foreign countries. A total of 3000 of the early AIM-9Es are still in Air Force inventory, along with 800 AIM 9Hs (principally a Navy version) and 14,000 AIM-9Js, which were brought on-line for the F-15. The AIM-9P is an improved version of the highly maneuverable AIM-9J, produced by conversion of AIM-9Js and Es. The AIM-9L is a 'third-generation' Sidewinder with new engines, im-

---

AIR-2A Genie
Manufacturer: McDonnell Douglas Astronautics
First deployment: 1957
Missile type: Nuclear-tipped air-to-air missile
Length: 9ft 7in
Maximum diameter: 1ft 5½in
Launch weight: 820lb
Speed: Mach 3
Range: 6 miles
Guidance: None (Fired automatically by Hughes Fire Control System in launching aircraft)
Warhead: Nuclear 1.5KT
Powerplant: (1) 36,000lb thrust Thiokol SR49 TC-1 solid-fuel

AIM-4G Super Falcon
Manufacturer: Hughes Aircraft
First deployment: 1960 (AIM-4A/C)
Missile type: Air-to-air missile
Length: 6ft 9in
Maximum diameter: 6.6in
Launch weight: 145lb
Speed: Mach 2.5
Range: 7 miles
Guidance: Infrared homing system
Warhead: 40lb high explosive
Powerplant: First stage: (1) 6000lb thrust Thiokol M46 solid fuel; Second stage: (1) 6000lb thrust Thiokol M46 solid fuel

---

AIM-7F/M Sparrow
Manufacturer: Raytheon/General Dynamics (Pomona)
First deployment: 1963, AIM-7D ; 1974, AIM-7F
Missile type: All-weather air-to-air missile
Length: 12ft
Maximum diameter: 8in
Launch weight: 500lb
Speed: Mach 3.5+
Range: 26 miles+
Guidance: Raytheon semiactive Doppler radar homing system
Warhead: High explosive
Powerplant: Hercules Mk58 Mod 0 boost-sustained

AIM-9L Sidewinder
Manufacturer: Naval Weapons Center
First deployment: 1953
Missile type: Close-range air-to-air missile
Length: 9ft 5in
Maximum diameter: 5in
Launch weight: 190lb
Speed: Mach 2.5
Range: 4.35 miles
Guidance: Solid-state infrared homing system
Warhead: 25lb high explosive
Powerplant: Rocketdyne/Bermite Mk36 Mod 7/8 solid-fuel

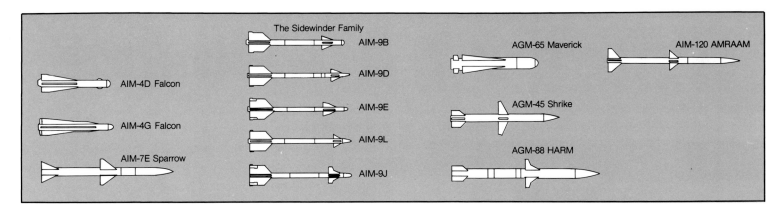

The Sidewinder Family

AIM-9B

AIM-9D

AIM-9E

AIM-9L

AIM-9J

AIM-4D Falcon

AIM-4G Falcon

AIM-7E Sparrow

AGM-65 Maverick

AGM-45 Shrike

AGM-88 HARM

AIM-120 AMRAAM

proved performance and maneuverability and improved tracking stability. The first of 15,000 of the new AIM-9M, an improved AIM-9L, went into production in 1982.

The **AGM-45 (Air-to-Ground Missile) Shrike** antiradiation missile, designed to automatically zero in on enemy radar sites, first entered service in 1965 against targets in North Vietnam. Since then more than 13,000 have been supplied to the Air Force.

The **AGM-65 Maverick** is a television-guided ground-attack missile with a 'launch and leave' capability, meaning that it can find the target on its own once launched. The Maverick was first used in Vietnam in 1972 and still equips all of TAC's first-line fighter-bomber and attack aircraft from the A-7 and A-10 to the F-111 and F-16.

The Texas Instruments **AGM-88 HARM (High Speed Anti-Radiation Missile)**, like the Shrike, is used against enemy radar sites and can cover a wide range of radar frequencies through programable digital processors in the avionics systems of both the missile and the launching aircraft. The HARM was designed for the F-4G 'Wild Weasel' but can also be used on the F-15 and F-16 as well as the B-52.

The General Dynamics **AGM-109H Tomahawk** is based on the Tomahawk cruise missile and is used in tactical nonnuclear operations where a subsonic standoff weapon is required for attacking heavily defended, high-value targets like enemy airbase runways.

The Hughes **AIM-120 AMRAAM (Advanced Medium Range Air-to-Air Missile)** is a radar-guided, all-environment intercept missile which will begin to replace the AIM-7 Sparrow as of 1986 aboard the F-15 and F-16. The AMRAAM has an inertial midcourse guidance system and active radar terminal homing, providing launch-and-manuever and launch-and-leave capabilities. The AIM-120 is superior to the earlier AIM-7 with respect to its warhead, velocity, range, low-altitude capability and electronic countermeasures.

Rockwell International's **GBU-15 (Glide Bomb Unit)** is described as an air-launched cruciform-wing glide bomb fitted with a television/infrared guidance system. It is basically a 'smart bomb,' whose guidance system gives it pinpoint accuracy whether dropped from five miles or a few hundred feet. The GBU-15 is a mid-1970s development of the earlier Pave Strike GBU-8 used in Vietnam. The GBU-15 offers two trajectories, a line-of-sight direct trajectory and an indirect trajectory in which the mid-course glide capability is brought into play. In this mode, the bomb can actually be guided to the target.

The latest twist in the arsenal of air-launched tactical missiles is the Vought **ALMV (Air Launched Miniature Vehicle)**, designed as an Anti-Satellite (ASAT) weapon that can be carried and launched by an F-15. Certain designated F-15s at designated TAC Air Defense bases will be equipped with this two-stage nonnuclear missile capable of destroying orbital altitude satellites in outer space.

AGM-45A Shrike
Manufacturer: Naval Weapons Center
First deployment: 1965
Missile type: Air-to-ground missile
Length: 10ft
Maximum diameter: 8in
Launch weight: 400lb
Speed: (classified)
Range: 3.5 miles
Guidance: Texas Instruments passive homing head
Warhead: 145lb high explosive/fragmentation
Powerplant: (1) Rocketdyne Mk39 Mod 7 or Aerojet General
    Mk53 solid-fuel

AGM-65A Maverick
Manufacturer: Hughes Aircraft
First deployment: 1971
Missile type: Air-to-ground 'launch & leave' missile
Length: 8ft 1in
Maximum diameter: 1ft
Launch weight: 462lb
Speed: (classified)
Range: (classified)
Guidance; Self-homing electro-optical system
Warhead: High explosive
Powerplant: Thiokol TX-481 solid-fuel

AIM-120A (AMRAAM)
Manufacturer: Hughes Aircraft
First deployment: 1985
Missile type: Advanced medium-range air-to-air missile
Length: 12ft
Maximum diameter: 7in
Launch weight: 327lb
Guidance: Inertial midcourse, with active radar terminal homing
Warhead: High explosive

AGM-88A HARM
Manufacturer: Texas Instruments
First deployment: 1983
Missile type: High-speed anti-radar missile
Length: 13ft 8½in
Maximum diameter: 10ft
Launch weight: 807lb
Speed: (classified)
Range: 10 miles
Guidance: Passive homing system, homes on radar emissions
Warhead: High explosive
Powerplant: First stage:dual thrust Thiokol smokeless solid-fuel

STRATEGIC AIR POWER IN THE US AIR FORCE

STRATEGIC AIR POWER

Strategic air power contrasts with tactical in that it is used against long-range targets that affect an enemy's *will* to wage war or long-term *ability* to wage war. Largely theoretical before World War II, strategic air power played a key role in the defeat of Germany and Japan. During the war, Britain's RAF and the USAAF were the major practitioners of strategic air power: the USAAF organized three numbered air forces, the Eighth and Fifteenth in Europe and the Twentieth in the Pacific, to carry out strategic bombing offensives.

After the war, to perpetuate its strategic bomber superiority, the USAAF created the Strategic Air Command (SAC) in 1946. Since then, while tactical air warfare has been a major part of nearly all postwar conflicts, strategic air power has been applied only sparingly. It was used by SAC in the 1972 *Linebacker II* operations over North Vietnam and by the RAF in the Falklands War of 1982, but scarcely anywhere else. Perhaps the main reason is that strategic air power has come, since World War II, to be associated with the massive strategic nuclear arsenals of the Soviet Union and the United States. It has taken on the aura of a 'doomsday' strategy. All the destructive power delivered by all

the strategic bombing offensives of World War II could be matched in a few seconds by a nuclear exchange between the superpowers. So massive is the potential firepower of these two arsenals that it could destroy not only the principals, but most of the known world as well. The world has been spared strategic nuclear warfare through US-Soviet recognition of the concept of Mutual Assured Destruction, with its appropriate acronym MAD. Nuclear war has been avoided, thus far, by balancing one arsenal against the other.

On the American side, the nuclear arsenal is in three parts, known as the *Triad*. One of these parts, Submarine Launched Ballistic Missiles (SLBM), is under control of the US Navy; manned bombers and Intercontinental Ballistic Missiles (ICBM) are under control of the US Air Force's Strategic Air Command.

THE STRATEGIC AIR COMMAND

The Strategic Air Command was created at the same time as the Tactical Air Command and the Air Defense Command (21 March 1946). It is the US Air Force's long-range strike force, deterring nuclear war by its readiness to fight a nuclear war and supporting other operations by maintaining heavy bombers for conventional bombing missions. SAC has

Below: SAC maintains bombers and missiles for long-range strike missions, but it also manages a fleet of high-performance reconnaissance aircraft, such as this super-secret SR-71 photographed by the author at Beale AFB, to gather the information needed to develop and update the strategic war plan.

provided bombers for service in both Korea and Southeast Asia, with bombers in Korea under FEAF Bomber Command control, but those in Southeast Asia under direct SAC control. Beginning in the 1980s some of SAC's bombers have been organized into a Strategic Projection Force (SPF) to provide massive conventional bombing capabilities in support of the Rapid Deployment Force (RDF).

With nearly 110,000 uniformed personnel, SAC is the largest single Major Command in the Air Force. In addition, it is the gaining command for 15,800 members of the Air National Guard and Air Force Reserve. The SAC Force is composed of over 1000 ICBMs, nearly 400 B-52 and B-1 long-range bombers, 60 FB-111 medium-range bombers and nearly 100 sophisticated U-2, TR-1 and SR-71 strategic reconnaissance aircraft. In addition to these, SAC manages the Air Force's entire fleet of over 600 KC-135 and KC-10 aerial refueling tankers.

About 30% of the bomber and tanker fleet are on a 24-hour ground alert, ready to react immediately in time of war. At the same time, SAC's ICBM force also maintains a 24-hour alert posture.

SAC is composed of three major components, the Eighth and Fifteenth Air Forces and the First Strategic Aerospace Division. Of the three major strategic air forces of World War II, the Eighth and Fifteenth were both assigned to SAC within six weeks of its creation while the Twentieth, having gone from direct JCS control to part of FEAF, remained under that Command until permanently disbanded in March 1955. The Second Air Force, one of the four continental numbered air forces of World War II, was reactivated in November 1949 and assigned to SAC as the home-front Third Air Force had been assigned to TAC. Until 1950 the three SAC numbered air forces were divided by type of aircraft. The Second was in charge of reconnaissance aircraft, the Eighth heavy (B-36) and some medium (B-29) bombers, and the Fifteenth medium bombers. In April 1950 SAC forces were realigned geographically. The Fifteenth (March AFB, California) would be in charge of SAC forces in the west, the Eighth (MacDill AFB, Texas) would supervise the central region while the Second (Barksdale AFB, Louisiana) controlled the east. In 1951 seven SAC Air Divisions were established under numbered-air-forces control, including two overseas, the Fifth at Rabat, French Morocco, and the Seventh at South Ruislip, England. In June 1954, with deactivation of the FEAF Bomber Command, SAC's Third Air Division was established at Andersen AFB on Guam, although the base was not transferred from FEAF to SAC until the following year.

In June 1955 Eighth Air Force Headquarters was moved to Westover AFB in Massachusetts, giving it control over SAC assets in the central and northeast states while the Second retained the southeast. In July 1957 the Sixteenth Air Force at Torrejon AB near Madrid, Spain, was assigned to SAC, assuming control of SAC operations in Spain and sharing with the Second control of Fifth Air Division operations in North Africa, which were fully integrated into the Sixteenth, as the Fifth was deactivated in 1958. The Seventh Air Division in England was also dissolved, but not until 1965. In April 1966, after nine years with SAC, the Sixteenth was transferred to USAFE; on 31 March 1970 the illustrious Eighth was deactivated at Westover AFB with all SAC's assets in the United States divided between the Second and Fifteenth Air Forces. It was the first time since 1949 that SAC had only two numbered air forces in the continental United States.

While the idea had been to eliminate the Eighth entirely, the plan was changed out of deference to the Eighth's long history, going back to its exploits during World War II in the skies over

The Commanders of the Strategic Air Command	
Gen George Kenney	Gen Bruce Holloway
21 Mar 1946–15 Oct 1948	1 Aug 1968–30 Apr 1972
Gen Curtis LeMay	Gen John Meyer
16 Oct 1948–30 June 1957	1 May 1972–31 July 1974
Gen Thomas Power	Gen Russell Dougherty
1 July 1957–30 Nov 1964	1 Aug 1974–31 July 1977
Gen John Ryan	Gen Richard Ellis
1 Dec 1964–31 Jan 1967	1 Aug 1977–1 Aug 1981
Gen Joseph Nazzaro	Gen Bennie Davis
1 Feb 1967–31 July 1968	1 Aug 1981–

Germany. Instead, the Eighth Air Force was re-established on 1 April 1970 at Andersen AFB, incorporating the Third Air Division, and given jurisdiction over the B-52 *Arc Light* raids against Southeast Asia that originated there. In January 1975 the Eighth was moved back to Barksdale AFB, where it replaced the Second Air Force which was deactivated.

The third building block of the present SAC, the First Strategic Aerospace Division (1STRAD), like the numbered air forces, reports directly to SAC headquarters. On 21 July 1961 the former First Missile Division became the first Strategic Aerospace Division based at Vandenberg AFB, California. The original concept had called for the First Missile Division to function as the keystone of the SAC ballistic missile force, comprised of a diverse conglomeration of missile units based around the country and operating various types of missiles. However, the Thor and Jupiter missiles had been deactivated, and by 1961 the Atlas and Titan units assigned to the First had been transferred to the Fifteenth Air Force.

Thus when the First Strategic Aerospace Division was born, its function was to control the missile test launches taking place at Vandenberg and to train missile crews for SAC. Since 1958 over 1500 launches have taken place at Vandenberg, largely under the auspices of 1STRAD. These have included the huge Titan IIID space booster, many Minuteman launches and recently the MX test program. As the host unit at Vandenberg, 1STRAD is host to the Air Force's Space and Missile Test Organization, an agency of the Air Force Systems Command (AFSC), conducting missile tests over the Pacific Ocean from its Western Space and Missile Center (WSMC). The WSMC's Western Test Range extends from Vandenberg across the Pacific and into the Indian Ocean. The Shuttle Activation Task Force (SATAF) at Vandenberg is responsible for the program making the base the western launch site for the Space Shuttle program.

STRATEGIC AIR COMMAND BASES

Offutt AFB (SAC Headquarters)
Location: 8 miles south of Omaha, Nebraska
Area: 1914 acres
Altitude: 1048ft
Personnel: 12,880 Military
      3348 Civilian (including 740 contract personnel)
The US Army's Fort Crook was activated on the site in 1888; in 1924 the landing field was renamed in honor of Lt Jarvis J Offutt, an Air Service pilot who died 13 August 1918 of injuries suffered during combat in World War I. In addition to being SAC's headquarters, the base is home to the 55th Strategic Recon Wing and the 544th Strategic Intelligence Wing – as such it is also home base for the *Looking Glass* Airborne Command Post. USAF Global Weather Central (MAC) is also at Offutt, as well as MAC's 3d Weather Wing.